An Anthology of Contemporary Bengali Plays
by Bratya Basu

An Anthology of Contemporary Bengali Plays by Bratya Basu

Edited by

NANDITA BANERJEE DHAWAN *and* SAM KOLODEZH

Translated by

MAINAK BANERJEE *and* ARNAB BANERJI

B L O O M S B U R Y

NEW DELHI • LONDON • OXFORD • NEW YORK • SYDNEY

BLOOMSBURY INDIA
Bloomsbury Publishing India Pvt. Ltd
Second Floor, LSC Building No. 4, DDA Complex, Pocket C–6&7,
Vasant Kunj, New Delhi 110070

BLOOMSBURY, BLOOMSBURY ACADEMIC INDIA and the Diana logo are trademarks of Bloomsbury Publishing Plc

First published in India 2024
First published in Great Britain 2023

Cover design: Jess Stevens

Cover image: The Masks, Ganesh Pyne, 1994, Tempera on canvas pasted on mount board, 53.6 × 58.5 cm © Mrs Meera Pyne

This edition published with permission from Bloomsbury Publishing Plc, 50 Bedford Square, London, WC1B3DP, UK

A catalogue record for this book is available from the British Library.
A catalog record for this book is available from the Library of Congress.

ISBN: 978-93-56409-31-6

Series: Methuen Drama Play Collections

Typeset by RefineCatch Limited, Bungay, Suffolk
Printed at Manipal Technologies Limited, Manipal

To find out more about our authors and books
visit www.bloomsbury.com and sign up for our newsletters

Contents

Introduction

This anthology of contemporary Bengali plays by Bratya Basu arrives at a moment in which Indian media is exploding on the global scene both in the diasporic community and beyond. Yet, even as Indian culture and media is becoming a more prominent part of global discourse, contemporary Indian playwrights are rarely translated for global markets. One of the reasons why Indian theatre has continued to remain on the margins of contemporary world theatre – whether as texts, theatrical performances, digital media, or as objects of academic scholarship – is its linguistic and cultural plurality. Every state has its own language, performance tradition and approach to theatre. Even postcolonial theatre studies, which are themselves subjected to a triple marginalization by genre, ideology and language, bypass contemporary Indian theatre because of its complex history, practices and varied influences that range from a spectrum of European and Anglo-American drama to the drama of classical, postclassical and colonial India. This anthology seeks to be one of hopefully many future collections of contemporary Indian playwrights that brings the world unique perspectives of everyday Indian culture often not captured in widely distributed films and television shows.

Bratya Basu is an award-winning playwright, actor, filmmaker and politician who has been the strongest and perhaps most innovative voice in the Bengali theatre scene for the past twenty years. Most recently, he received the Sahitya Akademi Award in 2021 from the Ministry of Culture, Government of India. He is the first Bengali playwright to have received the award in fifty-four years.

Basu remixes genres, styles, topics, cultures, theatrical conventions and production practices to invent a unique theatrical language and production methodology that is simultaneously Bengali and global – painting a picture of contemporary India at the palimpsestic nexus of tradition, modernity and explosive growth while also challenging Indian cultural myths and stereotypes within India and in the diasporic Indian community.

Basu is also unique as a playwright because he writes his plays in Bengali. He is exceptional in the Kolkata group theatre scene in that of the fifty plays that he has written, the majority of them are original works rather than adaptations of traditional Indian stories or plays from playwrights belonging to the traditional Western canon such as Shakespeare, Chekhov or Brecht.[1] All of the plays are written and originally performed and published in Bengali. Basu incorporates dialects from across Kolkata and West Bengal and remixes dialects incorporating the Hindi and English of Bollywood, Hollywood and the global theatre scene. Moreover, Basu dives deep into the less formal languages of his plays to more fully induce one into a subcultural experience: the language of physics, of cricket, of the Greek polis, of art history, of medicine and any of the other various languages that weave throughout his oeuvre.

1 The plays have been published in four volumes with the first volume published in November 2004 and the fourth volume in May 2022. English translations include *Quadrangle*, *Winkle Twinkle*, *Virus M*, *Hemlat, The Prince of Garanhata*, *The Black Hole*, *Rudhasangeet*, *The Contract Killer* and *Just Like Cinema*; and were published in an anthology of his works in 2015 in Bengal. See Basu (2004, 2010, 2016, 2022).

While Basu writes to revitalize the rich Bengali-language theatre tradition, he also writes with the goal of generating a more equitable and generative discourse between local Kolkata, regional Bengali, national Indian, and international global theatre traditions and markets. Translation, performance and publication are important for the dissemination and reception of original contemporary plays in diverse Indian languages to audiences in order to facilitate more dialogue about theatre within India and beyond its borders. Basu and we hope that practices of translation and dissemination can reconfigure globalization so that the global and the local are mutually constitutive to open more emancipatory spaces of theatrical expression and camaraderie, resulting in new theatre languages and epistemologies as they offer radical visions of the world.

Basu's work emerges from Kolkata's group theatre. The roots of Kolkata's group theatre go back to the end of the eighteenth century during the colonial period when Gerasim Stepanovich Lebedeff, a Russian musician learning Bengali, started the first Bengali-language theatre in 1795 where the first plays performed on a proscenium stage were mostly translations of English and European plays.[2] Interestingly, the first production by a Bengali was a play in the English language.

From the nineteenth century onwards, Bengali theatre history can be broken up into three phases constituted by two major shifts. First, the urban commercial theatre split from what was known as '*babu* theatre' of feudal landlords. In the mid-nineteenth century, rich and influential feudal landlords organized '*babu* theatre', which were private affairs where invitations were extended to selected audiences and ordinary people had no access to watch theatre. This was followed by the second phase when commercial theatre emerged in the late nineteenth century. During those times Calcutta (now Kolkata) and Bombay (now Mumbai) both had active and independent theatre cultures. This 'modern' phase shifted the traditional relationship between actors and audiences through two innovations: 1) the popularization of the proscenium stage with an emphasis on illusion and the fourth wall, and 2) the introduction of ticket sales for theatre productions. These two innovations changed the relationship of the audience with theatre forever (Karnad 1989). As urban theatre started to intervene actively against colonialism, Dwijendra Lal Ray and Girish Chandra Ghosh moved away from mythological themes that were pervasive in Bengali drama to powerful patriotic dramas. Girish Chandra Ghosh set up the National Theatre in 1872 which was commercial as a willing audience could enter the auditorium by buying tickets. The likes of Ghosh distanced themselves from the theatre produced by feudal landlords and became 'managers' of theatre alongside their roles as actors, directors and playwrights – accepting money and fame and introducing modern notions of celebrity to the theatre scene. Almost eighty years later, in the 1950s and 1960s, Bengali theatre entered a third phase and a new language of theatre was authored by the famous trio – Shambhu Mitra, Utpal Dutt and Ajitesh Bandyopadhyay – as they scripted the grand narrative called 'group theatre',

2 For a detailed history of Kolkata's group theatre see Banerji (2022); Banerjee (2021). Mukherjee (1982); Bharucha (1983).

made up largely of middle-class volunteers that worked in the theatre alongside regular jobs, with many forming their own theatre groups as they gained their own popularity and acclaim (Basu 2021; Chatterjee 2007; Banerjee 2021; Banerji 2022).

However, the history of Bengali urban theatre was one of exclusion. English-educated urban upper-middle-class Bengalis were looking for newer and less archaic amusements as they looked up to the European plays and their adaptations as 'high culture'. This was in contrast to the 'low culture' associated with 'licentious and voluptuous tastes' (Banerjee 1989: 131) of the 'vulgar' populace of lower orders (class, caste) in which women were active participants. Thus, the public theatre apparently seemed to have democratized the proscenium theatre under the mask of enlightened and sophisticated cultural activities of the *bhadralok* (Banerjee 1989; Kundu 2010).

The process of constructing symbols of 'low culture' continues in independent India where, for example, bar dancers/erotic dancers are culturally stigmatized and are labelled as symbols of moral perversion. There is feminist scholarship on how local and traditional performance practices of 'public' women in folk, tribal or popular cultures (such as *tamasha*, *nautanki*, *naach*, cabaret, bar dance, etc.) continue to disturb and subvert the normative structures of culture as 'high' and 'low' (Chakraborty and Tambe 2022). Autobiographies such as that by Binodini Dasi (Bhattacharya 1998) further reveal the dilemmas of theatre artists as women both from 'respectable' categories and those categorized as women of 'easy virtue' had different journeys of acceptance as they made public performances on stage. This is despite the fact that both Lebedeff and Nabin Chandra Basu, who is known for the first Bengali play (*Bidya-Sundar*) on a Calcutta stage, used actresses for female roles in theatre, a practice that was soon reversed (Chatterjee 2007).

In the 1990s, the economic liberalization policies in India led to both economic and cultural globalization and changed the theatre scene as much as it changed India. As India became a global destination for foreign investment in the 1990s, there was transnational corporate domination and 'cultural invasion' in India's television policies and airwaves as well. Global conglomerates soon realized that the local–global nexus was crucial for their profit-making and began producing content and products targeted towards the burgeoning middle classes.[3] With the liberalizing economy, consumption patterns of India's middle classes became symbolic of India's modernity as their politics and everyday practices played an important role in reproducing their privileged position even as structural inequalities were deepening, aggravated by the steady rise in the price of basic goods. Their social and cultural capital in terms of education, occupation, high incomes and political power were significant instruments in helping the dominant fractions of the middle classes to reproduce their hegemonic position (Fernandes and Heller 2006; Oza 206; Dhawan 2010). The middle-class consumers who made up a devoted theatre audience, now the primary consumers in the global market, had other attractions: visiting shopping malls, buying expensive

3 This group of the middle class, which scholars have referred to as the 'New Middle Class', is a socially diverse category whose boundaries are constantly being defined. For more details, see Fernandes and Heller (2006) and Dhawan (2010).

tickets to see movies in modern cinema multiplexes, and watching soap operas and global programmes on more than 200 television channels. The already massively popular television and film industries that were progressively marginalizing theatre culture since the mid-twentieth century became monolithic in the entertainment and cultural landscapes (Basu 2017b).

Basu first entered the Kolkata group theatre scene at the height of India's economic liberalization policies with the 1996 premiere of his first play, *Ashaleen*, which was described as the first postmodern Bengali play. In *Ashaleen*, as in his other works, he stands out with his pastiche approach, mixing the personal, political, aesthetic, pulp and highbrow through a self-reflexive approach that is integral to a feminist and post-structuralist methodology – simultaneously refracting himself and experiences through his characters as they reflect and refract through and around each other to create something resonant.

For him, theatre is personal. It is neither a religious shrine nor a political party office. It is instead an explosive and expansive crowd of subjectivities speaking for Basu and beyond him to the many crowds within us all (Basu 2017a). The personal and intersubjective approach that Basu brings to the theatre makes him stand out on the Bengali theatre scene. He also stands out because his original plays in Bengali comment directly on contemporary issues that challenge grand narratives of patriarchy, nationalism, religious dogmatism, middle-class respectability and political ideology, while eschewing dogmas of his own.

Power dynamics on and off the stage do not disappear. They are examined, contested, made malleable and played with in order to provide space and time for the possibility of new subjectivities. His plays focus especially on the hypocrisy and contradictions in the lives of the urban middle class through playing with what is spoken and what resonates in the silences and the gaps – inviting audiences to allow their own subjectivities, ideas, emotions and experiences to perform and write the performance. Such an approach allows Basu to both court and critique the middle class by pushing the boundaries of acceptable narratives in the theatre while drawing on the techniques and strategies of globalized entertainment to make both a theatre practice that is uniquely Bengali and theatre in general sustainable in the globalized world.

The changing economic and cultural context in the 1990s posed challenges to the structure and continued functioning of group theatre, which faced intense competition from globalized media and continued to be marginalized by the effects of economic liberalization. In response, Bratya Basu pioneered a critique of the grand narrative of group theatre to formulate what he calls 'company theatre', which combines aspects of commercial and group theatre into the following practices:

1. The work constructs a neo-creative commentary of time through an experimental theatrical language.
2. The company establishes connections with contemporary politics, markets and marketing strategies.
3. The company works with and depends on media outlets for marketing.
4. Actors are allowed to work with other directors from other groups.

5. The company pays the required taxes (entertainment/corporation) to the government following the tradition of group theatre while setting the price of tickets high following the tradition of commercial theatre.
6. The company is run by a 'Producer-Director' – a new synthesis between a group theatre director and a commercial theatre producer in which creative direction and market viability are synthesized.

(Basu 2017b: 131–50)

His concept has been criticized for undermining the formation of a solid front against private ownership and instead using the language of corporate investment and profit-making in the realm of theatre. Basu, however, exposes the primarily middle-class and individual enterprise of group theatre that is often couched in the garb of a utopian horizon of a fashionably proclaimed leftist cultural 'movement' of the so-called 'people's theatre'.[4] He moves beyond the confines of interpersonal conflicts and individual egos to attempt to make theatre an economically viable and a respectable profession in the existing socio-economic-political context.

Through his manifesto of 'company theatre', Basu questions the traditional binary of theory–practice in the contested territory of group theatre by using the intersectional experiences of his position of privilege as middle class and the marginalized standpoint of a theatre practitioner. The concept of company theatre enriches the discourse through which the 'core duality'[5] (Banerjee 2021: 15) of group theatre in Bengal can be analysed by using the feminist research method of 'breaking binaries' and pursuing critical self-reflexivity. Therefore, Basu's accounts of the 'real' world of theatre and negotiations with its contradictions and (im)possibilities are not a surrender to capital but a strategy for theatre, and especially non-commercial theatre, to overcome the challenges posed by globalization and open markets. He strives to find strategies for survival of theatre as a marginalized art form to survive in a neoliberal world in which global market forces reign over cultural production. He sees theatre as a primary index for social change and works towards keeping theatre traditions and practices relevant and evolving (Basu 2017b).

At the helm of his company, Kalindi Bratyajon, Basu has been advocating for theatre to be a viable space for professionals to enter and be taken seriously. Since forming Kalindi Bratyajon, he has produced at least one play a year until the pandemic paused theatre production around the world. Alongside theatre productions, the company has produced theatre festivals, run educational theatre workshops for children, created a

4 The concept of group theatre has drawn from the ideology of Indian People's Theatre Association (IPTA), formed in the 1940s, which was used as an explicitly political tool for communicating with the masses.

5 Banerjee (2021: 15) studies group theatre in Bengal between 1950 and 1980 as emerging from a core duality which as a 'space of political performance practice [is] marked by being constantly at the crossroads, torn between the complex and centrifugal pulls faced by a "middle-class art" theatre when it attempts to become an actual "theatre of the people"'. The likes of Ajitesh Bandyopadhyay of the well-known Bengali group theatre Nandikar took on the difficult project of having full-time theatre professionals and making theatre economically viable and politically commited to the cause of the masses (ibid.: 139).

theatre journal and facilitated lectures on theatre. At the same time, he has worked in the film industry, creating bridges between theatre and film practices. However, like his predecessors and fellow theatre practitioners, he has mourned the failure of owning an auditorium where he and his colleagues could do theatre without the pervasive pressures of finding theatre spaces and producing shows in an unstable environment (Banerji 2022). Basu therefore underlines the necessity for the state to plan measures to ensure sustainable theatre. Theatre practitioners like Basu emphasize the necessity of seeing theatre as a profession that is valued by especially middle-class society as much as professions such as doctor, engineer or academic. According to Basu, only then can a theatre-lover feel proud and confident to take it up as a possible livelihood and look forward to a sustainable future.

Alongside challenges he has faced as a producer and director, Basu has also faced many challenges in his trajectory as a theatre artist. His plays have both stirred up controversy and received accolades. While some of his plays such as *Winkle Twinkle*, *Hemlat: The Prince of Garanhata* and *Ruddhasangeet* amongst others have been criticized as anti-establishment and overly critical of the Left Front, he has been criticized for not writing enough political plays after entering parliamentary politics. Basu (2017a) has, however, refused to accept that he has ever written 'political' plays and he has always emphasized that party politics is just one component of the plays he has written. His entry into politics followed his active participation in the Singur-Nandigram movement against the Left Front government in West Bengal; he contested elections in 2011 and thereafter took on the responsibility as a minister of the present ruling party, Trinamool Congress, in West Bengal which had ousted the Left Front government from power after thirty-six years. As with his innovation of company theatre and his approach to playwriting, he has used his lived, complex and contradictory experiences of being part of the theatre–politics binary to conceptualize a vision for the sustainability of theatre that is grounded in self-reflexivity to point out how the intersecting, hegemonic and patriarchal structures of family, community and state construct the 'legitimately violent' in society. At the same time, he has remained stylistically playful as a playwright in order to produce affective experiences for audiences that trigger their own self-reflexivity.

Basu's plays emerge out of a pastiche of cinema, pop culture, Western theatre traditions, *rasa* aesthetics, postmodern conventions, Bengali language and dialects, and a remixing of time and space to comment on the most pressing cultural and sociopolitical issues of India, and especially Bengal today. His plays are often cinematic, incorporating techniques that can be found on Bollywood, Tollywood and Hollywood screens. Scene transitions often follow a zoom-in model in which objects such as photographs or letters initiate a scene transition. Multiple scenes sometimes occur simultaneously in a live-split screen. Music, and especially pop music or songs that are culturally and generationally relevant, often permeate the scripts.

More importantly, like Bollywood or Tollywood films and like classical Indian performances, the plays can be better understood through the aesthetic of *rasa*. Rasa is first described in Bharata Muni's *The Natyashastra* as 'the cumulative result of *vibhava* [stimulus], *anubhava* [involuntary reaction], and *vyabhicari bhava* [voluntary reaction]' (quoted in Shechner 2001: 29). Rasa literally translates to 'sap', 'essence', 'flavour' or 'taste' and Muni utilizes a food metaphor to describe *rasa* as the result of the cook, the diners and the food all interacting together to leave a lingering mouthfeel and taste once a meal is done. As a concept, *rasa* describes the overall affect and aesthetic produced through a sharing of emotion between audience and performer that is unified and one in which audience and performer also share in the medium of performance and participate in an emotional and physical exchange. There are eight *rasas*: *Vira* (energy, rigour), *Bhibhatsa* (disgust), *Bhayanaka* (dread), *Sringara* (eroticism, love), *Hasya* (humour), *Raudra* (rage), *Karuna* (compassion, pity) and *Adbhuta* (wonder, awe). Performance is then centred around transitions between emotions that create predominant moods and aesthetics to culminate in an intended audience experience rather than a fragmented collection of one's personal reading of a work that is less intentional. Such an approach is different from one found on traditional Western stages in which plays are often plot- or character-driven and audiences take on the roles of evaluators, judges or consumers.

Basu does not adhere strictly to *rasas*. His work can also be read through a postmodern lens in which plays are often written and performed to create shared experiences with audiences through a variety of techniques meant to intellectually, emotionally, physically and sometimes spiritually immerse the audience in the hyperreal world of the performance in order to create shared sense-making tools and shared meaning. He uses hyperrealism to create new realities by enhancing the black holes of life, by exploring its inaccessible spaces. Basu (2017a) talks about having to grow in an environment of dwarfed reality and it is through the lens of dwarfed reality that we have to analyse and deal with human relations, love and sexuality, as well as our (in) abilities. Whether understood through rasas by way of India's film industry, postmodern theatre or its attendant hyperrealism, Basu's plays work to produce predominant moods and leave the audience or reader within an affective sense and experience of the event of and the events within the performance. These moods, however, are almost never singular. They are explored through their many contradictory complexities. Yet even as these moods shape the plays and transfer well across cultures and traditions, the moods, the plays and the references all remain deeply Bengali.

The specificity of Basu's language is one of the key elements that make him a Bengali playwright that effectively captures the moods and movements of contemporary Bengal. However, the linguistic specificity of his plays is not rigid. It is instead playful and allows languages and dialects to move comfortably together whether disjunctively as juxtapositions, or conjunctively as complements. The combined playfulness and specificity of language is what allows for Basu's works to simultaneously be global and local – to be translated and provide a global audience with a taste of West Bengal and India while also allowing an audience or reader to move freely through the moods that the languages and the characters that reciprocally embody them create. The specificity of language alongside the postmodern remixing of sub-cultures and mediums that creates dynamic and immersive moods also allows Basu to explore issues that are overtly political such as the Indian middle class, gender and sexuality in India, mental health, the institution of marriage, the justice system, the 1947 partition, zealotry and religious dogmatism, among others, without prescribing a particular politics or valorizing a distinct identity. In fact, characters are often distant from the norm whether because they are strange, as in the case of the cricket-loving bumbling private-eye Chotok in *Who?*; from a distant time and place as in the case of the eponymous queen

Creusa, the Greek queen seeking justice and agency in *Creusa – The Queen*; polarizing as in the case of Muhammad Ali Jinnah in *The Final Night* or Devadatta in *The Penitence*; or alienated from themselves as in *The Black Hole*.

Structure of the book

This anthology of six selected plays written between 2000 and 2020 by Bratya Basu is divided into three sections with each section starting with a summary of the plays. The first section, titled 'Poignant Challenges, Soulful Remorse', examines power in Indian politics, religion and family while raising relevant questions about human agency and ethics with regard to the fault-lines in society. *Love in Times of Corona* (2020) imagines a Kolkata overtaken by pandemic and wild animals as families, governments and media fall apart. *The Penitence* (2016) takes the audience back to Gautam Buddha's *Mahaparinirvana* to examine the relationship between religion, violence and ethics in its historical contexts with contemporary relevance.

The second section, '(In)Visible Boundaries, (Un)Democratic Choices', explores the relationship among democracy, nation building and the role of women in intergenerational political struggle. *The Final Night* (2018) re-imagines the Indian nationalist Muhammed Ali Jinnah's final night in British India set within the tumultuous events of partition. The play revolves around emotional wounds between him and his daughter in the larger ethico-political imagination of leaving the injured nation to the newly created Pakistan. *Creusa – The Queen* (2019) is based on Greek mythology as it follows Queen Creusa through a murderous plot and an unrelenting challenge to the gods and patriarchy within democracy in her pursuit of social justice.

The third section, 'Intimately Political, Politically Intimate', navigates queer identity, mental health and the fabulation of modern Bengali life in a twenty-first-century India straddling the progressive politics that removed section 377 and Hindu nationalisms that stoke new conservatisms. *The Black Hole* follows Angshuman Banerjee's crisis of sexual identity down a black hole of absurdism, digital information overload and knowledge–power knots that make up the struggle of self-fashioning in the digital age. *Who?* is a psychocomic thriller that puts contemporary Bengali life under a microscope and deftly moves through topics of misogyny, mental health and cricket in an absurdist whodunnit that spotlights the hypocrisy of the middle-class Indian family.

References

Banerjee, Sumanta (1989). Marginalisation of Women's Popular Culture in Nineteenth Century Bengal in Kumkum. Sangari and Sudesh Vaid (eds), *Recasting Women: Essays in Colonial History*. New Delhi: Kali for Women.

Banerjee, Trina Nileena (2021). *Performing Silence: Women in the Group Theatre Movement in Bengal*. New Delhi: Oxford University Press.

Banerji, Arnab (2022). *Contemporary Group Theatre in Kolkata, India*. London: Routledge.

Basu, Bratya (2004). *Natak Samagra* [Collection of plays]. Kolkata: Ananda Publishers.

Basu, Bratya (2010). *Natak Samagra* [Collection of plays] (Vol. 2). Kolkata: Ananda Publishers.

Basu, Bratya (2016). *Natak Samagra* [Collection of plays] (Vol. 3). Kolkata: Ananda Publishers.

Basu, Bratya (2017a). *Sakkhatkar Sangraha* [Collection of Interviews]. Kolkata: Kolikata Letterpress.

Basu, Bratya (2017b). *Prasanga Theatre* [Through the Lens of Theatre]. Kolkata: Saptarshi Prakashan.

Basu, Bratya (2021). *Bangla Theatre: Oitijhya o Parampara* [Bengali Theatre: Tradition and Legacy]. Kolkata: Apan Path.

Basu, Bratya (2022). *Natak Samagra* [Collection of plays] (Vol. 4). Kolkata: Ananda Publishers.

Bharucha, Rustom (1983). *Rehearsals of Revolution: The Political Theatre of Bengal.* Honolulu: University of Hawaii Press.

Bhattacharya, Rimli (ed. and trans.) (1998). *Binodini Dasi: My Story and My Life as an Actress.* New Delhi: Kali for Women.

Chakraborty, Aishika and Tambe, Anagha (2022). Performing Art/Performing Labour: Gender, Body and the Politics of Culture. *Economic and Political Weekly*, *Review of Women's Studies*, 57(22), 28 May. https://www.epw.in/journal/2022/22/review-womens-studies/dancing-night-away.html

Chatterjee, Sudipto (2007). *The Colonial Staged: Theatre in Colonial Calcutta.* Calcutta: Seagull.

Dhawan, Nandita Banerjee (2010). The Married 'New Indian Woman': Hegemonic Aspirations in New Middle Class Politics? *South African Review of Sociology*, 41(3), 45–60. https://doi.org/10.1080/21528586.2010.516122

Fernandes, Leela and Heller, Patrick (2006). Hegemonic Aspirations: New Middle Class Politics and India's Democracy in Comparative Perspective. *Critical Asian Studies*, 38(4): 495–522. https://doi.org/10.1080/14672710601073028

Karnad, Girish (1989). Theatre in India. *Daedalus*, 118(4): 330–52.

Kundu, Manujendra (2010). Bengali Theatre: An Edifice on the Ashes of People's Culture. *Social Scientist*, 38(3/4): 55–73.

Mukherjee, Sushil Kumar (1982). *The Story of the Calcutta Theatres, 1753–1980.* Calcutta: K.P. Bagchi.

Oza, Rupal (2006). *The Making of Neoliberal India: Nationalism, Gender, and the Paradoxes of Globalization.* New Delhi: Women Unlimited.

Schechner, Richard (2001). Rasaesthetics. *TDR: The Drama Review*, 34(3): 27–50.

Section One
Poignant Challenges, Soulful Remorse

Summaries

Love in Times of Corona (2020)

Love in Times of Corona is a hyper real one-act play set in Kolkata, India, in May 2021 ravaged by Covid-19 with a death toll of millions drawing wild birds and animals to migrate for the feast of flesh lain in the streets before them. The play is a blend of satire, family drama, magical realism and parable that derides both global and local responses to the pandemic while addressing the anxieties and dangers accompanying mass illness, trauma and death in the twenty-first-century Anthropocene. It tackles themes such as the relationship between Indian nationalism and authoritarianism, the vulnerability of the elderly, media hypocrisy, the exploitation of migrant workers and class inequality.

The play opens with Bijoy and Sulagna, who live with Sulagna's aged mother, and their servant Gopal, who is eventually eaten by a roaming jaguar while trying to deliver food to the couple. As Bijoy and Sulagna's marital dynamics become more vicious and vulgar, so does Sulagna's treatment of her mother. Sulagna labels her mother as 'anti-national' and views her as a burden. As punishment for taking off her mask to eat, Sulgana decides to kill her mother with rat poison.

At the play's climax, Corona comes to visit Bijoy in his home, where Bijoy hosts Corona with tea and snacks. The conversation between Corona and Bijoy moves from the abrogation of rights in Kashmir, to the degradation of human values, to human-caused environmental destruction. Corona warns that he will continue returning as a god as long as humans continue their violent anthropocentrism. Bijoy and Sulgana dismiss the warnings of the virus, and Sulgana shoots at the immortal Corona. However, the bullet ends up killing her son instead, who has just arrived after walking as a migrant from California back to Kolkata.

Love in Times of Corona imagines a Kolkata overtaken by pandemic and wild animals as families, governments and media fall apart. The play's tragic conclusion highlights human agency in its self-destruction and the destruction of the world. At the same time, the play's multimedia elements offer an immersive audience experience in which they are implicated in the brutality, vapidity and artificiality of the characters facing the end of the world. The play paints an image of the dissolution of community that was present long before Covid-19 – the fault-lines of which continue to be exposed in the aftermath of the height of the pandemic.

The Penitence (2016)

The second play in this section, *The Penitence*, takes the audience back to Gautam Buddha's *Mahaparinirvana* to examine the relationship between religion, violence and ethics in its historical contexts with contemporary relevance. Poststructuralist scholars have critiqued the rational subject presupposed by the Enlightenment and the liberal tradition which excludes all that is emotional and non-rational. The play is a poststructuralist critique of the premise that religious assiduity in terms of submission, docility and lack of agency does not symbolize agentic capacity and is hence not revolutionary. The text of the play talks strongly in favour of multiple ways in which religious members entail agency in living their faiths. Thus, religious faith in an institutional setting cannot be limited to an individual(istic) religious ethos. We rather need to locate religious acts in their politico-historical context to understand their full meaning which can enable us to study how religious performances of true belief are tainted by material and sociopolitical complexities.

This historical fiction play takes place during Gautam Buddha's *Mahaparinirvana*, or moving on to *Nirvana*. Devdatta, an old monk and cousin of Gautam Buddha, comes to ask forgiveness from Buddha. Devdatta asks Buddha's loyalists, Sariputra and Moudgalyayana, to see Buddha; however, they are unsure that Buddha will agree to meet Devdatta. The majority of *The Penitence* oscillates between flashbacks of young Devdatta and his conversation with Buddha's two followers. The play offers a critique of the contemporary tie between Indian politics and religion by situating religion in a specific political and historical moment while addressing the fine lines between reason and faith, criticism and peace, and allegiance and resistance.

Devdatta recounts his jealousy towards Sariputra and Moudgalyayana because Buddha paid more attention to them. The young Devdatta was also jealous of Buddha's popularity and influence amongst Buddhist clans. He plans to kill Buddha by convincing the other monks to rebel against their leader. Through a series of political manipulations, Devdatta is successful in convincing a prince to kill his father, one of Buddha's great supporters, while Devdatta kills Buddha. The plan, however, ultimately fails because Devdatta fails to kill Buddha or to even succeed Buddha during the prince's reign because he fails to garner the support of the *bhikkus*, or monks. The monks, too, reject him because he fails to live by the principles that he espouses.

After a series of flashbacks and philosophical conversations between the three characters, the play ends with the screaming Devdatta calling Buddha merciless and unkind because he does not allow Devdatta to go near him on his deathbed. Moudgalyayana cheers at Buddha's decision. Through the character Devdatta in *The Penitence*, Basu engages with the negative virtues that infuriate the soul, with the vices that prevent the liberation of the soul and the pride and ego that often get in the way of meaningful change. Buddha, the liberated soul, is able to overcome all plans set to kill, belittle, and overpower him by his enemies. The debate between rationality and faith, criticality and peace, allegiance and resistance keeps returning in the philosophical discourse of the play. The play reveals that religion is entangled with the violent, social and political.

Translator's notes

Mainak Banerjee

Love in Times of Corona (Bengali: *Coronar Dingulite Prem*) pinpoints the degradation of the environmental system as a pitfall of impurities created by humankind. The playwright uses figurative and contemporary language to draw metaphors and similes in the play. His staccato technique of writing adds tension and suspense all around the drama. The etymology challenges the digital dictatorship and algorithm of the modern, scientific era. I have kept the typical Bengali idioms and phrases to convey the taste of raw Bengali culture.

The Penitence (Pali: *Anusochna*) digs deep into evaluating the ethical limits of forgiveness of great souls like the Buddha himself. Basu experiments with Pali, the only official language of Buddhist literature, Tripitaka. The reason why I have used the same Pali and Sanskrit words in the translation is to retain the same fervour with which the playwright creates the slow-burning tension in *The Penitence*. The language used here is calm yet violent. Sanskrit blended with Pali phonetics looms heavily in the dialogues of the characters, creating an atmosphere of theocratic dominance. Therefore, the linguistic pattern in the play perfectly corroborates the dilemma of explicit vengeance over meek atonement.

Basu's immaculate grasp over his mother tongue has time and again put me in tough and unfathomable situations as a translator. I have made efforts to ensure that the 'original' resonates with the 'translation'. In my effort to excite global readers, I have tried to keep it simple to unfurl Basu's versatility in the context of Bengal and Bengali.

Love in Times of Corona

Bratya Basu

April 2020

Translated by Mainak Banerjee

Female characters: 3

Male characters: 8

Country of origin: India

Original performance date: The play was written after the onset of the pandemic. It has not been performed as yet.

Characters

Bijoy *(male)*
Sulagna *(female)*
Runu *(male)*
Newsreader *(male)*
Newsreader *(female)*
Himanka *(male)*
Tansen *(male)*
Azhar *(male)*
Chilka *(female)*
Gahin *(male)*
Corona *(male)*

Drawing room of a middle-class family. A table, sofa, etc. placed downstage. A high platform upstage, with a television frame on it. A PPE[1]*-clad* **Newsreader (female)** *is seen reading the news on television. A suffocating moan is heard in the background. The* **Newsreader** *continues to read.*

Newsreader (female) According to the latest reports, the total number of people alive in our country has come down to merely two *lakhs* thirty-five thousand. Only two *lakhs* thirty-five thousand people are surviving in all. Not a single person is now alive in Spain and Italy is entirely desolate. Currently, the number of survivors in America is a sheer six *lakhs* and in China it is only nine *lakhs*. Today one *crore* thirty-three *lakhs* people are reported to have died in our country thus far. Crows, kites and vultures are seen to be flying above each street. In every locality dogs, foxes and other ferocious animals are roaming around to devour the innumerable dead bodies strewn across the streets. Animals having fled from the zoo are roaring across each and every lane corner. Snakes too have slithered out of their dens to strike on dead bodies or hunt rats and moles eating the guts spilling out of corpses. Even the owls and bats are flying around in open daylight. Heaps of human carcasses are piling up on the city streets. Nobody except me is alive in our channel. Perhaps I am that last bona fide person alive who, failing to ignore the greater social responsibility, has stayed back in my office for the last three days amid huge numbers of dead bodies. I am reading out news for you, I mean, for the remaining few thousands of people. I am sure you all will remember my sense of responsibility, my dutifulness and my acumen in rendering public service till the last moment. If you ever get together for a party or function or you go to a gymnasium or attend a casual gathering in the future, aside from your usual slandering and gossiping, shed at least a few drops of tears in remembrance of my superhuman effort in delivering services to you. And at the time of remembering such a responsible, dutiful newsreader like me in such parties, may you dither at least once while enjoying your jokes and making cheap fun about others. I wish you freeze for a second when you raise a toast by clinking your glasses filled with rum mixed with Thums Up or whiskey and soda. For once, may the background track of Daler Mehendi, '*Tunuk tunuk tun, tunuk tunuk tun . . .*',[2] being played through the huge black amplifier, be replaced by Manna Dey's compassionate tune, '*Manush khun hole pore manushi tar bichar kore, neito khunir map, tabe keno payna bichar nihato golap . . .*',[3] or,

---

1 Personal protective equipment, recommended for protection from Covid-19.

2 A Punjabi song sung by Daler Mehendi (1967–) where the words, 'Tunuk tunuk tun . . .' signify the sound when the musical instrument tumbi from the Punjab region of India is played. Daler Mehendi is an Indian (from the region of Punjab) singer, songwriter, author and record producer. He has helped to make Bhangra and Indian pop music popular worldwide. He is best known for his dance songs, voice, turban and long, flowing robes.

3 A Bengali song sung by Manna Dey, with a literal translation being, 'When a man is murdered, he is adjudicated by another man with no leniency shown towards the murderer; why is then justice denied to the trampled rose.' Manna Dey (1919–2013) was an internationally acclaimed and celebrated Indian playback singer, music director and a musician. As a classical vocalist, he belonged to the Bhendibazaar Gharana and was trained under Ustad Aman Ali Khan.

say, replaced by the track of Kishore Kumar in his admonishing tone, '*Ami nei, ami nei, vabtei byathay byathay mon . . .*'[4]

With Kishore Kumar's song on her lips, the **Newsreader** *suddenly passes away. With lights out, the suffocating groan in the background intensifies. It continues for some time. Then enter* **Bijoy** *and* **Sulagna** *from two sides of the stage.* **Bijoy** *is around forty-five to fifty years of age and* **Sulagna** *around forty to forty-two. They both are wearing protective equipment that looks exactly like the one used by Jude Law's character Alan Krumwiede in Steven Soderbergh's film* Contagion. **Bijoy** *and* **Sulagna** *glance at each other with suspicion and doubt.* **Bijoy** *nods his head with a query in his eyes and* **Sulagna** *gestures at him.*

Bijoy No, I am still alive.

Sulagna Have you taken any food? (**Bijoy** *nods yes.*) When did you last eat?

Bijoy Day before yesterday, in the morning! A slice of bread and a boiled potato. I closed the kitchen door, lifted open my headgear a little. Then added the potato in boiling water, and warmed the bread in the microwave oven.

Sulagna Got it!

Bijoy When did you eat last?

Sulagna I don't remember. I have even forgotten when I had my last period or when I last went to the loo. I can't seem to recollect when I last changed my clothes even. I am confused about everything, the moments, the dates, the days! I can't seem to remember anything.

Bijoy Please eat something. Otherwise, how will you survive?

Sulagna I will think about it later. We have almost exhausted our stock of food.

Bijoy I know. Yesterday I tried to call Gopal, he didn't take my call.

Sulagna Gopal! Huh! Do you think he is still alive? I don't think so.

Bijoy When did your mother eat last?

Sulagna No idea! I am going to her room often. No, not to see how she is doing, just to ensure she has not taken her mask off. She has aged and is always reluctant to wear it continuously.

Bijoy Reluctant? Then let her die! How does it make a difference? Your mother has lived long enough!

---

4 A Bengali song sung by Kishore Kumar which translates as, 'I am nowhere . . . I no more exist . . . even this thought makes my soul heavy . . .' Kishore Kumar (1929–87) was an Indian playback singer and actor. He is widely regarded as one of the greatest and most dynamic singers in the history of Indian music. He was one of the most popular singers in the Indian film industry, notable for his yodelling and ability to sing songs in different voices.

Sulagna Thereafter I get infected by her! And then the infection spreads to you. Is this what you want? Height of intelligence, Bijoy!

Bijoy But we are still living, Sulagna. Very much alive! Possibly we are the lone survivors in the locality or in this apartment. This lane is clogged up with dead bodies.

Sulagna Yes, we are still alive! But Bijoy, I want to live for some more time. I am sure by June or July of next year things will definitely get better. Or possibly by the year after that. Or the following year. Will the situation not improve? What do you think?

Bijoy (*nods*) That's what I know!

Sulagna It has to. We will again go on a tour to Europe or to Kovalam. Runu will come all the way from the USA to join us in London and all three of us will holiday in a resort. You will book a car in advance and the next morning we will again take a serpentine, sloping road to reach another hill, or enter a forest. We will disembark from a colourful train to visit a small European town; sitting on the shore of a crystal-clear lake, we will be able to again enjoy the view of the sun, setting in the horizon. Won't we, Bijoy?

Bijoy Of course we will.

Sulagna Is Runu available over the phone? Have you tried to reach him again?

Bijoy No. At times the phone goes on ringing, at other times I am getting a message 'out of range'. I can't understand. I doubt if he is still alive!

Sulagna Stop talking nonsense! My son has to be alive.

Bijoy Even I wish the same! But is anyone even alive in California now? I am yet to get an update about them.

Sulagna If we still exist, Runu has to be alive too.

Bijoy Fine. I agree with you. But we have to live as well, so let us arrange for some food.

Sulagna Don't be obsessed with food! Can't you spend a month without eating? Just one month? Japan is claiming to have almost discovered the medicine. They will take about another month or so. And then we will be able to use the medicine to combat Corona.

Bijoy Who is going to discover this medicine? Who? In Japan, in all probability some twenty thousand people are alive. Among them, we don't even know who are the scientists or the doctors, we have no clue about who are the clerks or the thugs or the scammers. Who do you think will save us? Japan? America? China or Germany?

Sulagna Or Namibia? Or will it be Bahrain or Brazil? Which country? Who are those people?

Bijoy All are dying, Sulagna. The stench of the human cadavers is sweeping across the globe. So, never cheat yourself! You may rest assured that nobody is going to save us. Not a soul! Nobody will descend from Mars like Daniken or like a god or like a ghoul to inform us, 'Hey, here is your medicine – take it twice a day, once in the morning and again before going to bed for three consecutive days to be completely cured of Covid-19.'

Sulagna Ah, stop jabbering! I know it all.

A noise is heard outside. Both of them become alert. **Bijoy** *gestures to* **Sulagna** *to stay quiet. Then he takes out a revolver from his pocket and aims it towards the door. After some time* **Bijoy** *puts his revolver back in his pocket and takes out a pair of binoculars. He scans the outside with them.*

Sulagna Is the face mask obstructing your view?

Bijoy *shakes his head in the negative and takes his eyes off from the binoculars.*

Bijoy Gopal!

Sulagna Who?

Bijoy Gopal. He has brought food for us.

Sulagna Is Gopal still alive? Oh God, it is unthinkable! But don't allow him to enter the house.

Bijoy Am I crazy? Get him over the phone and enquire what food he is carrying for us.

Sulagna *takes out her mobile phone and tries to contact Gopal.*

Sulagna Let me see if the network is available. Yes, it is still available. (*Speaks to Gopal over the phone.*) Yes, Gopal, are you still alive? No. I mean, God forbid, of course you will live!

Bijoy I know these 'Gopals'[5] are immortal. They have exceptionally high immunity.

Sulagna Ah, keep quiet! (*Over phone.*) Yes, what have you brought for us, Gopal? Okay . . . Maggi, eggs, coffee – good! What about chicken? Have you got chicken or some corn and peas? Oh, you couldn't get cheese, right? All workers in the mall at the end of this lane have died. The freezers there must be stuffed with all kinds of food. Why didn't you pick up some from there? Yes . . . hello, speak up.

Bijoy These 'Gopals' are endless. These 'Gopals' are perpetual. These 'Gopals' are like, '*Ora kaj kare, Rajchatra bhenge pore, ranodonka shabdo nahi tole* . . .

---

5 This is a character in children's literature created by Ishwarchandra Vidyasagar (1820–91), a nineteenth-century social reformer in colonial India. Gopal is the prototype of a 'good boy' (against the 'bad boy' Rakhal) who can adjust to any situation and serve people at the cost of his own life without questioning anything. (Vidyasagar, Ishwarchandra. (1987). *Varnaparichaya*, Part-1. Kolkata: Benimadhav Sil's Library.) Sibaji Bandyopadhyay (*The Gopal–Rakhal Dialectic: Colonialism and Children's Literature in Bengal*, translated by Rani Ray and Nivedita Sen, Tulika Books, 2017) has shown how Vidyasagar has constructed 'black' and 'white' categories of 'good boy' and 'bad boy' which are then used as a pretext to morally define what constitutes 'goodness' and what does not constitute 'goodness'. Basu uses the prototype of the nineteenth-century 'Gopal' here.

Raktomakha astra hate jato rakto ankhi, shishupathya kahinite thake mukh dhaki. Ora kaj kare deshe deshantore.'[6]

Sulagna Uff, will you stop?

Bijoy '*Mole, molantore. Ovide, Covide, jhate jhatantore. Mari moroke.*'[7]

Sulagna (*over phone*) Are there no vegetables left? Is banana stem available or maybe banana blossom or some cabbages? Hello, Gopal, is lettuce available for making stew? Gopal? We need some milk and cornflakes for breakfast. Hello, Gopal.

Call gets disconnected.

I lost him. Anyway forget it! Let's take whatever he has brought. Take out the bamboo stick.

Bijoy (*moves to the upstage*) Twig, oh my sweet twig! '*Gopal oti subodh balok.*'[8]

He takes out a ten-foot-long stick from under the platform kept at the upstage. He hangs a cloth bag at one end. He holds the other end of the stick and extends it out to the right wing. **Sulagna** *helps him. After some time* **Bijoy** *pulls the twig and receives the stocked bag.* **Bijoy** *hands over the bag to* **Sulagna** *and puts the stick back in place.* **Sulagna** *sits on the sofa and takes out sealed packets from the bag.* **Bijoy** *sits besides* **Sulagna**. *He fiddles with the packets. Suddenly they hear the roar of a tiger outside.* **Bijoy** *quickly gets up and fixes his eyes on the binoculars.*

Bijoy Jaguar! It's a black jaguar! Oh, it has attacked Gopal!

Sulagna What the hell! And what is Gopal doing there?

Bijoy (*starts a running commentary*) It is a jet-black jaguar which was brought from Singapore to our zoo six months ago. It has set itself free and moved out of the zoo now.

Sulagna Oh, cut the crap! Tell me what happened to Gopal?

Bijoy The jaguar has gnawed at Gopal's neck and the neck dangles on one side of his shoulder. The jaguar has glistening capitalist teeth, which resemble a shopping mall and shine like a moonlit lake. The deadly swing of the jaguar's paws has split apart Gopal's surplus labour, his bloody hard work, his guts, his cough-bile-faeces – these are all splattered on the footpath outside our apartment. Sulagna, please get your synthesizer ready. Hey, civilian, let us hear a song accompanying this death, in this precious moment when a member of the proletariat has been murdered.

---

6 This is an excerpt from a poem by Rabindranath Tagore: 'Their toil they put down . . . Royal parasols crumb, the war trumpet goes dumb . . . With blood-stained sword in hand with their bloody look, They hide face in the children's lesson book. They work from the nation to outside.' Rabindranath Tagore (1861–1941) is best known as a poet, and in 1913 was the first non-European writer and the first lyricist to be awarded the Nobel Prize for Literature. He is referred to as the 'Bard of Bengal'.

7 This can be translated as, 'their toil they put down in a mall and beyond a mall . . . in *Ovid* and in Covid . . . in the udder and beyond udder . . . during plague and during pestilence.'

8 'Gopal is a very sensible boy.' Refer to footnote 5.

Sulagna *swiftly takes out her synthesizer.*

Sulagna Which tune should I play?

Bijoy You play any tune of Mozart or else play '*shala lut liya jaan*'.[9] Let your finger play the tune of the musical melody like a supernatural tyke.

Sulagna Should I play, '*Dost dost na raha*'?[10] Or '*jakhan porbe na mor payer chinho ei pothe.*?'[11]

Bijoy No, you better play '*ache dukkho ache mrityu*'.[12] Hurry up!

Sulagna Okay.

She plays the tune of 'ache dukkho ache mrityu' on her synthesizer. **Bijoy** *continues his running commentary in his weird outfit as he looks through his binoculars.*

Bijoy Now, the jaguar has torn Gopal's clothes, gloves and mask into pieces. It has split open Gopal's chest right at the centre with the help of its claws. Thus, another poor man breathes his last. Did he die because of communalism or because of starvation? Is he the victim of a multinational conspiracy or a prey to the biological warfare between states? Or has he died in his bid to provide us with a service? I don't know yet but I must find out. At this moment I can see Gopal's woody rib cage, hoops of bloody red flesh, his entrails and scabies-affected skin, all splattered on the road. The jaguar has just now broken open Gopal's skull with its mighty paw. It is thoroughly enjoying himself as he licks the brain flakes trickling down the edge of the broken skull onto the road. So, even as we watch Gopal's death, we don't actually know the updated figures of deaths in our country caused by Corona, or the number of deaths due to attacks by tigers, hyenas, vultures and jaguars. We require data, more and more data. Hey, television, please update us. Oh, learned Google, Facebook, Twitter, WhatsApp, Instagram, provide us with the latest data. Let our bodies be injected with bomb data which are being hurled at us; let these data be fired at us from sten guns; let them invade us like splinters; let the data be vomited all over our bodies from an ailing liver, from stale, bitter undigested foods. I want the news of Gopal's death right at this moment. Let his mutilated body be draped with the national flag immediately. Let there be several debates on Gopal right now. Let there be national mourning now. But before that, Sulagna, come, let us observe a 'one-minute silence' for our loyal attendant, Gopal.

Sulagna *stops playing her synthesizer. She comes forward. One-minute silence. Then* **Bijoy** *and* **Sulagna** *start howling together. The tune of Daler Mehendi's 'Bolo tara rara' accompanies them in the background.* **Bijoy** *and* **Sulagna** *start a vulgar dance while they continue to cry. The music stops in a while. They start panting. But they continue bewailing. A tune from a television channel is heard in the background. A*

---

9 Lyrics of a popular Hindi film song, 'he has bloody looted my life'.
10 Lyrics of a popular Hindi Bollywood song, 'A friend is no more a friend'.
11 Lyrics of a popular Bengali song, 'When there will remain no sign of my footprints on this path'.
12 Lyrics of a Bengali song written by Rabindranath Tagore, 'Woe and death both exist'.

Newsreader (male) *appears at the platform placed at the upstage.* **Bijoy** *and* **Sulagna** *raise their heads slowly. They wipe their tears while they listen.*

Newsreader (male) Perhaps today is my last day too. Yet, I came because I could not refrain myself from reading the news. Though everybody in my family, starting from my *Chotokaka* to my *Rangamasi*, advised me not to go out, I came here from my sense of sheer responsibility to read the news bulletin. Right at this moment, the number of survivors in our country has reduced to just one *lakh* ninety-nine thousand. The only silver lining in the catastrophe is that three out of these one *lakh* ninety-nine thousand survivors have completely recuperated. They have risen upright from the heaps of human carcasses and have returned home on their own. It is being reported that before they passed out on the road, all of them took the medicine prescribed by Dr Himanka Palchoudhury. As reported by our special correspondent, about thirty-three individuals are gradually recovering after taking Himanka Palchoudhury's medicines. Therefore, we have decided to first congratulate Dr Palchoudhury in the presence of all of you who are still alive. And thereafter we want to conduct a brief interview with him. We request Dr Palchoudhury to join us please.

Himanka Palchoudhury *enters with a crutch. His whole body is wrapped up with bandage.*

Newsreader (male) Doctor, please be seated.

He presents **Dr Palchoudhury** *with a bouquet of flowers.*

Himanka Thank you, thank you, all!

Newsreader (male) Why have you wrapped up your entire body with bandages?

Himanka This is my new invention. Besides using a mask, if you wrap bandages all over your body then all kinds of virus will lose their strength to infect. Let me explain it in a layman's language for your better understanding. Let's say, if there is a liquid deficiency in your blood along with a simultaneous growth in fats, the growth inhibition in blood circulation causes hypoglycemia in your pulmonary system. If this is accompanied by a cardiac thrombosis in your portal vein, you will notice that your left eyebrow has suddenly started twitching. This is the preliminary symptom. Then you will assume for sure that it is happening due to the secretion from your pituitary gland. But that is not the case. It is actually one kind of thyroxin counter of your carbohydrate or protein intake during this period. If you add a little bit of iodine, two teaspoons of honey, a half spoon of Dettol and small pieces of Heparin tablet to a glass of water and drink it at that time, you will see that not only has your left eyebrow stopped twitching, even symptoms related to exophthalmic goitre, etc. are all gone. Now if you cover your body with bandages, you will find that the thyroxin production in your body is blocked; you are slowly recovering from the symptoms of thermocytes or, say, from basic prognosis of diseases like polycythemia, blood-stool, scabies, ringworms . . . what our mothers and grandmothers used to refer to as expansion of spleen and ringworm . . . all these symptoms will gradually vanish too. You are neither having to take any medicine for this, nor will you have to visit any nursing home. Do you understand now?

Newsreader (male) Excellent! No doctor could have made us understand more simply than the way you explained. Well, Dr Palchoudhury, how did you manage to save a few patients by temporarily arresting the infection of the Corona virus?

Himanka There is a story behind it. Can I share the story with you?

Newsreader (male) Of course, sir.

Himanka Will I be able to complete my story in one go? I hope you will not be taking any commercial break in between.

Newsreader (male) You must be joking, sir! Where are those advertisers now? To have commercial breaks you need to have bookings for advertisements. Those advertisers are probably all dead. We are continuing our channel only on humanitarian grounds. Do you understand my point, sir? Therefore, there will be no break in our broadcast now. But of course, in between, we may receive some phone-ins for public interest. Yes, doctor, please go on with your story.

Himanka A few days ago, a few of my final-year students approached me. They were doing research on another topic. But I observed a few interesting elements in their research which helped me a lot in developing my new treatment.

Newsreader (male) What is that new element? Can you please share with our audience?

Himanka The new element is (*pause*) *Sen & Martin's Question Bank* and *Answer Series.*[13] I have studied these two books meticulously and these have helped me in controlling the multiplication of Corona virus, to some extent. So, *Sen & Martin's* contribution towards my success is truly undeniable.

Newsreader (male) Magnificent!

Bijoy *calls up the channel.*

Newsreader (male) There is a phone-in. If you allow me, please . . .

Himanka *gives the go-ahead.* The **Newsreader** *receives the call.*

Newsreader (male) Who is on the line please? Please identify yourself.

Bijoy I am Bijoy Adhya. I have a query. *Namaskar,* Doctor *babu*!

Newsreader (male) *Namaskar*! Many congratulations for staying alive, Bijoy *babu*!

Bijoy Yes, my wife Sulagna and I are still alive. Though I don't know how long we are going to live, but I have a long-cherished wish I want to share with you all.

Himanka Yes, tell us. Please tell us what is bothering you the most now – is it your swollen leg or a throbbing headache, do you have an irritating cough or water deposition in lungs? What is it?

---

13 The playwright here sarcastically refers to a popular set of Question Bank and Answers advertised on electronic media. They claim to help students score very high marks in the conventional and competitive examination system in secondary, higher secondary and higher education.

Bijoy Oh no, nothing of that sort! All that happened to me at an early stage, within the first two months of lockdown. By the sixth month, these symptoms subsided as well. By the eighth month, my wife and I started crawling right from the morning. We crawled across our house continuously for almost three months. We even got cured of this disease within a year. Thereafter, we started laughing continuously for the next twenty-one days in succession. We somehow managed to sleep for only two hours at night and then laughed and laughed for the rest of the day and night. Usually I guffawed and Sulagna giggled. This bout of laughing gradually subsided. By the twenty-sixth day, we stopped laughing too. Now, we are suffering from . . .

Himanka What are you suffering from? Stomach ache or nausea?

Bijoy Not really! As I mentioned to you earlier, all that happened to us in the earlier phase.

Newsreader (male) Then what happened to you? Please tell us.

Bijoy I find it embarrassing to share with you. Well, my wife will tell you.

He hands over the phone to **Sulagna**.

Himanka Oh dear! Why are you feeling embarrassed? You know, shame is all about some kind of synthesis of chlorpropamide and diguanylate. Shall I make it easier for you to understand? If you don't take a steroid regularly, with the help of albumin you can gradually analyse in your own way any inflammation or let's say secretion of durabolin hormones from the pituitary gland. Thereafter, you will never feel ashamed again. Do you get me?

Newsreader (male) How wonderful! Nobody could have explained it so easily. Anyway, yes, Mrs Addhya, please go ahead.

Sulagna (*over phone*) No, actually my husband is keen to perform before you. I mean some kind of singing or recitation or at least narrating an audio drama or a making a short film at home . . .

Newsreader (male) Just a minute, just a minute! You must be some celebrities, I presume! If yes, we will broadcast it right away. Please tell us what you wish to present before us. Do you wish to recite a poem?

Bijoy (*snatches the phone from* **Sulagna**) No, no, we are no celebrities. But if you broadcast our series of programmes on your channel for the next few days, then the remaining survivors, as long as they are not dying, can enjoy it. I mean they can even watch it while dying. Though I have my doubts whether watching me reciting or singing or dancing at a stretch the viewers will remain alive anymore. Yet, if you please allow me to present something!

Newsreader (male) No, hang on. But you are not bigwigs. What is your status from where you want to perform?

Sulagna (*snatches the phone back from* **Bijoy**) Well, forget about singing or reciting. What if I cook now? We have just received vegetables from the market. The delivery boy has actually . . . anyway forget it! If I send a video of me cooking to your channel, will you televise it? Let's say mutton liver fry or raw banana curry or, say, a famous dietician-prescribed double-egg hodgepodge? Can I send them please?

Newsreader (male) No, no . . . Mr Adhya, Mrs Adhya. Please listen to me. To get these televised you need to do something great in your life. It's useless studying hard to become a doctor-engineer-bureaucrat. Sorry, *bhai*, if you are not celebrities we cannot televise your extra-curricular activities. You better go and exercise in a gym with rapt attention for a few days.

Bijoy (*furious, snatches back the phone again from* **Sulagna**) Why should I go to the gym? Which gym should I go to? How strange! The teachers are dead, officers have expired, clerks have died, professors are dead, even politicians are dead, as if dieticians and *gymwallahs* are the only exception? How can you really talk so weird? Anyway, what if I move round and round and sing that song, the one from the cinema, '*Baba Taraknath*'?[14] '*Bhole baba par lagao, trishuldhari shakti jagao, bom bom tarak bom, bhole bom tarak bom.*'[15] I will sing while going around in a circle, won't it be possible to show my performance even then? Hello, please let me know. (*Changes the audio call to video mode and sings.*) *Bom Bom tarak Bom, bhole bom tarak bom* . . . Eh! Can't you see my biceps? Triceps? You, bloody advising me to go to the gym!

Newsreader *disconnects the line. Exasperated,* **Bijoy** *puts the mobile phone aside.*

Newsreader (male) Okay, Dr Palchoudhury, many, many thanks to you! You may please leave now. We will now move on to our special programme, '*Kaltala*'. But since most of our competition-addict, argumentative and malevolent citizens are currently dead, we will be inviting our non-resident Bengali guests from different countries to join us. Let me introduce them one by one. We have *Shri* Tansen Tripathi, present in our studio at Tanzania, *Shrimati* Chilka Chakladar is joining us from our Studio in Chile. We have Azhar Janam present in our Azerbaijan studio, and our fourth and the last guest is from distant Greenland, Gahin Gangota. We welcome you all.

Everybody is now visible. Each one of the guests are sitting at four different positions upstage. All are wearing masks. After everybody finishes their formal greetings, **Bijoy** *in disgust switches off the television with the remote. Upstage goes to black.* **Bijoy** *and* **Sulagna** *glance at each other. Sign of deep hatred in their eyes. They turn their faces away from each other. They murmur.*

Bijoy Huh! have to go to the gym . . . gym! As if I am 'Jack and *Gym* went up the hill'.

---

14 A very popular Bengali mythological film released in 1977 devoted to Lord Siva. Taraknath is another name for Lord Siva, the Hindu deity.

15 This is a devotional song in the Bengali film *Baba Taraknath*. It signifies a prayer to Lord Shiva such that the devotee attains salvation, and praying that the Lord helps to arouse the strength within the devotee.

Sulagna Why? It's rather good advice. You can jolly well go to a gym. I told you repeatedly to at least set up a small gym at home. You could have done lightweight lifting in the morning or at least twenty-five sit-ups.

Bijoy (*shrieks*) Stop talking rubbish! I will go to the gym! Gym! Eh! Have I been bitten by a cur that in these times of Corona, I have to work out from early in the morning? Do sit-ups . . . and '*Kapalvati*'! Bloody shit!

Sulagna Why not? Such a lazy bug you are!

Bijoy What! Am I a lazy bug?

Sulagna You . . . you are a lethargic cheat!

Bijoy Me? Am I lethargic?

Sulagna What else? Such a pot-bellied indolent you are!

Bijoy Me? Am I a good for nothing? Don't you know how big a corporate honcho I am? It is my tireless hard work and excruciating slogging that has earned our paint and cement industry a prestigious rank in the world.

Sulagna All trash! You have always shied away from work in your life. You reach your office by 10 in the morning, and delegate your job to someone or other. You then enjoy fanning around from Chandigarh to China or from Tarakeswar[16] to Tatarstan. You are basically very clever, apathetic and street smart.

Bijoy And what about you? You may be a school teacher but you are ultimately a highly irresponsible, violent and selfish person. Even Runu used to avoid you in his childhood. If anybody at all should be given credit for his growing up, it's me.

Sulagna Don't talk crap! Sitting idle at home, you have lost it completely. He is solely responsible for Runu's growing up . . . huhh.

Bijoy Who else but me? Have you ever looked after your son? After returning home from school, you used to enjoy going to my club[17] or you would love spending your time working on a travel plan – finalizing our summer tour location – Japan or Zanzibar. You didn't even take care of your mother. Invariably, after returning from the club in the evening, I had no option but to prepare a diluted stew for your mother's dinner.

Sulagna For my mother? Oh shit . . . *Maa*!

Bijoy (*stunned*) What happened?

Sulagna Not heard anything from *Maa* for a long time. Wait! Let me check! I hope she has not taken off her mask!

Bijoy Okay! Go inside and check on her once!

---

16 A town in the Indian state of West Bengal where the Tarakeswar temple of Lord Shiva is a popular tourist spot.
17 Club is a recreation place.

The suffocating tune that was heard in the beginning returns. **Sulagna** *goes inside. She returns after some time.* **Bijoy** *stares at her.* **Sulagna** *gestures and asks* **Bijoy** *to keep quiet. She takes out a big syringe from under the sofa and goes inside.* **Sulagna** *comes out of the room tired after some time. She sits down on the sofa. Music fades out.* **Bijoy** *comes and sits in front of* **Sulagna**. *He raises his eyebrows to understand what happened.*

Bijoy What happened?

Sulagna *shuts her eyes. Remains silent*

Bijoy Tell me what happened?

Sulagna *opens her eyes. Looks at* **Bijoy** *and then sways her head sideways.*

Bijoy What? I can't get you.

Sulagna Taking her mask off . . . she was having stale grapes, two days old!

Bijoy What do you mean?

Sulagna What don't you understand? I advised her repeatedly not to take the mask off. How dare she joke around at this age! She wouldn't budge! She took her mask off to have grapes.

Bijoy What happened then?

Sulagna (*shows him an injection syringe*) I had kept this injection filled with rat-killing poison. I gave her a shot.

Bijoy What do you mean?

Sulagna She was ninety-two. I have three elder sisters. None of them will bear her responsibility. How long can this go on?

Bijoy You mean to say. Oh dear, you murdered your own mother?

Sulagna (*reacts crazily*) Why did she take off her mask? Do you know the implications of taking off the mask? I warned her so many times not to take it off! Not to take it off! If needed, you can die without food, die from suffocation or even die having a nightmare but you cannot afford to take your mask off. Why don't they listen to our advice? They are the real anti-nationals. They are anti-institution and anti-*fatwa*. They cannot follow any rule properly.

Bijoy (*shouts*) '*Fatwa*'? Against what?

Sulagna I believe if the state has issued a directive to wear a mask during the Corona epidemic, you have to obey it. For that, you have to wear it in the toilet as well. Before holding someone's hand too you have to sanitize your hand first. Even if you wish to kiss someone, you have to first cover yourself with plastic from head to toe. We cannot afford to flout any rule. Nobody can do it! Whoever decides to go against rules, rat-killing poison has to be injected in their nerves or veins – it is compulsory.

Bijoy So, you killed her? You just killed my respected, esteemed mother-in-law? Alas, who will cook *Katla macher muro* on *jamai shasti* for me? Who will treat me?

Sulagna Fuck you and fuck your *Katla macher muro*! What a ravenous glutton you have become!

Bijoy I can't even imagine! How could you murder my mum-in-law? Who will now cook *kochipathar jhol* for me? Who will prepare hot *Tangra* fish soup with spring onions for me?

Sulagna Shut up, Bijoy! Don't act like a buffoon! How on earth can you be so fussy about food! Such voracity does not suit your age.

Bijoy Alas! Oh my *Chittohara Chital macher muithya*,[18] oh my *Shlokmakha Sholmulo*,[19] oh my *Iliushonbistari Alishan Bhapa Ilish*[20] – where are you all today?

Sulagna If you spell out one more word, I will give you a jab of this rat-killing injection. Just shut up!

Bijoy *stops talking. His eyes widen as he looks at* **Sulagna**.

Sulagna Just tell me whether you agree to follow a system? In times of crisis, will you not abide by the directives of an institution? Will you not give your concurrence to each and every *fatwa*? Tell me? Yes, speak up!

Bijoy (*sigh*) Yes, Sulagna. I will surely accept each and every *fatwa*. I will accept each of these suffocating moments and will tamely embrace every noose of these ropes. I am in favour of abiding by all the statutes, *fatwas* and injunctions issued in regard to this. Like an obedient student, like a faithful dog, like a loyal employee, I promise to obey all the rules and regulations and I will obey them till I live.

Sulagna Good!

Silence for sometime. **Bijoy** *loses his cool again.*

Bijoy Absurd! Impossible! How long will we escape this horrible contamination? How many days? Another two days? Five days? Seven days? How long will all kinds of caution, vigil, our attire like a joker, tip-toeing our way around save us? Impossible! Absolutely impossible! Hence, as long as I am going to live, I will live on my own terms. I will live in my own way.

Sulagna What do you mean by 'my own way'?

Bijoy I mean, as I wish! I wish to live like a reckless wanton or an irresponsible reveller. You know, even I feel like inserting my hand inside somebody's dress or abusing someone left and right, randomly on Facebook.

---

18 The playwright uses the term 'distressed' (*Chittohara*) to describe the Bengali delicacy, *Chital macher muithya* made of knife fish balls because his mother-in-law, who used to cook the dish for him, is no more.

19 A Bengali delicacy made with catfish and radish. The term '*shlokmakha*' literally means 'verse-wrapped'. The playwright uses the trend in India to give delicacies in restaurants stylish names which rhyme well with the name of the recipe.

20 A Bengali delicacy made of baked hilsa fish. The term '*iliushonbistari*' is used to illustrate the grand and illusory nature of this delicacy. The playwright rhymes the term with the dish to create a stylish name for the delicacy.

Sulagna So, this is what you mean by living 'my own way'?

Bijoy What else do you expect? Who do you think is doing his job silently here? Who is going deep inside a jungle or on a mountain top to meditate quietly? Who? Nobody. People are either panting or screaming. They are either becoming heroes or abusers or revellers. Why can't I enjoy the sizzling hot bod of a hot girl? Why can't I? Why!?

Sulagna Stop it, don't shout. (*Pause.*) It is because, on seeing you, girls either start making fun of you or they get scared of you!

Bijoy It is because I have evolved like this. And it is you who have made me such a person. On seeing me, girls either run away from me or they start smirking. This disappoints me and this is my sexual frustration. A carnal distress. And you know you are the one responsible for this!

Sulagna (*pouts her lips*) All rot! All baseless assertions!

Bijoy Then, please allow me once to become a reveller. How I wish I could throw ugly, nasty tirades at others in place of my diplomatic, polished corporate language. You give me your permission, Sulagna. I will open a fake Facebook profile today in the name of 'Badchalan BIJOY'.[21] Then in the name of politics, in the name of culture, in the name of social reform, I will accomplish several personal agendas. Let me satiate my red-hot jealousy, raw irritation and all my failures in this way. Please grant me your permission once so that I can open a fake profile. Please.

Sulagna Are you nuts? Now keep your mouth shut! We cannot keep *Maa*'s body unattended like this. Didn't we have a big plastic bag in our kitchen? Let me find that first.

Bijoy But how will you put the body inside the bag all on your own?

Sulagna Who is going to do it alone? What are you there for?

She goes inside. **Bijoy** *waits there for some time with a bored face. He then puts the TV on with the remote.* **Tansen** *is seen shouting on the channel.*

Tansen Muslims . . . these Muslims are responsible for spreading Corona worldwide. In Kuwait, Dubai, Saudi Arabia and even in Pakistan – you will see the Corona outbreak is much less compared with Europe or America. But Muslims are solely responsible for spreading it in India.

Azhar What an amazing logic! Muslims are being held responsible only in India, not in Kuwait or Saudi Arabia. Even China is not coming up with such a weird logic.

Tansen (*almost on his feet*) Once again you are making a counter-argument! You know, if I give you one tight slap under your ear, all your arguments will fall flat!

Azhar (*stands up too*) You will also feel the flak if I hit you hard with my shoes!

Chilka I have already told you, this is not the right way to judge it. Corona is primarily a fallout of ever-increasing cases of torture and rape against women around the world.

---

21 Literally in Hindi 'Bastard Bijoy'.

Gahin *whispers something in the ear of the* **Newsreader** *mockingly.* **Chilka** *gets irritated watching* **Gahin**.

Chilka I have been noticing that whenever I am trying to explain something, you are chuckling and whispering something to the anchor. Why this insult? One Me too case against you, you will learn a lesson! Actually, you don't even have the minimum understanding of when and how women feel offended. This is the reason why scientists believe that the Corona virus is masculine.

Gahin You cannot insult a *dalit* like this, madam. Corona has invaded our society because of elite atrocities. You all are responsible for this. Women's discourteousness and their vulgar outfits are responsible for the Corona outbreak in our society.

Chilka Conservative debauches like you are the reason behind the rise in violence against women. This is why there is an increase in Corona infections. It is you who are exclusively responsible for Corona's incarnation.

Tansen I strongly object to this statement. Corona has been dominating our country from the times we have failed to protect cows in the north-east. Because of cows, because of cows like us, I mean the human race is at risk owing to the general threat that cows face as a species. Not a single cow thinks about a man, I . . . I mean not a single human being is worried about a cow. The sacred cows of our country . . .

Gahin No, no, it's not about cows. You must not sidetrack the issue. Ever since Marxism has been imperilled in this world, the human species has been facing extinction. If the Soviet Union had survived till now, China wouldn't have grown so strong. Observing China's ever-increasing supremacy, America and the Soviet Union would have reconciled by this time, instead of indulging in a Cold War. Had the Soviet Union survived, we would have directly challenged China's capitalist authoritarianism.

Azhar Oh no! He now wants history to roll backward. Do you have any clue about history? Zionists have invited Corona in this world. The source of Corona is Israel. Corona has enjoyed backing from America, right from its onset. Let us destroy this Zionist Corona forever!

Chilka Only men are responsible for this.

Tansen Muslims are responsible.

Gahin China is responsible.

Azhar Israel is responsible.

Newsreader (male) Please hold on for a minute. There is a phone-in. You all please be quiet. Hello! Yes, please speak up, we can hear you. Hello . . . will you all please stop for a moment? Hello . . . yes, brother, go on.

Bijoy *is glued to the television.* **Sulagna***'s voice is heard, 'Can you hear me, come inside.'* **Bijoy** *goes out of the right wing. The debate continues behind them. The* **Newsreader** *tries to pacify them. Sometimes he says, 'Hello, hello.' Sometime later,*

Bijoy *and* **Sulagna** *are seen dragging a body packed inside a chained heavy leather bag. They are both panting. In between,* **Sulagna** *turns the TV off with the remote.*

Bijoy What will you do with the body?

Sulagna We will dump it in front of our house.

Bijoy In the open daylight?

Sulagna None of our neighbours are alive. So, no one will notice it.

Bijoy And then?

Sulagna I think the black ferocious jaguar must be hiding behind the milk depot.

Bijoy Behind the milk depot! Or is it hiding inside the ATM[22] counter?

Sulagna Wherever it be, it must be hiding nearby. On spotting the body, the jaguar will pounce on it and savour it.

Bijoy Are you sure?

Sulagna Absolutely sure!

Bijoy Let's throw the body out then.

They both drag the body. **Bijoy** *stops.*

Bijoy Just a minute! Wouldn't it be better if vultures finish the body?

Sulagna Why?

Bijoy Even the bones will not be left behind then. There will be no clue left. I am concerned in case there is any investigation in your name when the situation normalizes.

Sulagna There are enough kites and vultures in the sky. I saw a big eagle on the road that day. It perched right at the corner of our lane.

Bijoy Yes, kites and vultures are there in abundance. They can also eat the body. Not a single bone will then be left unfinished. Let's finish our job then.

They start dragging the jacket but stop again.

Sulagna Hold on! Let me check if anybody is waiting outside. You wait here.

She goes outside and then returns.

It seems the Maitys of plot no. 12 at the entrance of our lane are still alive. The old man comes to the balcony at this hour daily. If he sees us together, he may suspect foul play. Hang on . . . give me some time to think.

Bijoy You cannot manage it alone.

---

22 Automated teller machine for financial transactions at any time.

Sulagna Oh, don't talk rubbish! You stay back. I will see to it.

She drags the leather bag out of their house. **Bijoy** *waits. He too goes outside once but turns back soon. He wonders what he should do now. He picks up the TV remote and then keeps it. He sits on the sofa. A young man comes from inside and takes a seat on the sofa opposite to* **Bijoy**. **Bijoy** *looks alarmed. The young man is aged around twenty to twenty-five.*

Bijoy Hey, who are you? What is going on here? Where are you from?

Corona I just came from inside.

Bijoy What do you mean? Who are you?

Corona I . . . I am Corona.

Bijoy (*almost jumps from his seat*) What?

Corona Yes, I mean Corona. When your old mother-in-law took off her mask, I was standing beside her. She coughed a bit. She had one grape. But when I was thinking of attacking her, your wife entered. But she again went out of the room in the next moment. Your mother-in-law was still without the mask. I again thought of jumping on her. When I was dilly-dallying, your wife returned and pushed an injection into her mother's neck. Your mother-in-law expired while having grapes.

Bijoy (*voicing his objection*) Hey, please tell me seriously, who are you?

Corona Why don't you trust me? Okay, take that weighty headgear off your head once. You will then realize who I am!

Bijoy No, no . . . let it be. (*Calls out.*) Can you hear me, Corona has dropped by, please get some tea and snacks for him.

Corona She can't hear you now. By this time, she must have reached the security room behind your flat with the dead body. Perhaps she will dump the body there. I will not have tea. In fact, I don't take tea.

Bijoy *Bhai*, you are much younger than me. At least you appear to be so.

Corona *Dada*, I can't reveal my age, I am not supposed to. But you may always address me as your younger brother.

Bijoy Hmm! But I have a doubt, *bhai*.

Corona What kind of doubt?

Bijoy I hope you are not coming from the Coffee House,[23] *bhai*?

Corona What do you mean?

---

23 Indian Coffee House is a restaurant chain in India run by a series of worker co-operative societies. The branch of Indian Coffee House in the College Street of Kolkata was established in 1876. It has been a place for intellectual discussions and exchange of knowledge among poets, students, cultural activists and academicians.

Bijoy I mean, once upon a time I frequented there. I have a strong hunch that you are from the Coffee House. Your voice, your style of talking, your shimmering eyes . . . shimmering flame of what we call . . . ashy, smoky eyes, occasional gnawing of your teeth – all these attributes in you resemble a Coffee House frequenter. So, Coffee House, right?

Corona How can you presume such a strange lie?

Bijoy I have a feeling that you will start telling me right now, 'If a one-year lockdown is leaving you so devastated, think about the situation in Kashmir[24] once! How are the people of Kashmir staying there one year after the other . . .'

Corona Yes, Kashmir. Right you are. You can at least use WiFi, data-card facility in your phone here. And in Kashmir – what have you done there? Can you now relate to the state of mind of the common people there?

Bijoy Yes . . . absolutely . . . this is what I was trying to tell you. Now you will switch over from Kashmir issue to the moral crisis of human society. You will now enter into a thorough discussion about the moral degradation of human beings. Am I right?

Corona Are we humans anymore? With the progress of your civilization . . .

Bijoy *and* **Corona** Humanity is gradually obliterating. It can be better described as extinct.

Corona *stops.*

Bijoy Correct you are! You will say next, 'Human greed, their fiery jealousy, their ungratefulness, and mutual violence have gradually made me descend on earth.' (**Bijoy** *is imitating someone's voice.*) Now you don't seem to be talking about inter-state wars. There are no armoured vehicles visible on the borders. No arms deals are being done. Words like opportunity, shares, profits have been done away with for the time being.

Corona Petrified, you are now sitting inside your room with your heads down. Your glittery eyes, bright faces, sparkling teeth and shining chins appear stained. You all are growing beards as if you have taken a vow before a mother goddess.

Bijoy (*politely*) Hmm . . .

Corona You have asphyxiated your conscience, and completely disregarded the word 'friendship'. You have abandoned the issue of relationships deep down in the ocean and have laid 'values' to rest in the freezer of a morgue.

---

24 Kashmir is currently the northernmost Indian state and is part of the union territory Jammu and Kashmir. It had been given the temporary special status by the 1954 presidential order under Article 370 of the Indian Constitution, an order revoked in 2019. During the revoking of the special status, the Indian government had blocked the use of the internet and invoked a curfew across the state. This resulted in debates around the basic democratic rights of citizens stated in the Indian constitution.

Bijoy (*politely*) *Bhai* Corona, you must be associated with some NGO or is it some club? Or at least, with a group theatre? You have to raise some donations, right? For a relief fund? Where is your receipt book? Tell me how much donation you need, I will give. Anyway I am not going to survive for long. Tell me, how much donation do you need?

Corona Which subscription? What funds are you talking about? (*Roars.*) I am hidden within human greed, distress and in his unfailing sins –

Bijoy (*covers his ears with his palms*) Lower your voice! My nerves are extremely weak. Don't scream at the top of your voice. I come under serious pressure.

Corona Your endless boasting of power, your meaningless arrogance and sense of insolence towards all has invited me to enter your world of rice-pulse-milk-drugs. The moment you try to breathe, I will enter your lungs. If you shake hands with anybody, I will stick on your fingers. If you attempt to make love to a woman I will swarm your bodies entirely.

Bijoy Calm down. Stop this knavery. There is no woman present in this room who you can impress. Do you get it?

Corona Don't you feel ashamed that you are living like this? You are living like a worm, like an insect, like a piece of shit.

Bijoy Can I offer you a microphone? I think I have one little microphone in my music system.

Corona Where has your towering authority gone now? What about your conserved will? Your incalculable wealth? And what about your power to neatly insult everybody under the mask of desperately securing your self-dignity?

Bijoy My goodness! What strong language! Hey *bhai* Coffee House, will you stop?

Corona Mankind's heart-rending crouching, lustful ugliness, intractable upbraiding and the vice of lechery . . . these are all . . .

Bijoy (*yells at him*) Stop it! If you utter another word, I will shoot you.

Corona Ha, ha, ha! Are you threatening me with a gun? ME? Do you think I am like your octogenarian mother-in-law who you can kill whenever you wish? Hear me out, Bijoy Adhya. A lot of water will definitely flow through the rivers, be it the Ganges or the Thames. One day, in all probability you will also discover a vaccine to kill me. But remember, every time you invite a destruction within you, I will be reborn as a retribution of nature, time and again, in the form of an epidemic or a plague, on this taintless fairy earth.

Bijoy (*claps*) Wonderful! Magnificent! Unique! Now you have cleared all my doubts. You were a member of a Natya Company. Am I right, *bhai*? No, this year the *Jatra* season is not looking bright at all.

Sulagna *enters. She is shocked to see* **Corona**.

Sulagna What the hell is going on here! Who is he?

Bijoy Let me introduce you to him. He is Mr Corona.

Sulagna What?

Bijoy Oh dear, he is Corona. Corona, my *bhai*, don't stare at a woman obliquely. She is your respected *boudi*. You rather take her blessing by touching her feet.

Sulagna Hey, don't you dare touch my feet. (*Towards* **Bijoy**.) You have called this contract killer to murder me, right? He must be a hired killer?

Corona (*chuckles*) Can I once touch your feet, *didi*? Only once?

Sulagna What? Do you intend to touch my feet? You flippant brat!

Bijoy He is not only flippant but over-smart too. These polished brats are the ones undoubtedly responsible for our society's degradation. You rather go home, *bhai*, and spend time on Facebook. Go and 'troll' others. What will you gain by smirking unnecessarily at this hour of danger?

Sulagna I know he is a killer! A bloody killer! You hid him inside the room. The moment I went out you two were planning to murder me.

Bijoy Killer? Can these be slayers? My foot! They are the left-over Corona who have no faith in human labour. They are social trash, for them human achievements are no good. They disregard success by calling it a fluke, and look down on hard-earned achievements as cheap vegetables bought from the market. Do you have any idea about them Sulagna? You really think they can be killers? Do they at all have any sacred instinct desirable in a killer? They are an utter disgrace. They are products of new colonies – pretend to be all-knowing, but are actually shallow, over-smart and abusive clowns. If I had to murder you, I would have hired a better-quality element.

Corona Why aren't you believing me? I am actually Corona. Okay, take off your masks for once.

Sulagna No way! (*Rushes towards* **Bijoy** *and takes the revolver out from his pocket.*) Corona! Huh! Are you Corona? When the entire world is trying desperately to develop a vaccine to kill you, you sitting on our sofa and fooling around, looking fit like a *Jivegaja*! You rascal!

Corona (*bursts into a roaring laughter*) Are you going to shoot me? Ha, ha, ha! Really? Shoot me? Truly, Seleucus,[25] how bizarre can the human species be.

---

25 Seleucus was the son of Antiochus, a general of Philip II of Macedonia, the father of Alexander the Great. Seleucus participated in the conquest of the Persian empire as one of Alexander's officers, and in 326 BCE he commanded the Macedonian infantry against King Porus of India in battle on the Hydaspes River. The celebrated playwright Dwijendralal Roy of Bengal, in his play *Chandragupta*, made the Greek emperor Alexander speak to his trusted general Seleucus about the phantasmagorical complexities of the Indian subcontinent, 'Truly, Seleucus, what a strange country this is!' This referred to the contradictions where although India is celebrated for the quality of cultural pluralism, its history is simultaneously well known for its lies, deceit, greed, violence and narcissism.

Bijoy (*covers his ears with his hands*) *Bhai*, I don't think you have ever enacted the role of conscience! You are in fact behaving like a true villain number one. What an ugly smile!

Sulagna Disgusting!

Corona Hey, you both have been insulting me for a long time! Am I a flippant brat? Am I a reveller? Am I social garbage? And what about you? You all are worse than fat, greedy, giant rats – always digging holes to preserve your logistics of influential power for the upcoming winters. If I am an unwanted waste, you are filthy idiots with dirty, faecal greed and cruel selfishness sticking all over your body.

Sulagna Shut up. You murderer, contract killer.

Right at that moment their son **Runu** *enters.* **Sulagna** *fires from her revolver. The bullet hits* **Runu** *after piercing through* **Corona**. **Runu** *falls. Blood spills out of his mouth.*

Runu *Maa*!

Corona *chuckles, shrugging his shoulders.*

Corona Now you see the result! You will go on killing your next generation like this before you can develop a vaccine. This is how your greed, high aspirations and undeserving brutal demands will transform your descendants to mere corpses and the mound of countless carcasses will be seen lying across a vast, sky-kissing desolated land forever.

Pause.

Yes. I have surely heard a similar dialogue in some opera before. That evening I enjoyed jumping from one lung to the other thereby contaminating countless people. Okay, I will leave now.

Corona *leaves.* **Bijoy** *and* **Sulagna** *sit near* **Runu**. *They start wailing.* **Runu** *tries hard to say something.*

Runu Six months ago, during the lockdown I left my home in California. I thought of walking down home. I walked to reach Canada first. I found nobody at the border. All had died. Then I walked towards the north of Canada through Nome of Alaska in America, and reached Gambell, the last point of Russia's Arctic Circle. From there I entered Russia. Thereafter crossing Shoa, Mongolia, China and Bhutan I finally reached Siliguri. From there I walked back home. I witnessed so many deaths, plague and epidemic with nasty struggles for survival on my way home. There were tonnes of carcasses lying on the road like dead fish. In the Canadian desert an arrogant rattlesnake was out there to sting me but I managed to escape. A monstrous white bear in Russia would have almost killed me had I not hidden myself and fled. In China I was attacked by a ferocious pangolin but I ran away. In Bhutan leopards attacked me but I took shelter in a backyard of a tea-garden and spent three consecutive days and nights lying under the star-studded sky. *Maa*, I have been walking for the last six months to come to see you. Believe me, *Baba*, I got so tired, yet I never gave up. I ran with all my strength. At times it felt as if my heart would pop out of my mouth, but I still didn't stop, *Baba*. *Maa*, I have returned to you both outdoing the big clawed eagle and falcon whirring above my head; I also overcame the group of hyenas and the pack of wild dogs running by my side. It's been six months. And both of you? You?

He dies. Music is heard. **Bijoy** *and* **Sulagna** *weep inconsolably. They take off their headgear. They take* **Runu***'s head on their laps. Curtain is dropped.*

The End.

Glossary

Baba: Father
Bhai: Younger; brother
Boudi: Sister-in-law
Chital macher muithya: A Bengali delicacy made of knife fish balls
Chotkaka: The youngest uncle
Dada: Elder brother
Dalit: Dalits, also known as 'Untouchables', are members of the lowest social group in the Hindu caste system. The word 'Dalit' means 'oppressed' or 'broken' and is the name members of this group gave themselves in the 1930s
Didi: Elder sister
Babu: A term used to pay respect either as a prefix or suffix to the name or job profile.
Fatwa: An Islamic legal pronouncement that can be given by experts in religious law The *fatwa* aims to resolve an issue between two parties in accordance with Islamic law
Gymwallah: A person who is associated with a gym. The suffix 'wallah' suggests the person associated with the subject of its prefix or the owner or the person who deals with the subject
Jamai Shasti: Jamai means son-in-law, Shasti means sixth. This is a ritual celebrated by Bengalis on the 'sixth' day of the Bengali calendar's Jyestha month. This festival is dedicated to the son-in-law and celebrates the bond between the mother-in-law and her son-in-law
Jatra: A popular musical folk-theatre form of Bengali theatre. It is said to have originated from the rise of Bhakti Movements of Shri Chaitanya, a preacher of Lord Krishna's ideology
Jive Gaja: A traditional and popular Bengali sweet
Kaltala: The surrounding area (Bengali Tal) of a roadside faucet (Bengali, Kal) where free drinking water is distributed. In the city these areas are seen crowded with people standing in a queue and obviously there will be some disagreement or argument or fighting among the persons after some time. Hence the kind of chaos created adjacent to this area is jokingly compared with other events where uncontrollable drama and pandemonium takes place
Kapalbhati: Kapalabhati is an important breathing technique in yoga which is believed to have magical curative effects. It is intended mainly for cleaning the sinuses, known to remove toxins and other waste materials from the body. It also increases the metabolic rate and hence supports weight loss
Katla macher muro: A popular Bengali delicacy made with head of Catla fish.
Kochipathar jhol: A popular Bengali delicacy, lamb curry
Lac: *Lac* or *lakh* in Indian Rupees. Equivalent to 0.1 million
Maa: Mother
Maity: Bengali surname
Namaskar: Made up of the root words *namas* which means 'bowing or homage' and *kara*, meaning 'doing', *Namaskar* is a greeting, often accompanied by a hand gesture in which the palms are together, used in Indian and other Southeast Asian cultures

Natya Company: The word *nāṭya* is derived from '*naṭ*' meaning to move or to act. It is a presentation on the stage of a play. The company which organizes or conducts the same performance professionally is known as Natya Company in Bengali

Rangamasi: *Ranga* in Bengali means very good looking. *Masi* is aunt

Shri: Mr

Shrimati: Mrs often abbreviated as Smt

Tangra: A kind of fish also called the Gangetic Mystus or Mystus Tengara that is part of the catfish family

Thums Up: An Indian multinational brand of cola. The logo is a red thumbs-up

The Penitence

Bratya Basu

August 2016

Translated by Mainak Banerjee

Male characters: 14

Female characters: 1

Country of origin: India

Original performance: 26 January 2017 in Kolkata

Characters

Sudarshan *(male)*
Sariputra *(male)*
Moudgalyayana *(male)*
Old Devadatta *(male)*
Middle-aged Devadatta *(male)*
Young Devadatta *(male)*
Utpalabarna *(female)*
Ajatashatru *(male)*
Kokalik *(male)*
Samudradatta *(male)*
Revat *(male)*
Subhadra *(male)*
Kolit *(male)*
Dharmadatta *(male)*
Ananda *(male)*

Scene One

Location: Kushinagar. Outside a Buddhist Sangha. A gong is seen at the corner of the stage. **Sariputra** *and* **Moudgalyayana** *are standing behind a charpoy.* **Devadatta** *is lying on it in a recumbent position.* **Devadatta***'s* shishya **Sudarshan** *is standing in front of him.* **Sariputra** *and* **Moudgalyayana** *are silent. They are looking on the other side.* **Sudarshan** *begins the conversation.*

Sudarshan *Guru* Devadatta, my mentor, is in a state of extreme penitence. His remorse is tearing him apart from within. He is well aware of the fact that his days are numbered on earth. So, he is feeling genuinely apologetic for his past malfeasance. He is now craving to meet Lord Buddha once, only once. Respected *shishya* Sariputra and respected *shishya* Moudgalyayana, please be merciful on him! Kindly make some arrangement for *Guru* Devadatta to meet Lord Buddha once.

Silence.

Sariputra Hey, *bhikkhu*, dear *shishya* Sudarshan, you must be aware that true friends and kinsmen are those whose association brings warmth in a relationship and who do not disown their dear ones at the time of any predicament. *Bhikkhu* Devadatta was a cousin of Buddha and Yashodhara's son.

Moudgalyayana Nevertheless, he is indebted to Buddha. You must clear the air, Sariputra. Talk straight! Devadatta acquired a reputable stratum in society with the help of Lord *Tathagata*'s kind blessings. Despite this, he continued to feel jealous of our Lord throughout his life.

Sudarshan *Bhante* Moudgalyayana, *Bhikkhu* Devadatta is now facing death. A deadly disease has taken control over his body. Before the great Lord Buddha passes into *Mahaparinirvana*, *Bhikkhu* Devadatta is keen to see him once. Is it not possible to meet him even once?

Sariputra *Shishya* Sudarshan, three months ago at Vaishali[1], Lord Amitabha had declared that at the third hour of tonight in the month of *Magh*, when the full moon is on the sky, he would leave his body [*deha tyag*],[2] Yesterday in the afternoon when the sun was tilting towards the west, we, the chief *Bhikkhus* from all monasteries, have arrived here in this small city named Kushinagar.

Moudgalyayana *Abhuso* Ananda had said, 'The city, Kushinagar is small, just like the stem of a large tree. This small city is not a suitable place to host the congregation for the *Mahaparinirvana* of our great Lord. Your lordship *Tathagata*, if at all you wish to leave the material world, the most suitable of all places would be either the palace of Shravasti or Champa. We request you to choose one of those.'

---

1 Vaishali was an ancient city in present day Bihar, India. Here, Gautama Buddha preached his last sermon before his death in *c*. 483 BCE.

2 In Buddhism, the term '*deha tyag*' (lit. translation, 'leave the body') is used to imply that the soul/spirit is eternal but the body is transient. Death can be a liberation from the cycle of birth, death and rebirth. This depends on the kinds of good or evil actions or karma performed by an individual in this life or previous lives.

Sariputra Yet, Lord Buddha has selected Kushinagar as a desirable spot for his final departure because this remarkable city was a renowned and abounding place in ancient times. This land is the repository of the finest resources. So, tonight at the third hour, he will begin his heavenly journey. At this hour, placing a proposal before our Lord Buddha about *Bhikkhu* Devadatta's desire to see him once is almost impossible, Sudarshan.

Moudgalyayana Moreover, after the reckless behaviour of *Bhikkhu* Devadatta towards our Lord Buddha, with the wrath that his endless conspiracies and resentments have spewed on our benevolent master throughout his life, it is most unlikely that Lord Buddha will meet him at this hour.

Silence. **Old Devadatta** *struggles to somehow get up from his charpoy.*

Old Devadatta Hey, *Thera* Moudgalyayana, hey, *Thera* Sariputra, it is well known that the consequences of this-worldly actions are in the hands of the divine.[3] So, I don't expect returns for what I have done anymore. All I can say now is that the twigs of remorse are not like other feelings. Appraising the magnanimity of *Prabhu* Buddha's virtues is beyond me. It is like the impossibility of measuring the enormity of sea using water reservoirs. But I am also approaching death. Will our god of compassion still deny meeting me even once?

Theri Utpalabarna *comes out of the monastery and stands in front of* **Devadatta**.

Utpalabarna No, *Bhikkhu* Devadatta, you cannot meet Lord Buddha. Today is the day of his *Mahaprayana*. He has decided to deliver his religious sermon to the *Malla* Princes of Kushinagar at the first hour of night. Before that the Lord of Mercy is now meditating. Therefore, please give up on your idea of meeting him.

Old Devadatta Oh, *Theri* Utpalabarna, please have mercy on me. I have heard that your ravishing beauty was the reason for your father's apprehension that if he offered you [in marriage] to any prince or a qualified man, the other aspirants, blinded by envy, might bring harm to you and your father. So, he thought that if you accepted the *Bhikkhuni dharma* the issue could be resolved at its root. He had sought your opinion about accepting the vocation of a *Bhikkhuni*.

Utpalabarna True. But, *Bhikkhu* Devadatta, well before my father approached me, I had emotionally prepared myself. As a matter of fact, I knew that if I had an aspiration in life at all, it was to become a member of the *Bhikkhuni Sangha*. If I had any cherished desire, it was only to follow the path shown by Lord *Tathagata*.

Old Devadatta I am aware of it, *Theri*. But what I intend to say is different. I wish to explain that the only vice on earth that your father was thoroughly aware about was envy and its ill-effect.

Sariputra *Bhikkhu* Devadatta, this is not unknown to any wise man or householder. The only difference is that the wise man, being fully aware of its nature, can overcome jealousy while an honest householder cannot. He can only become fearful about this.

---

3 *Fol devayotto*.

Moudgalyayana The fear of *Theri* Utpalabarna's father was thus never illogical.

Utpalabarna No. Wait please. I think *Bhikkhu* Devadatta is hinting at something else.

Old Devadatta Right you are, *Theri*. I mean to say that envy is a true reality. Just like lust, anger, infatuation and intoxication. All men are not wise. Despite knowing that overcoming vices is the eternal philosophy of mankind, not everybody is capable of existing in the higher level. I have been obsessively vulnerable to the clutches of the mammoth, real and unimpeded vice of jealousy. I was swept away by its negative and infectious rage which bred extreme hatred within me. Of course there was a reason behind it.

Utpalabarna Reason? What could be the reason behind it? His highness's heavenly charm? His actions and practices? Or was it his worldwide fame? Or if you think it was something else, please elaborate.

Old Devadatta Sure, *Theri*. You know I am the blood-brother of Yashodhara, Buddha is therefore my cousin. Consequently, I was certain about my superiority in the *Sangha* over Buddha's disciples Sariputra and Moudgalyayana. But my belief was mistaken. I observed they were enjoying a better standing than me in the Sangha. This lit up a caustic fire within me, *Theri*. I wondered whether my competence was even less than theirs. Was I even more inferior than them?

Sariputra *Bhikkhu*, please don't get perturbed.

Old Devadatta No, *Ther* Sariputra, please allow me to explain. I was aware that in respect of humanity *Ther* Sariputra was superior to me, and *Ther* Moudgalyayan surpassed me in terms of his potential for labour. But I believed that my strength lay in possessing the blended potential of both these qualities. So, then? I realized later, *Theri* Utpalabarna, that humanity devoid of diligence was of no real worth and compassionless labour was undoubtedly useless. That I was lacking in both these virtues immediately caught the attention of the intelligent genius named Buddha.

Moudgalyayana Then that must have been the end to all problems. Your enlightenment must have opened the door to your logical self.

Old Devadatta Yes it happened, but much later. *Ther* Sariputra, *Ther* Moudgalyayana, at that time logic was not driving me. Instead, I was overwhelmingly pained by the realization that my childhood friend Buddhadeb believed that my level of work, competence, assiduity and talent was inferior to that of my compatriots. The audacity of his classification was enraging me. The snobbishness of his deliberation was wounding me deep within as I experienced vengeance and an inferiority complex at the same time.

Moudgalyayana That is when you sought the help of Prince Ajatashatru. Am I right, *Bhikkhu* Devadatta?

Old Devadatta Prince. Prince Ajatashatru. Exactly. He was, I don't know why, loyal to me from his infancy. And right from his childhood his relationship with his father was that of conflict. That is, he grew up opposing *Maharaja* Bimbisara.

Prince Ajatashatru *is seen stage right. A sword is hanging from his waist.* **Young Devadatta** *is seen standing beside him. Music is played. Other characters disappear from the scene. Both of them are on the corner of a palace.*

Young Devadatta *Vatsa* Ajatashatru!

Ajatashatru Order me, *Prabhu.*

Young Devadatta Don't you want to annihilate the hypocrite Buddhadeb? Don't you think the unstinted generosity that King Bimbisara has showered upon Buddha is absolutely needless? Had any less intelligent person received such favours, even he would have reached the apogee of his fame. Don't you feel so?

Ajatashatru Yes I do, *Prabhu.* I think a person who empathizes with other's pain, one who remains composed even after being emotionally torn, and who gets really weary of waiting for the right time for his own rise – actually he is like sugar cane. Now if this sugar cane becomes an outcaste amid adversity and cannot grow, is the sugar cane to blame or is it the fault of the scorching desert?

Young Devadatta Your father, King Bimbisara, is that arid desert. His obsessive love for Buddha has made him absolutely indifferent to his son's prosperity. One's life becomes blessed when he does not have to pay regular visits to a rich man's house, and he does not have to bear the pain of estrangement, and when the term helplessness too is absolutely absent in his life. Buddha's mortal life has been adorned by none other than King Bimbisara. These three hindrances have never worn him out. So, he has been able to effortlessly theorise his defunct and useless philosophy.

Ajatashatru Moreover, he is so dazzled in awe of Buddha that when my mother Khema, inspired by the divine Buddha, decided to sacrifice her domestic life to embrace the life of a *Bhikkhuni* and sought my father's permission to embrace *Pabbajja*, my father consented happily! *Acharya* Devadatta, I am myself a witness to this incident. Whereas my mother, Queen Khema, had all along avoided Buddha before that.

Young Devadatta It was quite natural. She had heard that finding imperfection in beauty was Buddha's nature. But *Maharani*'s glamour was celebrated across the world. And the same *Maharani* Khema, after getting a glimpse of Buddha, informed your father that she will either embrace the life of a *Bhikkhuni*, or else pursue *nirvana.*

Ajatashatru The day is still clear in my memory. After visiting *Benubana*, *Maa* returned to *Andarmahal*. That day she met the hypocrite Buddha for the first time. After coming back to the palace, when she encountered my father, oh *Acharya* Devadatta, I noticed for the first time, yes for the first time, that my mother did not pay obeisance to my father by offering *pranam.*[4] For the first time in her life. My father guessed that *Maa* had achieved her cherished . . . what is it called . . . yes, *Arhata. Arhata!!* Ahhh . . .! In a wink – the palace, her husband and her son –

4 The ritual of paying respect to a respectable individual by lying face down on the ground with arms outstretched towards their feet.

everything seemed untrue. Nevertheless, my father, my well-sighted and yet blinded father, enquired of my mother whether she had been blessed to earn Buddha's *darshan*. My mother, my only support, my *maa*, confirmed that she had seen the fraud Buddha not with her eyes but through her heart and soul. She explained that Buddha's *darshan* was infinitely superior to King Bimbisara's vision.

Young Devadatta I know, *Vatsa*. The next day, *Maharani* Khema completed the rituals of *Upasampada* to attain the faculty of *Bhikkhuni*. King Bimbisara ceremoniously sent your mother to Buddha, to the so-called *Bhikkhuni Sangha*.

Ajatashatru That fellow Buddha is not just a hypocrite but he is indeed a licentious individual. A woman is nothing but a bowl of *Ghrita* for him, and he himself is burning coal. If my father was a prudent man, he would never have allowed *Ghrita* to be placed near burning coal. King Bimbisara can never be pardoned, especially for this crime of his. At least I won't be able to forgive him ever in my lifetime.

Young Devadatta *Vatsa*, you kill Bimbisara. Thereafter I will kill Buddha. You are the best suited to find a place in the king's court of law and I am worthy of the rank of *Sangha*-Chief. A broken crystal sphere can never be mended, *Vatsa*. You have become emotionally detached from your father. Moreover, who does not accept the ephemeral moments of cloud shadow, devil-attraction, woman's youth and fresh crops. Their glamour is bound to culminate. Buddha's glory in this state is a matter of the past. *Vatsa*, just like a crystal-less crown does not exist, similarly action without authority can never be successful. Never ever!

Ajatashatru *Acharya*, what you are saying is correct.

Young Devadatta Can a person freezing in the winters ever get relief through moon rays? Can sunlight be dear to one drenched in sweat? So, how can you reach your goal without killing, *Vatsa* Ajatashatru? Moreover, forgiving a friend or a foe is a divine act of a saint. But, being a prince, if you show such a lenient virtue to your father, you will be committing a grievous sin. *Vatsa*, who does not know that a merciful king should definitely be repudiated just like an omnivorous Brahmin, an obstinate wife, an evil associate, an arrogant servant and an indifferent employee. King Bimbisara is infected by a disease named 'mercy', which can be an adornment of a saint, but never of a king.

Ajatashatru But he is acknowledged and appraised as a mighty king by the people. What if something 'untoward' happens in the state after his assassination, *Acharya*? Will we be able to cope with that?

Young Devadatta Nothing 'untoward' will happen, my child. A collective is the sum total of individuals. Their focus is individual self-interest, they do not put in their efforts to prioritize collective interest. They are fully aware that the big upright trees are uprooted during a severe storm, not the grassy herbs. So, believe me when I say this, *Vatsa*, the time is ripe for you to let the storm within you gather steam. The townsmen will soon be busy enjoying and merry-making in the forthcoming *Basantotsava*. This is the perfect opportunity to assassinate King Bimbisara, *Vatsa*.

Sound of heavy storm. Stops. When lights go on, we see the Bhikkhu Sangha at Kushinagar. **Utpalabarna** *speaks.* **Old Devadatta** *is seen with her.*

Utpalabarna Thereafter, Ajatashatru murdered Bimbisara during the festival. Am I right?

Old Devadatta *nods in agreement. Music is heard. Upstage Ajatashatru is seen to kill Bimbisara. Music fades out in sometime. Bhikkhu Sangha is seen again.* **Old Devadatta** *speaks.*

Old Devadatta The son killed the father. Ajatashatru occupied the throne and I became the chief counsellor.

Ajatashatru *and* **Young Devadatta** *appear again upstage.*

Old Devadatta It went exactly the way I had planned. By the grace of king, I decided to take control over the *Sangha*. I noticed that Sariputra, Moudgalyayan and Ananda outrightly defied the king and his power; they disregarded their self-interests as well. The solitary influence on them was that of Buddha. They only recognized Buddha.

Ajatashatru *speaks upstage.* **Young Devadatta** *stands with him.*

Ajatashatru The bunch of fools! The imbecile *Bhikkhus*! They are still unable to comprehend that Bimbisara is no more their king. I am the emperor now. Hence if *Sangha* does not obey my nominated representative, they will get no financial support of the state treasury. Such a big institution with innumerable members! How will the *Bhikkhu Sangha* manage to gather resources for all their expenditures?

Young Devadatta I am sure they also realize that. Yet they are of the opinion that in times of need they will beg alms to run the institution. They would rather lead an austere life than sacrifice the path and ideology of Buddha.

Ajatashatru What a ridiculous and audacious bunch of *Bhikkhus* they are! Don't they realize that the course of a society, nation and its politics is dependent on the present moment. The 'past' is not relevant in politics. Those who do not realize the value of the present moment of time are brainless idiots. The ones who trivialize royal favours will have to remain penniless forever. Even the wife of a pauper disowns him. How do they expect to run the *Sangha* without seeking help from the royal state? Impossible!

Young Devadatta Your honour, they consider Buddha as their final path to fulfilment. He is their ultimate support. They don't understand, *shastra*. They are unable to perceive that youth, monetary assets, intimate alliances and *Gurus'* advice is all in fact transient. During travel, a wayfarer takes rest under the shadow of a tree and then resumes his journey. So is the meeting between a master and his disciple in this world. River water always flows ahead. It never retracts its path. *Gurus* are changeable, it is crucial to opt for a new *Guru* – this bunch of fools do not even understand this proclamation.

Ajatashatru Then what is the way out? You have to grab that position by any means, *Acharya*. None but you can take control of the *Bhikkhu Sangha*. Otherwise, how will I establish my absolute authority over the empire?

Young Devadatta I have thought of an alternative. Hey, King of Kings, Ajatashatru, when the first seed of a human foetus appears in a mother's womb, his rhythmic and vivid journey towards death begins right at that very moment. Lord Buddha has sermonized that skin, nerves, fat, blood, bones, muscles, hair, etc. are constitutive unholy elements of the human body. It is therefore important to let oneself evolve beyond the human body to get the taste of barrenness in life. Hey, master, today I have therefore decided to bestow upon him a similar experience.

Ajatashatru What is that!

Young Devadatta What does that mean? (*Calls out.*) Shishya Kokalik.

Disciple of **Devadatta**, **Kokalik** *appears.*

Young Devadatta Emperor, please be informed that he is Kokalik. He is a *Bhikkhu* of the *Sangha* but my ardent follower. Kokalik is among the few in the *Sangha* who believes in Devadatta's superiority, not of Buddha. I have therefore entrusted him with this extremely crucial responsibility. Kokalik, explain your plan of action before the King Ajatashatru. Place your proposal without any fear.

Kokalik Respected King, we are a handful, we are a minority in the *Sangha*, but we all wish to see Buddha destroyed. We want him dead. Only his death can transform our lives from ignorant darkness to enlightenment.

Ajatashatru Even I wish the same. Tell me how you intend to eliminate him. But you have to be very careful. Buddha's death can lead to unrest in the kingdom. So, you have to execute this silently and secretly.

Kokalik That is how we have planned *Aryashreshtha*. (*Pause.*) My lord, I have hired an anonymous archer from Champa who has a record of hitting each of his targets unerringly. The tip of his arrowheads is smeared with the deadly venom of the poisonous cobra. According to records, this archer has never missed his targets even once in his lifetime. His services are expensive. We had to spend a huge amount of money to finalize the contract with him.

Young Devadatta Ah! King Ajatashatru will take care of the costs. Kokalik, you better describe the rest of your plan to the king.

Kokalik Tomorrow is *Baishakhi Purnima*. On this day, Buddha visits *Jetavana* at dawn, all alone. He sits under *Bodhidruma* to meditate. He does not even allow any *Sramana* to accompany him during this visit. It is supposedly at some *Brahma Muhurta* on this day that *Bodhisattva* had attained *Asavakshyaya*. An attainment that permanently cleanses the human mind from vices like greed, anger, obsession. So, on every full moon night of *Baishakhi*, a special seating arrangement is made under the tree *Bodhidruma* for Buddha to meditate. He will go there tomorrow again. Definitely. As he begins his solitary journey towards *Jetavana* at *Brahma Muhurta*, our mystic, anonymous archer from *Champa* will follow him throughout – bending his body forward like a coil, hiding behind the rows of *Jambu* trees, stealthily moving like a worm through the leaves of the *Betas* tree. Buddha will take his seat for meditation. The archer will also bend and sit in the shadow of a nearby tree. The assassin will pull his bow string made of strands of deer skin backwards and drag his unbent arrow till his ear before he releases it. The arrow will penetrate the bare chest of the hypocrite Buddha, immersed in meditation, and thus pierce his heart. Ha . . . We will also accomplish our long cherished, coveted goal. Hey, King, this is our strategy. *Tathagata* will finally get killed at the hands of young *Bhikkhus*.

Everybody disappears. The mystic archer of **Champa** *is seen alone. He comes downstage and sits with his back to the audience. He is carrying the arrow cover on his shoulder. Has the deer-bow in his hand. He pulls out an arrow from the case, fits it with his bow and pulls it. The shadow of meditative Buddha is seen on the cyclorama. Music is heard. Curtain is dropped.*

Interval.

Scene Two

Curtain goes up with a heavy tune of music. The Bhikkhu Sangha of Kushinagar appears. **Old Devadatta, Sudarshan, Sariputra, Moudgalyayana** *and* **Theri Utpalabarna** *are present. Music subsides. Silence. A sound emanates from a gong.* **Sudarshan** *breaks the silence.*

Sudarshan Everybody knows that when the secret assassin looked through the bow sight, he had aimed the arrow on the meditative Buddha. As the rising Sun dispersed its red glow onto the luminous white dawn, the assassin, under the lightning-struck blue sky, experienced a sudden tremor within. He felt, what was he about to do? Suddenly, *Tathagata*'s meditation got interrupted and he too saw the secret killer. Amitava smiled gently at the slayer, and the weapon slipped and fell from the archer's hand. Buddha realized that he too was like Angulimala,[5] who had attained *Arhata* in a flash. Buddha said, 'Dear assassin, my dear murderer, I will never again be reborn in the cycle of mortal life. But you are yet to step into the stage of last birth and hence still in the race. You are dynamic in the wheel-of-life.' On hearing this, the assassin fell on his feet. Buddha granted him disciplehood and took him to the monastery of Jetavana.

Silence. **Old Devadatta** *takes a seat on the charpoy. Seems abstracted.*

Old Devadatta *Sangha.* My *Sangha.* I have grown up here. I can still hear the floating sound of the ringing bell from the balcony, rows of bare compartments – a long and narrow balcony connecting all the rooms in the front, equidistantly placed faucets, corridors, arches, *chaitya*, *stupa*, all enclosed by a big vertical wall – Oh, my *Sangha*. When I grew up, I expected to achieve my due rank. In my conscience, I always compared myself with Buddha. Where did Buddha fare better than me? Why are the number of his disciples greater than mine? Is it due to his profound outreach or because of his polite behaviour? What was making such a difference? I did not understand. Is it due to his knowledge? But I do have the power of imagination which is superior to knowledge. So, what is it? Is it his intellect? Wisdom? But intellect is an

---

5 Angulimala was a murderer who supposedly lived during the times of Buddha. He was known to wear a garland (*mala*) of fingers (*anguli*) that he severed from his victims. After an encounter with Buddha, he became an *arhat*.

abstraction, and so is wisdom. Again, who does not know that human society has failed to distinguish between wisdom and cleverness until now. Moreover, when it comes to kicking up controversies and generating disputes, Buddha is a novice in my comparison. In matters of oratory skills, Buddha himself admitted that noise was a cause of major disturbance for a fatigued and resting individual. Also, controversy was a big deterrent for a spiritually awakened person.

Moudgalyayana How does it make a difference? This was well explained by our Lord at the end of the first round of meditation. He reminded us that on mastering this quality, the mind would reach a stage where it will be free from debates and judgements; instead the power of concentration of the mind will result in joy, tranquility, and content.

Old Devadatta Ah ha! What does this imply? This suggests that Buddha does not want to face any dispute. He is against debates. Therefore, he does not believe in logic and reasoning. So, he maintains silence when I question him.

Sariputra *Bhikkhu* Devadatta, you are . . .

Old Devadatta Ah ha! That was what I used to think. I used to construct a kind of logic in my mind. What else! Otherwise, how would I prove my authenticity to myself, Sariputra? How would I prove my supremacy over Buddha from my heart within? So, when the undercover archer also surrendered meekly before our Lord, claws of vengeance tore me apart. I again called on Kokalik –

Young Devadatta *and* **Kokalik** *appear.*

Kokalik *Acharya*, there is news for you. Tomorrow Buddha will travel from *Baishali* to the palace. He will be accompanied by several *Sramanas* of the *Sangha*. They will have to cross two hillocks on their way. When Buddha will cross the first one to ascend the second hillock, there is a mountain pass in between. We will hide behind the top of the second hill prior to his arrival. We will have a huge and heavy rock ready for him. The moment Buddha reaches the mountain pass, we will push the rock downhill, aiming at him. A heavy clanging sound of the rolling rock will reverberate around the hill. Chrrrr . . . chrrrr. The rock will roll downward toppling over grassy land and stony path of the inclined plane. It will directly land on Buddha's head. His head will get crushed under the rock. On the desolate, secluded valley will lie the tall, majestic body of Buddha covered in his loincloth, completely unaided. Let us go, my Lord. The sun is about to set. Let us begin our journey right away. Then we will be able to reach our destination before dawn.

Young Devadatta *and* **Kokalik** *leave. Theri* **Utpalabarna** *speaks.*

Utpalabarna And you failed to carry out this plan too, right?

Old Devadatta Yes. The huge rock we had gathered to hit our target broke down into a thousand small pieces right in front of our eyes. At that point of time, Buddha was crossing the mountain pass. Unscathed, he traversed the path conveniently. He was followed by innumerous *Sramanas*. Kokalik and I exchanged glances. On top of the deserted, rough hillock, two exasperated heads turned facing each other as they watched in dismay the queues of *Sramanas* walking through and the brown clothes of the *Bhikkhus* gathering grey dusts as they marched on the soiled roads.

Sariputra What happened after that?

Old Devadatta Then I sought the help of Nalagiri.

Moudgalyayana Nalagiri?

Old Devadatta A giant elephant, the most favoured vehicle of King Ajatashatru. He used to ride on it when he went for hunting.

Nalagiri's shadow appears on the cyclorama behind.

Old Devadatta It was of course Ajatashatru's plan. He said –

Ajatashatru *and* **Young Devadatta** *appear upstage.*

Ajatashatru *Acharya*, I think that anyone with a human figure will get hypnotized when he comes in front of Buddha. I will intoxicate Nalagiri with some drugs, *Acharya*. When Buddha will enter the palace city to gather daily alms, this big goliath Nalagiri will trample him under its feet.

Young Devadatta Great, then feed it with the strongest drugs. Let the intoxicant overflow through its head, cheek and trunk. Let the sound of a heavy blow of his earlobe supersede the sound of a *Dunduvi*. Instruct all the elephant keepers to steer clear of its way. Let the arrogant, intoxicated Nalagiri disobey them today. Untie the *Dindima* and *Porshun* from its back in one jerk. Insert thorns in the pierced rings on its skin. Fill the bundles of *vindipal* with thorns too. Sharpen its edge. Sharpen it more. The more drunk Nalagiri gets, the more it will trumpet. The loathsome foam will trickle down profusely from its two conch-white tusks. Its two calm eyes will turn crooked and riotous. Its glance will turn bloody red. A terrible rage will overpower it. Now pull and uncouple the iron clasps tied to its legs. Let us all hear the jingling sound . . . *jhanjhan* . . . *jhanjhan*. Hey, you, amateur elephant keepers, now all of you lift up the *vindipal* in unison on your heads and with full force strike it on the big head of Nalagiri. Now move away. Move back. You all clear the way.

Elephant trumpet is heard. The rumbling sound of Nalagiri running is heard. The elephant is seen in the cyclorama. It disappears in the distance. Blackout. Nalagiri's roaring trumpet is still audible. Lights are on. Bhikkhu Sangha is visible. All are present. Music fades out. **Old Devadatta** *speaks.*

Old Devadatta *Ther* Sariputra, *Ther* Moudgalyayana, do you recollect what happened that day?

They remain unresponsive.

You repeatedly pleaded with Buddha to not take the same route where Nalagiri was seen. Yet he chose the same route.

Sariputra Yes, I do remember. I remember holding his two tender hands and requesting to my Lord, 'Oh my Lord, my beloved *Tathagata*, please don't go near the rogue elephant. This creature is not human and moreover it is completely intoxicated. It will not recognise you, *Prabhu*.'

Moudgalyayana Said the master, one who has life has ignorance as well as wisdom. Even a man lives in an inebriated state throughout his life. Sometimes this inebriation is his pride, sometimes his vice and at other times it is bestiality. If the adjective 'beastly' can be applicable for a human being, then why can't we add the word 'human' to an animal?'

Sariputra While we were busy listening to his advice, Nalagiri suddenly appeared at the bend of the road like a comet. The elephant was standing only around fifty steps away from us. It was looking dangerously furious. Being scared, Moudgalyayana and I moved away. Right at that moment a petrified woman accidentally dropped her baby from her lap on the road. Just imagine, how ominous the sight of an intoxicated elephant was that a mother too could drop her infant and run away for life.

Old Devadatta Right you are! I sent Kokalik and another attendant Samudradatta behind Nalagiri to witness the killing of Buddha. They too had reported the incident of the infant's frightening cry to me.

Utpalabarna And what happened then?

Old Devadatta (*glances at her, smiles*) Thereafter?

Young Devadatta Give me an update.

Kokalik *Acharya*, what we saw today is simply unbelievable.

Young Devadatta Why? What happened? Didn't Nalagiri kill the hypocrite?

Kokalik Kill? (*Scoffs.*) My dear colleague Samudradatta, you better narrate the full story to *Acharya*.

Samudradatta When Nalagiri came within a distance of only ten hands from Buddhadeb and five hands away from the infant, it hesitated for a moment. We clearly noticed it. After taking its eyes off from Buddha, it doubled its speed and ran towards the infant. The shrieking and yelling of his mother escalated urgently. The infant's name was 'Bijoy'. His mother was seen howling, 'Bijoy, my dear baby Bijoy!' But Nalagiri didn't pay any heed to her cry. In an electrifying speed it appeared in front of Bijoy. When it was lifting its pillar-like left leg above Bijoy's head, Buddha's voice was heard that very moment.

Kokalik Buddha said, *Vatsa* Nalagiri, you have been intoxicated and sent to kill me. Neither to destroy urban lives nor to kill anyone else. So, *Vatsa*, spare the infant Bijoy and instead come to me.

Samudradatta *Acharya* Devadatta, when his distinctly uttered voice entered the inebriated elephant's ear, we observed a magic spell, my Lord. Nalagiri's left leg, which was lifted in air, came down slowly and touched the ground. Its fiery red eyes became gentle and calm again. Its airborne trunk became flaccid magically. The elephant then picked up the infant Bijoy gently with its trunk and returned him to his mother. Unbelievable, *Acharya*! Just unbelievable!

Kokalik Therafter, Nalagiri came forward calmly and stood still before Buddha. The divine glow emanating from Buddha seemed to be steadily taming Nalagiri. Lowering its trunk, it stooped before Buddha in such a manner so as to convey its loving obeisance to him. We have failed this time too, my Lord. Winning seems elusive for us, *Acharya*.

Silence for sometime. **Young Devadatta** *screams in frustration. He throws away utensils near him. He attacks* **Kokalik** *and* **Samudradatta**. *They cry out in fear. After sometime young* **Devadatta** *lies down tired.* **Samudradatta** *calls him after sometime.*

Samudradatta *Acharya*, please don't be angry with us. Please adopt a new strategy, *Acharya.*

Kokalik It is impossible not only for the king but also for the royal council or any of us to plan a strategy and harm Buddha. At the most we can vent out our grudge against him by mocking or bad mouthing him in our own circle. But we don't benefit from it. *Acharya*, if anything has to be done, please use your intelligence to plan. We are fascinated by your ruthless psyche, my Lord and request you not to suppress this strength in you.

Samudradatta *Prabhu*, only you can do this. Please formulate another strategy and allow us to execute your command.

Kokalik Even after observing Buddha in person and realizing his greatness, if we can still oppose him, there must be many others in the *Sangha* who are anti-Buddha. We are somehow unable to identify them.

Samudradatta We know that even sandalwood trees have snakes hiding in their roots, flowers are swarmed by poisonous bees, antelopes stay near tree-branches and bears live on top. So, surely there must be people around Buddha who, owing to the lack of factual knowledge and wisdom, are unable to become actual Buddha-opposers.

Kokalik *Prabhu*, please rise up to the occasion. Have courage and bring back your lost enthusiasm. Come let us destroy Buddha.

Devadatta *gets up and looks at them. Then he drags them by their hands and exits from the right wing. Music starts. A few* Sramanas *of the Bhikkhu Sangha appear. Ther* **Revat** *leads them. They sit to meditate. The meditation continues for sometime. Then from the last wing upstage enter middle-aged* **Devadatta**, **Kokalik** *and* **Samudradatta**. **Revat** *opens his eyes. Their presence catches his attention. He•is visibly surprised.* **Revat** *and other* Sramanas *get up slowly. Rumbling heard.* **Revat** *raises his hand and quietens them.*

Revat What happened, *Bhante* Devadatta? Why have you set your feet in the *Sangha* after such a long gap? Have you forgotten your way?

Middle-aged Devadatta No. Where is your Lord Buddha, *Abhuso* Revat?

Revat Some *Bhikkhus* of *Vajji*[6] clan have come from *Licchavi*. They have some doubts in their minds. Lord Buddha has joined them in a discussion in the garden outside the *Sangha*.

---

6 Sanskrit – *Vriji*.

Middle-aged Devadatta So, Buddha is again at it, busy eating their heads off with his blend of useless and fabricated jargons. I really wonder, *Abhuso* Revat, how do you tolerate his fake and fallacious lectures for days together?

Revat (*chuckles*) *Bhante* Devadatta, your anti-Buddhist stand has acquired a legendary status now. I think it is imprudent to oppose him so sternly now.

Middle-aged Devadatta Am I being stern? *Abhuso* Revat, one who does not merely want to be a part of this huge population will definitely be stern with himself. And that is what should be done. Your pastor is of the opinion that friendliness, affability, public service and sympathy are the only values that should be pursued to instill in your life.

Subhadra (*a* **Sramana**) Exactly, that is just, *Bhante* Devadatta. An act of salvation is possible only by living a virtuous life.

Middle-aged Devadatta (*sneers*) *Abhuso* Revat, these docile and cowardly buffalos have learnt all this since their childhood to shape only tyrants in our society. A dictator! And to dislodge these dictators from power we need people who are more intelligent than them. We have to gradually create a repository of such individuals to ensure that one dictator dies in the hands of innumerable other dictators.

Subhadra Decadence and killing are the essence of your contemplation, *Bhante* Devadatta. We do not have anything to learn from you.

Middle-aged Devadatta Hey, kid Sramana, don't even try to learn anything from me. It is beyond your means.

(*To* **Revat**.) Don't you think, *Abhuso* Revat, those who survive without undergoing self-decay are not worthy of respect anyway? Don't you think that contempt is the only objective of this world? *Abhuso* Revat, I hate those who set their sight on a life which excludes the experience of self-decay and self-destruction. I have deep hatred even for those who are scared to burn themselves out and live without the goal of failure.

Revat *Bhante* Devadatta . . .

Middle-aged Devadatta Learn to scorch yourself from within, *Abhuso* Revat. Learn to degenerate yourself. The cattle herd you have been producing generation after generation are destined to achieve nothing more than unquestionable allegiance. They have shining exteriors but they lead gross lives with stupid self-deception till they encounter death exactly like unquestioning buffaloes. Hey preachers of peace, you are actually scared to pull out the turmoil going on within you. You wither away carrying these unrests and agitations in your veins, arteries and guts all through your life. Your servitude is nothing but an outcome of your incompetence and laziness.

A few Sramanas *listen to* **Devadatta** *with rapt attention. They get excited.*

Middle-aged Devadatta If your sacrifice, your tranquility, your worship and determination, are true to your heart, then allow me to add five more precepts to the *Sangha* regulations. If you have the desired level of competence, incorporate these rules into the main policy of the *Sangha*.

Kolit (*a* **Sramana**) Yes, *Bhante* Devadatta, we are willing to listen. Please explain your rules before us. If there is any deficiency in our guiding principles, we should surely rectify.

Sariputra *and* **Moudgalyayana** *appear.*

Sariputra What is going on here, *Abhuso* Revat? What is it?

Revat *Bhante* Devadatta has entered our monastery all of a sudden, and is now trying to circulate a few rules here. He wants to present them before everyone right now.

Moudgalyayana We are not interested in listening to you. The proposal that *Bhikkhu* Devadatta wants to present must definitely be a byproduct of his evil thought.

Middle-aged Devadatta You imbecile, Moudgalyayana. Success in this world is always a byproduct of some kind of wickedness. Only deception can take you to the peak of power. Honesty cannot do so. Without an accord between rigorous hard work and a fanatic-autocratic mind, you can never gain success in this rotten world.

Sariputra We are least interested in listening to your flimsy philosophy. You please leave –

Kolit No, we are interested. You please continue, *Abhuso* Devadatta. You please explain the rules that you want us to execute.

Four to five Sramanas *say, 'We are ready to listen to your proposal.'*

Subhadra We do not want to hear. Those who are interested to listen to these destructive propositions should go out of the *Sangha*.

He is supported by two Sramanas.

Kolit *Sramana* Subhadra, who are you to ask *Abhuso* Devadatta to go out of the *Sangha* premises?

Kolit *and* **Subhadra** *get involved in an argument. They engage in a brawl. A few of them also get involved in a fight.* **Sariputra**, **Moudgalyayana** *and* **Revat** *try to stop them.* **Kokalik** *and* **Samudradatta** *are seen to instigate the fighters.* **Devadatta** *is seen to howl continuously. The situation comes under control after some time.* **Sariputra** *nurses* **Subhadra** *and* **Moudgalyayana** *takes care of* **Kolit**. **Revat** *speaks.*

Revat Please tell us, *Bhante* Devadatta. Now you please explain the set of rules you were referring to.

Middle-aged Devadatta Yes, please calm down. Even a saint cannot tolerate a conflicting opinion. But it should be given a patient hearing. Only then can the universe run. Otherwise, the world would have come to a halt by now.

Revat Please come to the point, *Bhante*. There is no need to make a prelude.

Middle-aged Devadatta I propose that from today onwards in the Sangh,
One: Buddhist *Bhikkhus* shall always stay in the forest. They cannot stay in the cities or villages anymore.

I propose, from today onwards in the Sangh,
Two: The only means of support of the *Bhikkhus* will be the alms they collect. They shall never accept any invitation for having food from anyone.

I propose, from today onwards in the Sangh,
Three: The *Bhikkhus* shall wear only forsaken clothes, they shall never accept any clothes from the common people.

I propose, from today onwards in the Sangh,
Four: The *Bhikkhus* shall stay under the trees throughout their lives, they shall never spend their nights under any other roof.

I propose, from today onwards in the Sangh,
Five: The *Bhikkhus* shall remain vegetarian all their lives, they shall not eat fish or meat even once.

Many Bhikkhus *cheer. A few* Bhikkhus *protest. But it is obvious that most of the* Bhikkhus *support* **Devadatta**. **Kokalik** *tells* **Samudradatta**.

Kokalik *Acharya* Devadatta himself does not follow these rules, *Abhuso* Samudradatta.

Samudradatta *laughs.* **Kokalik** *joins him. Music is heard. Blackout. The monastery of Kushinagar appears again.* **Old Devadatta**, **Sudarshan**, **Sariputra**, **Moudgalyayana** *and Theri* **Utpalabarna** *are seen. Music fades out. Silence for some time.* **Utpalabarna** *breaks the silence.*

Utpalabarna You deliberately placed those proposals in front of them. Am I correct, *Bhikkhu* Devadatta?

Old Devadatta (*nods in agreement*) Yes, I was sure that most of the *Bhikkhus* would fail to follow these sermons in their everyday lives. But those who are unable to follow these rules, since they are driven by their inherent desire to perform useless sacrifices, they will believe in the illusion that they are capable of abiding by these rules in their lives. This would certainly be a crucial self-purifying process for them. Moreover, the percepts sounded worthy as well.

Sariputra So worthy that when Lord Buddha heard them, even he showered praise on *Bhikkhu* Devadatta's proposals as valuable.

Moudgalyayana Yes, but he also said that it is not easy for everybody in the *Sangha* to observe these rules obediently. Only a few will be capable of following this.

Sariputra Expectedly, there was a dispute in the group. Buddha became despicable to many of the *Bhikkhus*. Some changed sides and became disciples of Devadatta. And *Bhikkhu* Devadatta, you left the *Sangha* with them.

Old Devadatta Yes. When we were taking a rest at a distance away from the town, you all appeared there all of a sudden. *Shishya* Sariputra and *Shishya* Moudgalyayana, who sent you after us? Was it Lord Buddha?

Sariputra Not at all. We, for the first time in our lives, followed you without taking prior approval from him.

Old Devadatta (*chuckles*) And I had thought you followed us with the intent to join our group. And that you were willing to accept my tutelage.

Blackout. Light is put on. Outside the town. **Middle-aged Devadatta**, **Kokalik**, **Samudradatta** *and a group of* Sramanas *are seen.* **Sariputra** *and* **Moudgalyayana** *are standing there.*

Middle-aged Devadatta Please tell us. Please share your opinion with us. We are eager to hear you out.

Moudgalyayana You tell them, *Abhuso* Sariputra.

Sariputra Are you giving me the permission, Lord Devadatta?

Middle-aged Devadatta Of course, yes. I told you that I am eager to listen to you. Please feel free to tell us, Sariputra. Please go ahead.

Sariputra Hey *Bhikkhus*, please ask yourselves whether you took the correct decision by leaving Lord Buddha. Please enquire from *Bhikkhu* Devadatta whether he himself is ready to practise the sermons proposed by him throughout his life. Out of all the rules that Devadatta has proposed, has he practised even one of those conventions in his own life so far?

Middle-aged Devadatta Hey, what are you saying, Shishya Sariputra?

Kolit No, please allow him to speak. We are ready to hear his views. Listening is an important part of democracy. This is what you have taught us *Acharya* Devadatta.

Dharmadatta (*another* Sramana) Absolutely correct. *Abhuso* Sariputra, you please continue. We need to hear you out also. We are eager to know.

Sariputra *(continues)* We all know that *Abhuso* Devadatta is a strict non-vegetarian. He does not shy away from expressing such feelings in public as well. The cloth he wears is far superior than what we wear. He is wearing a loincloth made of muslin. It has been gifted to him by the King Ajatashatru. Therefore, *Abhuso* Devadatta leads a sybaritic life, he craves for fancy clothes and all earthly pleasures. So, how can one who preaches something that he does not himself practis, become your *Acharya*? Please consider this before you take a final decision.

Moudgalyayana Therefore, you are left with only one path before you. The spiritual path shown by our Lord Buddha. According to him, life is ephemeral and so is power or authority. He says, this universe is eternally a prey to old age and death. And if you can comprehend that, at least don't keep any arrogance about power within you. Don't you please forget that you all are *Arhata*. Buddha's first aphorism for you is that he is the best even among the best, who even after eternally absorbing all miseries, trivializes them and continues to convey messages of peace for everyone else.

Sariputra My dear *Sramanas*, please learn to assess yourselves. You will then be able to understand Lord Buddha. You will realize that whatever little you have achieved in your life and whatever you could do is nothing other than the spirit of *Tathagata.*

There is rambling among the Sramanas. *They immediately realize their mistake.*

Dharmadatta We want to go back. *Abhuso* Sariputra, we want to return to our *Sangha.*

Kolit We will not spend even a single moment with such a double-standard, impious person. Let us go back to our *Sangha*. Let's go back right away.

All agree collectively. They all leave. **Moudgalyayana** *leads them.* **Sariputra** *follows at the end. He stares at* **Devadatta** *before leaving.* **Middle-aged Devadatta** *stays back with* **Kokalik** *and* **Samudradatta**. **Devadatta** *remains speechless. After some time* **Kokalik** *bursts in anger.*

Kokalik We have lost everything . . . everything. (**To Middle-aged Devadatta.**) It is all due to your stupidity. You . . . you are absolutely useless. All our efforts have gone down the drain. We have been destroyed. Despite enjoying the blessings of King Ajatashatru, we could do nothing.

(*To* **Devadatta.**) You are obnoxious, audacious, stupid, crass.

Samudradatta (*he tries to stop* **Kokalik**) Ah, Kokalik lower your voice!

Kokalik Lower my voice? How long will we continue to do that? We lost all the enthusiasm in our lives because of this humbug zealot. The archer, Nalagiri – we lost on everything . . . all! And this stupidity again today. Egoistic brute!

Samudradatta Have you lost it, *Abhuso* Kokalik? He is after all our *Acharya*!

Kokalik *Acharya*? Huh! He is hypocrital, brainless and absolutely worthless. He cannot even present a counter-logic when needed. All that we had planned for so long just went down the river *Bitasta*. All because of him. Snooty, powerless, rascal!

Samudradatta Kokalik . . .

Kokalik *pushes* **Samudradatta** *off his way. He rushes towards* **Devadatta** *and kicks his chest.* **Middle-aged Devadatta** *vomits blood as he falls on the ground.* **Kokalik** *leaves.* **Samudradatta** *runs to* **Devadatta***'s help. Light goes off. Music is heard. Lights are on. Outside the monastery at Kushinagar.* **Old Devadatta** *speaks.*

Old Devadatta Now I understand what Kokalik did to me was right. I was not only trying to murder my master, I was also trying to destroy my sense of gratitude. Whatever fame and virtue I attained in my life was undoubtedly due to Lord Buddha. And I was rejecting him. This means that I was trampling my past away, I was crushing my gratefulness. My immediate instinct was driving me to react so irresponsibly. And if I can reject my own *Guru*, why can Kokalik not do the same with me?

Sariputra It's alright. You please stop *Bhikkhu*! You are suffering.

Old Devadatta No my dear, I am not suffering. Please allow me to speak, *Abhuso* Sariputra. I have been really sick during the last three months. I am aware that within a very short time my mortal body will permanently leave this illuminated-moonlit-starry universe. I will enter into an eternal slumber. Before my exit I have realized that *moksha* is the ultimate truth of life.

Moudgalyayana Right you are. Everything in this world is impermanent. The reforms that destroy all convictions are indeed transient. You are now on the verge of a real trance, *Bhikkhu*.

Sariputra Precisely like our Lord.

Old Devadatta So, you know, I am suffering from self-torment since the last few days. Before the infallible moment snatches me away, can't I get a glimpse of the omniscient once? Just once? Then came the news that you all have come to Kushinagar. This is the place where Buddha will gain *Mahaparinirvana* tonight. The news made me very restless. I requested a few of my followers to take me near Buddha. Just once. I am yearning for his glimpse once and wish to convey my regards to him. But . . .

Utpalabarna But. But what, *Bhikkhu*?

Old Devadatta *remains silent.*

Sudarshan Everybody refused. They said it was impossible for them. Especially, on being instigated by *Acharya* Devadatta, the ill-treatment they had meted out repeatedly to Lord *Tathagata* resulted in a loss of their face which prevented them from even going near the Lord. However, I thought, whether it was his sin or goodness, whether he disseminated wisdom or folly, prudence or imprudence, he is after all my *Acharya*, my *Guru*. It is under his supervision that I have grown since my childhood. All the good or bad that I have achieved in my life has been possible only due to his blessings. How can I ignore his last wish? Therefore, I accompanied him very early in the morning today.

Utpalabarna You have done the right thing, *Vatsa*. What you did is right!

Middle Aged Devadatta *Theri*, you please tell me can't this doddering, dying person be allowed to meet Buddha once?

Moudgalyayana How will you prove that you do not have any other motive behind this meeting? How can you assure us that you are not hiding any arm inside your girdle which can prove fatal to Buddha?

Sariputra Ah! *Abhuso* Moudgalyayana, can't you see that Devadatta is now completely infirm. He lacks even the minimum physical strength needed to use weapons.

Old Devadatta *still comes forward. He raises his two arms. Intends to take his clothes off.*

Utpalabarna You may stop here *Bhikkhu*. Let me go inside. It is the second hour of the night. Lord Buddha had instructed *Ther* Ananda to send *Sramana* Subhadra to him as he has some queries for the Lord. *Ther* Ananda had forbidden Subhadra to go near our Lord. Yet Lord Buddha said, 'Ananda, don't stop Subhadra from coming to me. I wish to tell him something.' After listening to *Prabhu*'s aphorism, Subhadra will attain *Arhata*. Then will approach the most awaited third hour of the night. Let me go and talk to *Prabhu* first. Let me see if he agrees to meet you.

Old Devadatta *nods.* **Utpalabarna** *leaves. Music is played.* **Moudgalyayana** *comes near* **Old Devadatta**.

Moudgalyayana Please tell me honestly *Bhikkhu*, are you really feeling remorseful or is it another ploy of yours?

Sariputra Ah, *Abhuso* . . .

Moudgalyayana I don't trust him, *Abhuso*. The way he has continued his harsh slandering, insults and secret assaults, he has become completely unreliable. Moreover, we have also been victims of his vile attacks, *Abhuso*. Just because we follow Buddha's philosophy, and since Buddha is our *Guru*, he has convinced his followers to rain attacks on us. He has thus lost all his credibility to be trusted again. Correct me if you disagree with me, *Bhikkhu*.

Sariputra *Bhikkhu* Devadatta, *Abhuso* Moudhalyayana is talking to you. *Bhikkhu* Devadatta, can't you hear him?

Old Devadatta *looks up at them. Smiles gently. Remains silent.* **Moudgalyayana** *suddenly attacks* **Old Devadatta**.

Moudgalyayana You have to tell me. Even if you opt to behave like a deaf and dumb person, I am not going to spare you. You have to tell me.

Old Devadatta *falls on the ground.* **Moudgalyayana** *forcibly sits on him. Disciple* **Ananda** *enters.*

Ananda Ah, *Abhuso* Moudgalyayana, please set him free.

Moudgalyayana *leaves him and gets up.* **Sariputra** *goes near* **Ananda**.

Sariputra (*anxiously*) *Abhuso* Ananda, what message has our *Prabhu Tathagata* left for you?

Ananda *swings his head sideways.* **Old Devadatta** *gets up and looks at* **Ananda**.

Ananda *Prabhu* will not meet *Bhikkhu* Devadatta.

Moudgalyayana *cheers in joy.*

Sariputra What exactly did our *Prabhu* convey?

Ananda *Prabhu* elucidated that the person who had insistently tried to convince Buddha to implement five new commandments in the *Sangha* has done nothing exemplary later such that his outbreak of sheer penitence makes him eligible to meet Buddha and seek his blessings.

Moudgalyayana *again cheers in merriment.*

Ananda *Abhuso* Sariputra, *Abhuso* Moudgalyayana, you please go inside. We are already in the third hour of the night. He has just delivered his final statement from his mortal body. Now he will sit for his meditation.

Old Devadatta What is it? What is *Prabhu*'s final command, *Ther* Ananda?

Ananda *Prabhu* expressed, 'Hey, *Bhikkhu* community, here is my last advice for you – the nature of all substances is to be annulled. So, be composed and concentrate wholeheartedly for your accomplishment.'

Sariputra *starts mourning.* **Moudgalyayana** *joins him. Ther* **Ananda** *raises his hand.*

Ananda You please go inside, *Abhuso*. The moon is right up in the middle of the sky. Else you will not be able to get a glimpse of our *Prabhu*.

Sariputra *and* **Moudgalyayana** *hastily go inside.* **Ananda** *was about to leave. At the last moment, he turns towards* **Old Devadatta** *and approaches him.*

Ananda *Bhante* Devadatta, please don't try to forcefully barge inside the *Sangharam*. *Prabhu* Buddha has instructed me that if you defy his request to return, or if you try to enter the *Sangharam* forcibly, he will leave his mortal remain before you can reach him. You will not get to see him. He has not forgiven you. He has not forgiven you at all.

Ananda *enters* **Sangharam**. *A few* Sramanas *enter.* **Old Devadatta** *screams.*

Old Devadatta Even I am on my way to breathe my last. Today I am going to die. Shall the Lord not allow me to go near him once, only once?

Old Devadatta *is surrounded by the* Sramanas.

Old Devadatta (*loudly*) Merciless! Unkind! Didn't I qualify for receiving the bestowal of his compassion at least today? *Prabhu*, why have I, even on my final day been debarred from your touch of kindness? Why?

Old Devadatta *laments. Music is heard.* Sramanas *move around him in a circle. Someone hits the gong. Music is heard. Curtain falls.*

The End.

Glossary

Abhuso: A contracted form of *āyusmanto* (Pali). Friend, a form of polite address 'friend, brother, sir', usually in conversation between *bhikkhus*

Acharya: A Hindu or Buddhist spiritual teacher or leader

Amitabha: One with boundless splendour. Sanskrit: 'Infinite Light' also called Amitayus ('Infinite Life') in Mahayana Buddhism. The title is most commonly used for Gautama Buddha

Andarmahal: Inner apartment

Arhata: 'One who is worthy' in Sanskrit, Pali *arahant*. In Buddhism, a perfected person, one who has gained insight into the true nature of existence and has achieved spiritual enlightenment

Aryashreshtha: *Arya* means respected person in Sanskrit. *Aryashreshtha*, the most respected and most superior among the *Aryas*

Asavakshyaya: Mental effluent, pollutant or fermentation. Four qualities – sensuality, views, becoming and ignorance – that 'flow out' of the mind and create the flood of the round of death and rebirth

Baishakhi Purnima: Full moon night in the Bengali month Baishakh, The first month of the Bengali Calendar

Basantotsava: *Basant* is a month in the Bengali calendar implying the spring season. *Utsav* literally means the 'celebration of spring'. The beautiful tradition of celebrating spring with a festival in Bengal was first started by Nobel Laureate Rabindranath Tagore, at Vishwabharati Shantiniketan, the university founded by him

Betas: Wild *Beta* species of tree can be found throughout the Atlantic coast of Europe, the Mediterranean coastline, the Near East and parts of Asia including India. The best-known member is the common beet, *Beta vulgaris*, but several other species are recognized

Bhante: Venerable sir. *Bhante*, sometimes also called *Bhadanta*, is a respectful title used to address Buddhist monks and superiors in the Theravada tradition

Bhikkhu/Bhikkhuni: *Bhikku*, (Pāli), feminine *bhikkunī*, Sanskrit *bhikṣu*, or (feminine) *bhikṣuṇī*. In Buddhism, one who has renounced worldly life and joined the mendicant and contemplative community

Bodhidruma: The Bodhi Tree ('tree of awakening'), also called the Bodhi Fig Tree or Bo Tree, is a large sacred fig tree (*Ficus religiosa*) located in Bodh Gaya, Bihar, India. Siddhartha Gautama, the spiritual teacher who became known as the Buddha, is said to have attained enlightenment after meditating beneath one such tree for forty-nine days

Bodhisattva: In Buddhism, a *bodhisattva* or *bodhisatva* is any person who is on the path towards *bodhi* ('awakening') or Buddhahood

Brahma Muhurta: One hour thirty-six minutes before sunrise

Chaitya: *Caitya* (Sanskrit) refers to a 'temple', and in a broader sense represents 'devotional place' or 'residence of God'

Dindima: A musical instrument, a kind of small drum or tabor

Dunduvi: A musical instrument used in the early Vedic times both in war and peace

Ghrita: Butter from which water and milk solids have been removed, so that only the butterfat remains

Guru: Spiritual teacher in Sanskrit

Jambu: Berry tree

Jetavana: Jetavana (lit. 'Jeta's grove') was one of the most famous of the Buddhist monasteries in India (present-day Uttar Pradesh). It was the second monastery donated to Gautama Buddha after the Venuvana in Rajgir. The monastery was given to him by his chief male patron, Anathapindika

Licchavi: (also spelled Lichchhavi). A powerful tribe of India in the time of the Buddha. They were certainly khattiyas, for on that ground they claimed a share of the Buddhas relics. They settled (sixth to fifth century BCE) on the north bank of the Ganges River in what is now Bihar state in India; their capital city was at Vaishali

Magh month: Tenth month of a Bengali year. It is one of the months of the winter season

Mahaparinirvana: The Buddhist term 'Mahaparinirvana', meaning 'great, complete Nirvana'. The word 'Mahaparinirvana' usually refers to the ultimate state of Nirvana (everlasting, highest peace and happiness) entered by an Awakened Being (Buddha) or 'arhat' at the moment of physical death, when the mundane skandhas (constituent elements of the ordinary body and mind) are shed and only the Buddhic skandhas remain (this in Mahayana Buddhism)

Mahaprayana: Holy Death

Nirvana: (Sanskrit nirvana) Liberation; literally, the 'unbinding' of the mind from the mental effluents, defilements and the round of rebirth, and from all that can be described or defined. As this term also denotes the extinguishing of a fire, it carries the connotations of stilling, cooling and peace. 'Total nirvana' in some contexts denotes the experience of Awakening; in others, the final passing away of an arahant

Pabbajja: (Pali: going forth) A novice in the wanderer's life. From home to the homeless life, introduction to the life of a *Bhikkhuni*

Prabhu: A term most commonly translated as 'master' or 'prince'. It can also be translated to mean 'omnipresent', 'creator of the universe'

Sangha: *Sangha*, meaning 'company' or 'community', refers to the monastic communities of monks and nuns across the Buddhist world. The *Sangha* has kept Buddhist texts safe over the centuries and has interpreted and taught Buddhist philosophy

Shastra: Scriptures

Stupa: A stupa is a Buddhist shrine used for meditation. A stupa (Sanskrit: lit. 'heap') is a mound-like or hemispherical structure containing relics

Tathagata: (Pali) One of the titles of a buddha and the one most frequently employed by the historical Buddha, Siddhartha Gautama, when referring to himself. The term is often thought to mean either 'one who has thus gone' (*tathā-gata*), 'one who has thus come' (*tathā-āgata*), or sometimes 'one who has thus not gone' (*tathā-agata*). This is interpreted as signifying that the *Tathāgata* is beyond all coming and going – beyond all transitory phenomena

Thera (masculine), Theri (feminine): 'Elder'. An honorific title automatically conferred upon a *bhikkhu* of at least ten years' standing. Theravāda is a major branch of Buddhism having the Pali canon (*tipitaka*) as their canonical literature, which includes the *vinaya-pitaka* (monastic rules), the *sutta-pitaka* (Buddhist sermons) and the *abhidhamma-pitaka* (philosophy and psychology)

Upasampada: (Pali) Buddhist rite of higher ordination, by which a novice becomes a monk. Ordination is not necessarily permanent and, in some countries, may be repeated in a monk's lifetime

Vajji: (Pali, Sanskrit – *Vriji*) *Vajji* or *Vṛiji* was a confederacy of neighbouring clans including the Licchavis and one of the principal Mahajanapadas of Ancient India. The area they ruled constitutes the region of Mithila in northern Bihar and their capital was the city of Vaishali

Vatsa: *Vatsa* or *Vamsa* (Pali and Ardhamagadhi: *Vaccha*, literally 'calf') *Vatsa* is used in Indian culture as a beloved son

Vindipal: An ancient missile, used during the armed confrontation

Section Two

(In)Visible Boundaries, (Un)Democratic Choices

Summaries

The Final Night

The play imagines Muhammad Ali Jinnah's final night in 1947 India before he leaves for Pakistan – taking place at the intersection of history and imagination, where the playwright articulates the conditions for delving into debates on interpersonal gendered relationships both within the family and in the public sphere in pre-independent and independent India. *The Final Night* challenges the official histories of India and Pakistan, which cast him as a villain and a founding father respectively. The plot revolves around Muhammad, his absent-present wife who is referred to throughout, his daughter Dina Wadia and his younger sister Fatima Jinnah who all discuss colonial India's past and independent India's future alongside their own past and future. The play offers a window into the emotional life of Muhammad and the strong women that guide him as he transforms from the 'best ambassador of Hindu–Muslim unity' in colonial India into an advocate for a separate Muslim state post-independence. The characters assess the role of violence and probe their own emotional states as they recount their roles as victims, aggressors, bystanders and witnesses to India's religious and ethnic fault lines under British colonial rule.

The mood or tone explored throughout the piece is loss. Yet within this context, loss becomes a complex event that encompasses grief and love across various planes: marriage, nation, religion, family, history, culture and memory through a lens that is at once post-colonial and beyond the postcolonial as the subcontinent equally celebrates and mourns seventy-five years after partition. Through the distance created by the figure of Jinnah, Basu is able to play out both the real and imagined loss Jinnah felt in a historical context as well as the real and imagined loss felt by Indians today navigating the aftermath of colonialism and the new movements of contemporary India that play out at the intersections of religion, gender, propriety and identity as articulated by Nandita Dhawan.[1]

Dina, as the representative of the next generation, probes into the 'personal as political' to search for the (im)possibilities of a feminist ethico-political imagination in the history and destiny of the new nations. The discussion and conflict between generations reveals how personal emotions and private family dynamics become the sites of political struggle in each character's individual life and in their varied roles in creating the future of India and Pakistan. Dina dreams of a future with an ethics of care, connectivity and empathy realized by ideals of trust, peace and friendship – a future that resists the structures and aesthetics of patriarchy couched in religious and cultural hegemony.

Creusa – The Queen

Creusa – The Queen is a Bengali adaptation of Euripides' *Ion* that draws parallels between Athens, the first known democracy, and contemporary India, the world's

---

1 Dhawan, N. B. 2020. 'Bratya Basu's "The Final Night": The (im)possibility of gender equality and religious plurality', *Asian Journal of Women's Studies*, Vol. 26, No. 3, 365–82. https://doi.org/10.1080/12259276.2020.1820158.

largest democracy. The play depicts the contradictions of democracy in an attempt to trace its constraints and articulate the messy relationships between love and politics, each framed as both personal and political concepts that interrogate both justice and the role of religion in the public sphere.

The plot follows King Xuthus and Queen Creusa, who visit the oracle of Apollo to ask for a child who will be the heir to the throne of Athens. The oracle prophecies that they will soon bear a male child, but he warns them that until the prophecy comes true, they must follow Apollo's commandment and adopt an orphan of Apollo's temple and crown him the prince of Athens. While the king happily agrees, the queen rejects the commandment and conspires with her servant Danius to kill Ion during the adoption ceremony. Creusa's and Danius' treachery is exposed and they face the Athenian courts. The trial exposes Creusa's tumultuous past and she realizes that Ion is her child.

Creusa is a strong and fearless queen who challenges both social and divine hierarchies. She ridicules her husband for his cowardice and his willingness to submit to the gods' exploitation of humans. A voice of resistance to the patriarchal designs of both democracy and autocracy, Creusa questions the ethical and political worldviews of the Athenian polis to unsuccessfully subvert democratic processes for her own ends. Her characterization lays bare the gendered violence imbedded in the social contract of democracy through a peek into the invisible sexual contract used to reinforce patriarchy.

Creusa becomes the representative of all women in liberal democracies who aim to fight against being blamed for their 'disorders' which result in ruining the state. She is the archetype of the weak and oppressed on earth who believe in re-writing their destiny by questioning the perpetual superiority of Gods. Her embodied entity sharply questions the hierarchical divine–human relationship of authority-obligation to redefine the paradigm of justice in a democratic state. The play showcases the contradictions and overlaps between domestic and civil life to deconstruct the gendered dichotomies of the 'public' and 'private' spheres. Creusa's standpoint in the narrative exposes ways in which the public–private realms are mutually constitutive in defining the *legitimate* in society. Basu provides an opportunity to re-visit the democratic practices in *real* spaces by unveiling the vantage point of the excluded in Creusa's struggle for justice such that her subordinate and undervalued position in society can be overcome. In her desperation to disrupt and redefine the gendered binaries of care and justice, Creusa represents both order and disorder; rationality and emotion; mind and body; morality and immorality; passion and apathy.

Translator's notes

Mainak Banerjee

The Final Night (Bengali: *Antim Raat*) revisits the political debates of partition, nostalgia of freedom, birth of new nations and pains of humanity. The language used reflects the erudite and aristocratic identity of the characters who have been inheritors of English education. Jinnah's deliberation embodies authority and power whereas his daughter Dina voices the language of equality and social justice.

In the play ***Creusa – The Queen*** (Bengali: *Rani Creusa*), the playwright creates an inimitable style depicting royal language which is neither histrionic nor melodramatic. Intertwining subplots and ideas of ancient Western and Eastern plays and verses, he adorns his wit and wisdom in Bengali language and culture. To my mind, Elizabethan English language is best fitted in the first half of the play with a colossal Greek visual in the background while the language in the later part of the play is politico-legal language suited for modern democracy. Coining his own words in the poetry of Rabindranath Tagore, Basu brings here his legato approach to language in the final section of the play.

In the Indian epic *Mahabharata*, Kunti, the proud mother of five Pandavas (her five sons), finds Karna, Kunti's long-lost son, as the biggest threat of Pandavas because he takes the side of their enemies Kauravas in the epic battle. Nobel laureate poet Rabindranath Tagore beautifully pens down the affective exchange between Kunti and her newly 'discovered' son in *Karna–Kunti Sangbad* and his verse has touched numerous souls across the world. The playwright has drawn a poetic simile between Karna–Kunti and Ion–Creusa to depict the relationship of a mother and a child long lost or abandoned. My special thanks to Ketaki Kushari Dyson for her translation of *Karna–Kunti Samvad* written by Rabindranath Tagore.

The Final Night

Bratya Basu
April 2020

Translated by Mainak Banerjee

Female characters: 2

Male characters: 1

Country of origin: India

Original performance date: The play was written after the onset of the pandemic. It has not been performed as yet.

Characters

Muhammad Ali Jinnah *(male)*
Fatima Jinnah *(female)*
Dina Wadia *(female)*

Act One

Muhammad Ali Jinnah*'s three-storeyed house at Mumbai's (erstwhile Bombay) Malabar Hill's South Court residence. A chamber cum drawing room on first floor. A table and a chair are centre stage and a book rack behind it. All placed by the window. Book rack is piled with legal books. A few racks are empty. A closed cabinet is attached to the rack. Seating arrangements for a couple of persons in front of the table. A black telephone is placed on it. Two small sofas and a table are seen downstage left. A few fully taped packing boxes are seen scattered at the upstage. It is evident that some books are crammed into them. When the stage is illuminated after the curtain is raised, seventy-one-year-old* **Jinnah** *is seen talking to somebody over the telephone. He is wearing a three-piece suit and sitting on a chair with a burning cigar held between his fingers. Time: 6 p.m. Date: 5 August 1947.*

Jinnah (*over telephone*) Yes, I will be reaching Delhi tomorrow. So what? No, I don't have time tomorrow. I have a busy schedule. I will be finally leaving for Karachi day after tomorrow. Ask Liaquat to meet me there. Tomorrow morning, I have an appointment with *Baralat* . . . No, no, I won't be able to meet in the evening. My health does not permit. I cannot take much stress anymore. Liaquat is aware of my physical condition quite well . . . you are again talking about cabinet ministry. Who has asked him to strain his brain over it? I will take care of it. I have my plans. (*Calms down.*) See, Khalique, I already have decided who will be our Labour Minister and Law Minister. I will declare it in due course of time. Tell Liaquat to concentrate on his own job. Ask him to run through the arrangements of the oath-taking ceremony so that nothing untoward happens. Is it okay? Now don't force me to talk much. That's all for now.

Hangs up the phone, puts out his cigar. Lights a cigarette. Gets up and stretches himself. He scans around the room and then calls out loud:

Fatima, Fati.

Jinnah*'s sister* **Fatima** *enters with medicines and a glass of water in her hands. She is fifry-four years old.* **Jinnah** *is visibly surprised.*

Jinnah Why are you bringing my medicines? Where is Abul?

Fatima I have sent him to the kitchen. Your steak is almost ready in the oven. I told Abul to check it once.

Jinnah (*takes his medicines*) I have my doubts. Abul is a righteous Muslim. He never tasted a pork steak in his life. He does not have any inkling about how much exactly it needs to be grilled. Let Gauhar do the cooking.

Swallows a pill.

Fatima Did you get the steak from Crawford market?

Jinnah Yes. I was passing by the Crawford market, on my way back home. I felt tempted. So, I sent Sikander to pick it up.

Fatima Did you stop your car on the way?

Jinnah Hmm.

Fatima How strange you are! What if people spotted you?

Jinnah How would they recognize me? I was in my Packard. They could have spotted me, but identifying me would not have been easy. Moreover, I was sitting with my head down. Is this the new medicine?

Fatima Yes. We received it last week. Dr Patel has advised you to take it once a day, two hours before dinner.

Jinnah Patel is never going to accept that medicines cannot heal a lung abscess.

Fatima How ridiculous! But it can at least reduce the pain.

Jinnah Yes, it may reduce the pain a bit.

Stubs the cigarette in the ashtray. Readies to light another one. **Fatima** *snatches it from his hand.*

Fatima What the hell are you doing?

Fatima Dr Patel has set a limit for you. You are not supposed to have more than twenty cigarettes a day. Yet you are smoking one after the other.

Jinnah Fatima, we already have talked about it many times. You will not poke your nose in my private affair. I don't like to whine about it repeatedly.

Snatches back the cigarette from her, lights it up and then opens the drawer.

Fatima Where did you go today? After returning home from the airport, you just offloaded your luggage and went out again. You didn't even take rest.

Jinnah (*searches his drawer for a paper*) What to do? The flight was late by twenty minutes. You know well that I am very particular about time. But you first tell me, what made you stay back home? You could have easily paid a visit to your old chamber at Malad. In all probability, you may not get the opportunity to visit this place again.

Fatima Let it be. That chamber was closed years back. I heard that the person who bought it from me had sold it to the owner of a saloon. (*Pause.*) What's the point in visiting the place again? The more you forget the past, the better. I have got everything packed in the afternoon.

Jinnah Hmm. (*With a paper in his hand.*) Now lend me your ears. Tell me how well I have written this draft. I will deliver this speech on the 11th at Karachi. Let me read it out.

Fatima (*suddenly lobs a question*) You visited Ruttie's grave today in the morning, right?

Jinnah (*feigns as if he could not hear anything.*) See, in the second stanza, I write, 'Remember, you are now a part of a sovereign constitutional power.' Here I have replaced the word, 'power' with 'body'. Again, say . . .

Fatima Am I right? You did visit Ruttie's grave?

Jinnah In the end I have written, similar to the different sects in the Muslim community like Pathan, Punjabi, Shia, Sunni, etc. there are divisions among the Hindus too, like Brahmin, Vaishnaba, Kshatriya, Bengali, Madrasi, etc.

Fatima *Bhaiya*!

Jinnah Here I am in double mind about whether I am correct in mentioning Bengalis after Brahmin or Kshatriya. Because, you see 'Bengali Brahmins' and 'Bengali Muslims' can co-exist. Isn't it? So . . .

Fatima (*raising her voice*) I am asking you something, *Bhaiya*.

Silence. **Jinnah** *turns towards* **Fatima**.

Jinnah (*simpers*) *Bhaiya*?

Fatima Yes, you are my *Bhaiya*.

Jinnah And you are my *Behen*. Aren't you?

Their gazes are fixed at each other. There is a momentary silence. **Jinnah** *breaks the silence.*

Jinnah Yes, I went to Mazgaon today in the afternoon and then finished the rest of my jobs.

Pause.

It was cloudy. When I crossed Byculla station the familiar fishy smell hit me. And when I crossed Tarana, the waves of the Arabian Sea caught my attention, that rocky terrain . . . (*Becomes distracted.*)

Yes, Fati, I did pay a visit to her grave at Mazgaon.

Fatima That is why, despite having a busy schedule, you came rushing from Delhi to Bombay. I kept wondering why you were so interested in coming to Bombay all of a sudden. You said that you had to pick up some important items from your South Court residence.

Jinnah Of course, yes, these books and some odds and ends . . .

Pause.

I am not sure whether I will ever be able to return to Bombay again!

Ambles towards the window.

Bombay. This city is my existence, Fatima. The Malabar hills, quiet sea, Nariman point, Churchgate, Victoria Terminus, attending Bombay High court daily walking by the Fashion Street, nightlong drafting of *Vakalatnamas* . . . this city has wrung my desire out of me. I have bared my soul to this city. This city has also given me a lot in return. A lot.

(*Suddenly gets angry.*) Even if you wish, your past cannot be wiped out in a flash, Fati. Life is not a blackboard where 'yesterday' can be wiped out crystal clean with a duster in a jiffy.

Fatima Okay, alright. I understand. Why are you talking unnecessarily today? Weird!

Jinnah Hmm. I am talking too much, am I? As a matter of fact, I am leaving this city for good and I will never return to Bombay from Karachi again. I know. Yet it is giving me a weird feeling. Anyway, it's pointless to be so emotional. You are correct.

Fatima You still do remember about my dental clinic, *Bhaiya*? You arranged it all for me.

Jinnah (*parks himself in the chair*) Of course, I remember it. Anyway, tell Gauhar not to grill the steak anymore. Go and check it yourself. And send some coffee for me. I am feeling fatigued. Let me amend the draft in the meantime. You may go now.

Fatima *stands still.* **Jinnah** *pays her a glance.*

Fatima Which flowers did you offer at Ruttie's grave? Her favourite, chrysanthemum?

Jinnah I can't recollect. A child was selling flowers outside Church Glory. I took whatever I got from him to lay on her grave. You go now. By the way, there is a *Complete Shakespeare* by Cambridge on the rack beside my bedroom. Get it packed. I will have a look at the rest of the books later and choose the ones to carry. Oh, by the way . . .

Pauses.

Fatima What is it?

Jinnah I have already packed all my suits sometime back. There are some more dresses in the wardrobe . . .

Pauses. **Fatima** *smiles.*

Fatima I know. You mean Ruttie's gowns and skirts, right? I have laid those in order on your bed.

Jinnah Oh have you?

Fatima Yes, in the afternoon itself. I am not sure in which of your bags should I pack them.

Jinnah Let me decide that. Nobody should touch them. I will figure out where to pack them.

Fatima Alright, I am sending your coffee.

She leaves. **Jinnah** *appears distracted again. The next moment he concentrates on the draft. Starts dialling a number on the phone.*

Jinnah Hello, get me to Pirzada. Yes. (*Waits. Then starts speaking.*) Pirzada, pass on the message to the secretary of *Baralaat* that I have decided to take an early morning flight on the 7th, I mean the day after tomorrow, to reach Karachi . . . Yes, I know *Baralaat* is apprised of this; however, listen to me carefully. Yesterday, in Delhi he had offered to lend me his personal aircraft to fly to Karachi. In that case, we need to prepare a list of passengers who can accompany me and Fatima on board. You instruct Chagla to prepare a list and keep it ready. He should get it vetted by me after I reach Delhi tomorrow morning . . . What, I don't get you? Who will not follow instructions? Your instructions? Secretary to Mountbatten? Yes, I know, he is the *Baralaat*! So what? Pirzada, don't you forget that you too are the ADC of the first Governor General of Pakistan. Am I clear? Bye.

Disconnects the phone. Peers outside and is surprised. **Dina Wadia**, **Jinnah***'s daughter, enters. She is twenty-seven years of age. A tall, good-looking woman. A basket in one hand.* **Jinnah** *overcomes the initial awe and then composes himself.*

Jinnah Mrs Wadia, you?

Dina *Ji*, it is me, Mr Grey Wolf. How are you doing? Heard you had set your foot in my city this morning?

Jinnah (*looks at her*) Your city?

Dina Of course, it's my city. I have been here for nearly ten years.

Jinnah Hmm . . . indeed. By the way, who informed you about my arrival in Bombay?

Dina What are you saying? Does it require any source to know where and in which city *Quaid-e-Azam* is staying? The entire country knows this. I got the information in the afternoon itself.

Jinnah No, no. I have come to Bombay just for a day. I have come without informing anybody else. I will go back to Delhi tomorrow and fly to Karachi the day after. For good.

Dina I know. (*Slightly raises the basket.*) Where shall I keep it?

Jinnah What is there in it?

Dina Got some good fruits near Mangladas. Peach, karonda, carambola. I brought some for you. Now this . . . by the way, where is *Fufi*?

Jinnah She is inside. (*Presses the bell.*) But why did you have to carry this upstairs? Where is your driver?

Dina He is waiting downstairs. Your security stopped him from entering the house, so I thought of carrying it myself. It is not that heavy.

Jinnah Do you have any purple jamun in your basket? Let me try one.

Dina I think I have. I bought a platter of fruits.

Opens the lid of the basket, picks up one jamun and hands it over to **Jinnah**. **Jinnah** *takes a bite.* **Fatima** *enters with a tray in her hand. A flask and a few cups are placed on the tray.* **Fatima** *is also surprised to see* **Dina**.

Fatima Oh, you?

Dina Yes *Fufi*, it's me. I heard you all have come today. So, I thought of meeting you. I wonder when we will meet again . . .

Pauses. Shows her the basket.

Where should I keep it, *Fufi*?

Fatima Give it to me. I will take care of it. Hope you will have dinner with us?

Dina No, no. My son will start crying. I slipped out of my house when he fell asleep. After getting up he will definitely be on the lookout for me.

Fatima How old is Nus now?

Dina He is three and half years old. *Fufi,* give me some coffee please?

Jinnah Of course, here it is.

Tries to pour coffee in her cup clumsily. **Fatima** *goes to help him quickly.*

Fatima You won't be able to pour it properly. Let me do it.

She pours coffee in the cup.

Jinnah Tell Abul to bring one more cup.

Fatima You carry on. Let me take the fruit basket inside. Here is your coffee.

Hands over the cup to **Dina**.

Fatima You stay here. Let me go to the kitchen. Don't you want to take some food?

Dina Don't worry, *Fufi*. I will stay here for a while and then leave. Since I came rushing, I could not bring anything for you.

Fatima Oh, come on. What will you bring for me? It means a lot that you have come.

She goes inside with the basket. **Jinnah** *lights a cigarette.*

Jinnah Why does Nus sleep so late? What does he do in the afternoon?

Dina Usually he sleeps in the afternoon. A teacher visits him every evening. Yesterday night he felt a bit feverish. Worn out, he has fallen asleep today.

Jinnah Oh, then you could have brought him along tonight.

Dina I did think about it. It's been a long time since you have seen him. But he has been snappish today. I thought you may be busy as well, so . . .

Jinnah Has he become naughty nowadays?

Dina He keeps quiet in front of me. Otherwise, he is very skittish.

Jinnah Hope he is concentrating well in his studies?

Dina Yes, he is.

Jinnah My house looks so messy now. You must have noticed. Almost everything is packed. No, I have already sent a big chunk of my belongings to Karachi a month back. And some have been sent to my house at Aurangzeb road. A few things are lying in this house. So, tell me what should I gift to Nus? I can send it through you.

Dina You don't need to send anything to him. He has plenty of toys. He does not require anything now.

Looks at **Jinnah**.

Dina Have you come to Bombay again just for this reason, Grey Wolf? Just to empty your house?

Jinnah *looks at* **Dina**.

Jinnah How does it bother you, Mrs Wadia? Does it really make a difference to you as to when and where your *Abbu* goes?

Dina I keep myself abreast of every move you make, Grey Wolf. Not even a year has passed since you had a meeting with Jawahar uncle here in this house.

Jinnah All of India knows about that. Ten days from today, the whole of Pakistan will keep an update about me as well. How does that even bother you?

Dina (*replies gently*) We are meeting after so many days, is it necessary for you to be difficult with me even today?

Jinnah *stares. Intends to reply. Remains quiet.*

Dina Anyway, congratulations, A*bbu*! You could make it possible. Nobody but you have been able to singlehandedly build a country like this. Now you can declare unhesitatingly that you have your two children – Dina and Pakistan.

Jinnah I am leaving for Karachi the day after tomorrow. I am considering going on *Baralaat*'s personal aircraft. They are planning to welcome me there.

Dina Hmm. Then, what are you doing here today, in Bombay instead of Delhi?

Jinnah As I said, I came here to have a last look at this house and to take away whatever light and paltry is left – some of my books and some old files, etc. That's it.

Dina *looks at* **Jinnah** *for some time. Then suddenly enquires.*

Dina Did you visit my *Ammi*'s grave today, Grey Wolf? Somebody informed me. He supposedly saw you at Mazgaon.

Jinnah *looks at* **Dina** *for sometime.*

Dina That is why you came here, am I right? Because you will probably never be able to come here again. So, you wished to place flowers on my *Ammi*'s grave for one last time, right?

Fatima *enters with her cup of coffee.*

Fatima I have asked Gauhar to quickly prepare a few keema-chops for you. Once done, I will go and get it. Let me serve you some more coffee.

Pours some coffee for **Dina**.

Fatima Cookies are out of stock. Abul did not buy any. I have settled Abul's salary, *Bhaiya*. Tomorrow morning, he will move to his home at Worli.

Jinnah I had asked Abul to reach Delhi after a couple of days and also offered to arrange a flat for him right beside Gauhar's flat at Karachi. But Abul is not ready to leave Bombay. He says that he can't leave his ancestral home. Old school of thought! Look at me, even I am leaving my South Court residence but he can't leave his shanty. They do not understand the significance of Pakistan.

Sips from his cup.

How old is this house after all? It just seems that day. When Balley told me that it would cost around two lakhs of Rupees to build the house, many of my friends in the court were awestruck.

Just imagine, how much the current value of the house at Mount Pleasant Road would be? Don't you forget that it is in South Bombay! And the beautiful Arabian Sea is visible right there.

Dina Are you planning to dispose of this house too, *Abbu*?

Jinnah What will I do with this? I have already sold off my four other houses. The last one bungalow at Aurangzeb Road in Delhi was also purchased by my client, *Sardar* Baisakh Singh. I am planning to give him the offer of this house . . .

Dina You mean to say . . .

Jinnah No, I have not finalized on it yet. But if I finally decide it will be him.

Chuckles.

Baisakh Singh! He is now dreaming that like Shobha Singh, he will also bag the title 'Sir' from the British.

(*Speaks to himself.*) If the history of Delhi is ever written, the names of five Sikh Sardars who laid the foundations of New Delhi have to be incorporated in it.

He stubs out the cigarette.

Dina Don't sell this house, *Abbu*.

Jinnah What do you mean? What are you trying to say?

Dina Don't sell this house. I mean, let this house remain.

Jinnah What do you mean by let this remain? Who will take care of this house?

Dina You have so many contacts. Ask the independent Indian government to make some arrangement for this house.

Jinnah Are you crazy? Who do I make such a request to now? And as matter of fact why should they, in the first place, entertain me? No, no, this cannot be!

Dina I am your only daughter, *Abbu*. I am pleading you not to sell this house. Please don't do this. This will not be a right decision on your part.

Silence.

Jinnah But tell me why? Do you want to stay over here?

Dina No. The house at Marine Drive, which I now own after my divorce with Nevile, is no less than the house where Nevile stays.

Jinnah Oh yes. You are right. I am really sorry, Mrs Wadia. Please forgive me for asking whether you want to stay in this house.

Dina *Abbu*, if you always behave like this . . .

I just wish to tell you one right thing at the right moment.

Jinnah (*interrupts*) This house belongs to your *Fufi* in accordance with the will that I made eight years ago. Accordingly, Fatima is the legitimate owner of this house now. If Fati concurs with your request then this house will not be sold.

Dina *looks at* **Fatima**.

Fatima *Bhaiya*, you are fully aware that this house is formally in my name, but your decision will be final. But I primarily agree with Dina. If it is Dina's wish, don't sell this house, *Bhaiya*.

Jinnah I . . .

Fatima This is your lucky house, *Bhaiya*. Just imagine, what an important role this house has played for the last ten years in your professional and political life, and even in the course of you gaining Pakistan. Keep this house, *Bhaiya*.

Jinnah Fati, the day after tomorrow we . . .

Dina I believe when you stood in front of *Ammi*'s grave at Mazgaon, *Ammi* must have suggested the same.

Jinnah *glances at his daughter for a moment and then dials a number.*

Jinnah Hello operator, get me Jawaharlal.

Hangs up the phone. Silence. **Jinnah** *strolls towards the cabinet behind him. He takes out bottles of whiskey, wine and some glasses. While arranging them on the table he gazes at* **Dina**.

Jinnah Mrs Wadia you were saying something, sometime ago?

Dina What did I say?

Jinnah No, you were saying that you came here to tell me the right thing at the right time.

Dina Yes, I did. Do you have any objection to what I said, *Abbu*?

Jinnah No, your timing is impeccable when it comes to saying the right thing at the right moment.

I had asked you during your marriage that out of lakhs of Muslims staying in our country you failed to find even one educated man to marry, such that you had to finally marry a Parsi. What was your response?

Fatima (*chuckles*) *Bhaiya*, undeniably, your daughter's reply could not have been more apt.

Jinnah (*as if trying to recollect*) 'There was no dearth of beautiful, modern Muslim girls in the country. Still, why did you marry a Parsi woman, Grey Wolf?'

Fatima *bursts into laughter.* **Jinnah** *reprimands her.*

Jinnah Don't laugh, Fati.

Pours whiskey from the bottle. Prepares a peg of wine for **Dina**.

Cheers. (*Sips from his glass.*) Right thing at the right time. Hmm . . . Fati, you all forget that Ruttie converted her religion before we got married. She even changed her name.

Dina Yes, *Ammi* became Mariam.

(*Looks at* **Jinnah**.) Even I changed my religion before marrying. So, there's no difference, it's one all. *Abbu*, you had taught me during my childhood that religion cannot be the only identity of a human being.

Jinnah (*gets angry*) No need to remind me what I used to teach you when you were a child, Mrs Wadia.

Jinnah of the past can never ever be the same as Jinnah at present. Never. It is not desirable as well.

Phone starts ringing, **Jinnah** *receives the call.*

Hello, Jawahar. This is me. Yes, please listen. I need a help from you. Hello, I am calling from Bombay. I will not dispose of my South Court house here. I will be glad if your government acquires this house after the 15th of this month. Hello . . . no, I am not saying that. You can use this for setting up a foreign consulate, preferably a European country. I don't want you to allocate it for any south-east Asian country. Please do this favour for me. Jawahar, I have never asked you for anything. You are the first Prime Minister of your country and I am also the first Governor General of my country. I request you to please honour my plea. . . what? . . . pardon me, can't hear you, Hello? What did you say? You will think over it? Okay, please do think about it. Alright, I am leaving it to you. Thanks, Jawahar. Thank you. Sorry to bother you! Okay, Jawahar, bye.

Puts the phone down. **Fatima** *gets up.*

Fatima Great, this matter seems to have been taken care of. Let me go and check what Gauhar is doing with the fries.

She goes inside and **Jinnah** *raises a toast with* **Dina**.

Dina How are you keeping, *Abbu*? Do you still drink daily?

Jinnah (*smiles*) Forget about my health! Now, I am doing better. I mean, definitely better than last year. But I drink less these days. Don't you know what happened to me when I was returning to Delhi from Shimla?

Dina What?

Jinnah I fell so sick in the train that Dr Patel had to be given a call midway. The train was pulled up at a station to take him on board. Patel advised me not to disembark from the train at Dadar as thousands of League supporters were waiting for me at the station. So, I was taken to Kalyan. From the station I was taken straight to the hospital. They did an x-ray on me. Their apprehension (*pointing towards his lungs*) was found to be true. You know, Patel advised me to go to a sanatorium for three months. (*Scoffs.*) The gink is after all a Hindu. He knew if Jinnah is shunted to a hospital for three months, Pakistan will also be delayed. But he is a renowned doctor. I can't do without him.

(*Pauses. Then snarls.*) I am not like Maulana Azad to defer all my meetings after dusk.

Dina *Abbu*, you take good care of yourself. Your new country seriously needs you.

Jinnah Is this also pointing out the right thing at the right moment, Mrs Wadia?

Dina What I am saying is undoubtedly the right thing. But I am not sure whether this is the right time for it.

Fatima *enters with food. She serves it to* **Jinnah** *and* **Dina**. *Gives them spoons, forks and napkins. She also takes some for herself.* **Jinnah** *takes a bite at the fries.*

Jinnah Thanks, Fatima. Gauhar has prepared this well. What about my steak?

Fatima It will take a little more time. He has done some processing on the raw steak.

Jinnah Yes, that is what he is supposed to do. Do you know where he worked as a chef? Imperial Hotel.

Dina You have made him accompany you to Bombay? As your cook?

Jinnah Of course! Who else but Gauhar can cook healthy food for me?

Fatima What an example of a healthy food. Your *Abbu* is still having steak every night. I insist that he has some boiled vegetables too but who cares.

She sways her head sideways. **Jinnah** *prepares another peg.*

Jinnah This is how *Quaid-e-Azam* will lead his life, Fati. I have lived like this forever and can't change my habits at this age. Huh . . . boiled vegetables. If vegetables are what I have to eat then why at all, at the dawn of civilization, did we descend from trees?

Fatima *and* **Dina** *giggle.* **Jinnah** *goes to pour more wine for* **Dina**. **Dina** *refuses. She is yet to finish her wine in the glass.*

Jinnah Well, Mrs Wadia, your South Court residence then remains. Though I am not sure whether Jawahar will honour my request. But he is a gentleman like me. I hope he will not place this house under the Enemy Property Act.

Dina What is the Enemy Property Act?

Jinnah (*smiles*) Yes, this Act exists. Last week I was going through it in the latest edition of Crowley's. Jawahar is also a distinguished barrister. Well, not as celebrated as me, he has not even practised law, but I am sure he will consult this book. I too will need to read more on the issue. Let's see. (*Changes his tone.*)

By the way, I have kept your request, Mrs Wadia.

Now, will you honour my request? Or will you continue to be arrogant with me, as ever before?

Fatima Oh, not again, *Bhaiya*! You can never forget who had done what in the past. Try to ignore the past. Even with your own daughter you will . . . strange.

Jinnah Fati, my memory is my biggest weakness. I wish to wipe it off, but I cannot. I don't know why? What's the matter? Why have you fallen silent, Mrs Wadia?

Dina You are a formidable barrister, *Abbu*. Your appearance petrifies your opponents in court. So, I am wondering what you are up to now. As a matter of fact, I am also a little scared.

Jinnah You are your father's daughter indeed. You never give your word in one go. You are an astute lady, really. (**Dina** *smiles.*) Well, well.

Fatima Dina, don't decline your *Abbu*'s request. Please do agree with what he says, sweetheart.

Dina But if he does not open up on what he wants, how will I understand?

Fatima Yes, please tell her, *Bhaiya*. I am also getting curious.

Jinnah It's pretty simple! As a president, I believe it is my duty to know when the daughter of *Quaid-e-Azam* will first set her foot on independent Pakistan.

Dina (*mumbles*) Pakistan . . . independent Pakistan! (*Looks at* **Jinnah**.) Have you given any thought, *Abbu*, on how the flag of independent Pakistan will look?

Jinnah (*smiles*) Surely. Do you want to have a look at it?

Takes out the flag of Pakistan from his drawer, shows it to **Dina**.

Jinnah Please note, six days from today, on the 11th, this flag is going to get unanimous approval in our new house of parliament. Look at this green portion, it represents our unconditional loyalty to Islam. And mind this white part which signifies that in our new country rights of minorities will be secured.

Dina It bears a close resemblance to the flag of your Muslim League.

Jinnah (*sneers*) Do you really think in the absence of the Muslim League or, as a matter of fact, without the person sitting opposite to you, Pakistan would have been possible? So, how else should the flag of the independent country look like? Amiruddin Kidwai has designed this flag and handed it over to me. Our new ministry is going to take the oath on 14 August standing under this flag. Tell me, how does it look?

Dina Superb. It is really noteworthy that this flag is ensuring the safety of the minority communities. What can be more beautiful? But, *Abbu*, will the safety of the minority communities actually be protected in your country? Or, will it merely remain as a symbol on this flag?

Jinnah The telephone is right here on the table. Just call your Jawahar uncle and enquire from him that I have heard your independent country is going to be secular. Will people from all religions get equal rights and respect in your country?

Dina Why should I call him? I will ask him directly whenever I get an opportunity to meet him.

She takes out an Indian national flag from her sling bag.

Even I have one with me, *Abbu*.

Jinnah What a surprise! Where did you get this?

Pause.

Of course, they got the approval on their flag on the 22nd of last month itself. It is now available everywhere.

Dina Right you are. I have collected one too.

Jinnah But the fact that their tri-colour resembles the flag of the Congress, didn't that raise a query in your mind? All your enquiries and suspicions are held only against your *Abbu*, right?

Stops, stares at **Dina** *with suspicion.*

Jinnah Why have you brought the Indian flag with you here? What will you do with it?

Dina *chuckles.* **Jinnah** *looks uncomfortable.*

Dina Nothing special. Coming 14 August at 12 o'clock midnight, that is when it will be 15 August . . .

Jinnah You mean, on your birthday?

Dina Exactly, *Abbu*. It will be my twenty-eighth birthday on 15 August 1947. *Abbu*, I will hoist both these flags (*takes Pakistan's flag from* **Jinnah**) on the terrace of my Marine Drive apartment, exactly at midnight, all by myself. By that time my son Nus will have fallen asleep in my room. Many cars will zoom past my flat, honking and celebrating as they head towards Nariman Point. Noise and cheers of celebration will fill the air around. I will quietly hoist both the flags on the rooftop of my apartment. Tears may well up in my eyes but I will raise the slogans all by myself, '*Mera Bharat Mahan*' and '*Pakistan Zindabad*'.

Jinnah (*becomes irate and back Pakistan's flag from* **Dina***'s hand*) Yes, this is exactly what I feared. This means that you will not visit Pakistan, am I right? You will continue your fight with your *Abbu* in this case too?

Dina *Abbu*, I am a non-Muslim now. What will be my social identity in Pakistan? You all first decide what status will you grant to the non-Muslim women in your country? Thereafter I will definitely pay a visit to your country. (*Smiles.*) Otherwise, why won't I visit a country founded by my Grey Wolf? I will surely go there.

Fatima Well, what about this country? If this country does not grant you citizenship, what will you do then?

Dina Why won't they, *Fufi*? I have been staying here for so many years. My husband and my son belong here as well. Why won't I get citizenship?

Jinnah You leave it to me to decide about the fate of your social status in Pakistan. You don't have to get involved in it. Let me first reach there, let me settle down, then I will certainly make an arrangement.

Dina *Abbu*, I will not go there. If needed, I will rather get settled in New York or London, but I will not be a part of this bizarre division. Besides this, what will my Nus's fate be? Neville will not allow him to leave anyway.

Jinnah Right! Absolutely right! Sometimes I forget that now you are MrsWadia. Even after your break-up from Neville, you are still Mrs Wadia! Even after your husband has converted from Zoroastrianism to Christianity, you remain the same Mrs Wadia. Even after your *Abbu* has created a new country, you still remain Mrs Wadia.

Dina Neville will be reconverted to Zoroastrianism, *Abbu*. He intimated to me the other day. He will not remain a Christian for long.

Jinnah Oh, really? Why on earth does your husband, Mr Wadia, change his religion like a train changing tracks at a junction?

Dina *Abbu*, you are yet to read Neville's mind. He does not care much about religion. He loves experimenting. He is keen to study different religions.

Fatima Then you ask him to embrace Islam to bury the hatchet on this issue once and for all.

Dina It's absolutely his personal choice. Why should I advise him on this? And even if he finally accepts Islam as his religion, I will never change mine. So, you see the issue of my social identity in Pakistan still remains unresolved.

Jinnah I have already told you to leave it to me.

Fatima But why will you not accept Islam? Your ex-husband, being a Parsi can change his religion, and you can't even after you get a divorce from him?

Dina No, I can't. My *Ammi* converted her religion from Parsi to Muslim, I have converted from Muslim to Parsi. I have repaid my debt to the Parsi community on my *Ammi*'s behalf.

Jinnah Your mother's influence is reflecting in your action. But you are forgetting that during the time you were growing up your mother was not fully well. If she has spoken to you about repaying her debt it must have been her lamentation during ill-health, and might as well be an outcome of her complex vengeance on me.

Dina (*visibly irritated*) You cannot simplify it like this . . .

Fatima *rises from her chair.*

Fatima It's getting late. You better have your dinner here, Dina. Let me go to the kitchen and instruct Gauhar to prepare dinner.

Dina Drop the idea, *Fufi*. I have taken enough food and will skip dinner.

Fatima Then you can at least have some soup. Allow me some time.

She goes inside. **Dina** *gets up and pours some wine in her glass. She goes towards the window.*

Dina My city, Bombay, looks so magnificent. See the flickering lights on the Malabar Hill, a couple of cars are seen spiralling up the hill from time to time. The quiet Arabian Sea is seen beneath with some people probably gossiping on its banks, saline sea waves are wetting their feet at intervals. At this hour it seems as if no violence is happening in any part of the world, there is no skirmish anywhere.

Jinnah But how untrue it is. Can your poetic composition change the outside world? It cannot. A bomb thrown from any part of the world can explode on those sitting and gossiping on the edge of the Arabian Sea. Just as your insight induces some truth, so is there a lurking reality on the other side as well. Always.

Dina *Abbu*, if *Ammi* had at any time complained against you to me, please don't curse her. Please don't forget that when you both got married, she was only eighteen and you were forty-two.

Jinnah She was only sixteen when we fell in love, Mrs Wadia.

Dina I know that. *Ammi* shared every minute detail with me. She shared with me the details of her *Abbu*, your erstwhile client and how close a relationship you two shared as friends. You all once made a trip to Darjeeling when *Ammi* was really young. She told me how she became attracted towards you there and also the story of her expressing her feelings to you. She told me everything. Under the spell of sickness *Ammi* used to share every detail with me. I was also very young to understand everything. For me it was a flight to a strange fancy – as if my *Ammi* was my daughter and I became my *Ammi*'s mother. Probably she felt relaxed by venting it out. Sometimes bewildered, I used to give her a patient hearing and make a few comments. All those conversations may sound meaningless and stupid but I still feel that *Ammi* experienced a sense of peace when I used to console her with my childish words.

Jinnah That was your *Ammi*'s biggest ammo. She was capable of creating such an impact in people's minds that in no time they adjudged her to be a hapless woman with the mind of an innocent child.

Dina That's exactly how my *Ammi* was, *Abbu*. And you know very well that she was fiercely emotional. Otherwise just imagine, a sixteen-year-old girl, while cutting the cake on her birthday, declared in front of her relatives and guests that if she had to marry at all, she would marry none other than 'J' – I will marry the most famous lawyer of India, Mohammad Ali Jinnah.

Jinnah (*indistinct voice*) Yes, the venue was Hotel Taj Mahal! And a few days before that I had put up a proposal before my friend, my would be father-in-law, Dinesh Petit – If you do not have any objection to inter-religious marriage and if your progressiveness is not just an eyewash, I want to marry your daughter Rattanbai Petit.

(*Pours some whiskey.*) Progressive. Huh . . . secular! Secular Dinesh Petit severed such a long relationship with me forever, in a whisker, just over a marriage proposal.

Dina He might have objected to the age difference you had with *Ammi*. Otherwise, he may have agreed to your proposal.

Jinnah No, he would have never agreed. If that had been the case, our relationship should have become normal after our marriage or after your birth. But that didn't happen.

Your *Nana* lived for four more years after your *Ammi*'s death. He did not even give me a call once. (*Pause.*) Your country has reminded me time and again from my childhood that it does not matter whether you are accomplished or rich or educated a person, you should not ultimately forget that you are actually a Muslim. Most of the times I have ignored these insults and indifferences shown towards me. But there are few wounds which never heal up, Mrs Wadia. This was definitely one of those wounds.

Otherwise, your *Nana*, Dinesh Petit, was such a nice person, so fun loving and jovial, the idea of a Muslim son-in-law made him . . .

Stops. **Dina** *goes near* **Jinnah**.

Dina It's okay, *Abbu*. You are still my Grey Wolf. Please don't feel bad, it makes me miserable. (*Changing the tone of her voice.*) Tell me, *Abbu*, you were not allowed to meet *Ammi* for two years, from when she was sixteen years old till she was eighteen. How did you both manage to keep in touch with each other during that time?

Jinnah What difference will it make? It seems to have happened in another age altogether. I hardly remember those days.

Smiles and then speaks indifferently.

When she was alone at her home, your *Ammi* and I talked over the telephone. Your *Ammi* used to give me a missed call. The time she would call was pre-decided. I used to wait for the phone to ring. Then I would return her call. We continued like this for two years. Once after returning from his office your *Nana* caught your *Ammi* almost red handed while we were talking. However, I immediately changed the tone of my voice while he was on the phone. Dear, don't you forget that when I was studying Law in London, I used to watch Shakespearean theatre every day. Dinesh Petit was unaware of how hard I had worked to become an actor. So, I decided to apply my acting skills there.

He starts laughing, **Dina** *joins him.* **Fatima** *enters.*

Fatima (*to* **Dina**) I have asked him to prepare a light soup for you. Once ready, I will serve it with a yummy bread. Before you leave you must have it.

Turns towards **Jinnah**.

Fatima *Bhaiya*, your steak is nearly ready.

(**Dina** *nods.*)

Fatima What is *Dinu* talking about, *Bhaiya*?

Jinnah (*glances at* **Fatima** *then turns towards* **Dina**) You are advocating so much on behalf of your *Ammi*, but do you know that you did not have a formal name till you were nine years old? We used to call you by any name of our choice. When we were about to send you to a school, we realized that you did not have a good name. You were finally named after your *Nani*. It was your *Ammi*'s decision. But it was me who first noticed that you did not have a good name.

Dina If you were the first person to notice it, you could have easily done it a few years earlier to save my *Ammi* from this burden. Isn't it?

Jinnah Yes, I am fully aware of it. A deceased person is always beautiful and one who is alive is by default the accused. Who does not know this? If I had died instead of your *Ammi* in your childhood, the arguments would have gone in my favour. Isn't it?

Fatima *Bhaiya*, how absurd can you be.

Jinnah (*agitated*) Mrs Wadia you must remember, even if I did not want to live, I had to live for the sake of history, to set foot on the new nation the day after tomorrow. History has always remained indifferent to trivial human weal and woe. It tears apart silly emotions, pleasures and despairs to move forward.

Dina That is history's misfortune. I don't believe history is so cruel and blunt. It keeps a record of human sorrow, joy and everything else, just that it is not always vocal about it.

Fatima Dina, please stop. *Bhaiya* will get agitated soon. I plead with you to not poke him.

Jinnah (*still agitated*) Mrs Wadia, you have become so weird. You neither keep any contact with me nor do you care whether I am alive or dead. Just because you heard that I had gone to offer flowers on your *Ammi*'s grave, you come all the way to my house after years to give me a piece of your mind.

Dina It is not I, *Abbu*, it is you who severed relationship with me after my marriage. And I haven't come here to give you a piece of my mind at all.

Fatima Dina, my dear, please stop now.

Jinnah What else have you done? Without prior appointment you have come to my house, just to let me know that you will not set foot in my newly built country and instead you will stay back in my enemy country! If needed, you will rather settle abroad than go to the nation I have founded. Against whom are you declaring *Jihad*? Do you think I don't understand anything?

Fatima *Bhaiya*, you please calm down.

Jinnah Your *Ammi* passed away when you were only ten. For the next three years your world encircled around me, Mrs Wadia. Even when you were in London with me. But after returning from London you somehow changed.

Dina And at that time, I never enjoyed your company for two consecutive days at home or in my life . . .

Jinnah I had no other choice. I do not see any justification in your getting so agitated with me for this reason. Since then, your mind became so detached from me that it has never healed. You seemed to have accepted your *Ammi*'s brief about me from within. Your feelings have always been targeted against me, against your own *Abbu*.

Dina No, it is not as you think.

Jinnah How dare you accuse me on so many accounts after coming to my house? Remember, I am the *Quaid-e-Azam*. The entire world's attention is now on me. And you have come here to express your apathy in accompanying me to Pakistan, the nation that I have built myself.

Dina My *Ammi*, I mean your wife, would have expressed the same feelings had she been alive, *Abbu*.

Jinnah (*exploding in anger*) Dina.

Dina At least that is what I feel. And you know quite well that what I am saying is right.

Fatima *becomes speechless.* **Jinnah** *keeps looking at his daughter. Then he restrains his anger. He moves towards the table and dials on the phone.*

Jinnah Operator. You leave it, I will call him directly.

Dials a number and waits for the response.

Hello, am I speaking to Neville? Neville Wadia? This is Jinnah speaking, Mohammad Ali Jinnah. Yes, please listen. Your ex-wife has come to my house. I have something important to discuss with you. I want to do that in the presence of both of you. Can you please come over to my Malabar Hill's South Court house now? I hope, like other *Bombaites* you too are aware of the location of my residence . . . Yes, thank you. Please do come. We are waiting for you.

Hangs up the phone. **Dina** *stands up.*

Dina What have you done?

Jinnah Now, if you call him and ask him not to come, I will call him tomorrow, and again the day after tomorrow. I will keep on calling him till I am able to convince you about the relation I shared with your *Ammi* in his presence.

Dina *Abbu*, Neville is no more my husband. It's been three years. He does not care about us anymore. We are done with our relationship.

Jinnah Mrs Wadia, your mother too is no more a part of this world. If she can still continue to stand between us, then even I have every right to call your ex-husband and speak my mind out according to my convenience. Do you follow me?

Dina Do you want to take revenge on me, *Abbu*? Are you still struggling to overcome your trifling sense of vengeance?

Jinnah Have you been able to overcome this? Who has been capable of doing so in this universe? Can anyone forget an insult? We are no gods, MrsWadia.

We are human beings, made of flesh and blood, not with smoke and dust. The whole world is driven by these diatribes, their impressions and their retributions. Those who want to add a different perspective to it, they are either damn liars or they deceive themselves.

Dina Please ask Neville not to come, *Abbu*. You are being unfair by inviting him here.

Jinnah I will not stop him. My ex-son-in-law should turn up here.

Dina You are behaving like a child, *Abbu*. Just tell him not to drop in. We do not need him here.

Fatima *Bhaiya*, ask him not to come. It is pointless now. You will fall sick.

Glancing at both of them **Jinnah** *moves towards the telephone, dials.*

Jinnah Hello, operator, connect me to the last dialled number.

He waits, holding the receiver in one hand. **Fatima** *and* **Dina** *watch* **Jinnah**. *Music is heard. Curtain falls.*

Interval.

Act Two

Curtain is raised after music fades out. It is late into the night. The first-floor room of **Jinnah** *appears again.* **Dina** *is reading a book sitting on a sofa.* **Fatima** *enters. They both are wearing similar clothes.*

Fatima Tell me, how did you find Gauhar's cooking?

Dina The soup was delectable, *Fufi*. It was spicy and yet so light.

Fatima He cooks really well. Which book are you reading now?

Dina Mulk Raj Anand's new novel, *The Big Heart*. Have you read it?

Fatima When was this published? I haven't seen it.

Dina A few days back. I bought it in London.

Fatima I read a book recently, *Kali Salwar*. Begum Rana suggested it. It is written by Sadat Hossain Manto. It is extremely obscene. I have asked *Bhaiya* to impose an outright ban on this kind of writing and writer in independent Pakistan.

Dina You found the book obscene?

Fatima What else? Every other sentence has vulgar words and settings. What is the point in writing about a prostitute's solitude?

Dina I loved *Kali Salwar*. I have also read his collection of short stories, *Dhuan*. Adequately realistic writing. He is probably a young writer. There is an aggression in his writing.

Fatima I don't know. I cannot understand what is the need to attack in literature.

Jinnah *enters wearing a Sherwani and a Jinnah cap.*

Jinnah Who has attacked whom?

Fatima We were discussing a writer.

Jinnah You all have a lot of spare time to read books and all. I don't have so much time in hand. I rather spend time reading books on law. But Dina from her early age has enjoyed reading literature.

Dina I didn't have any choice. It was difficult spending time alone. Books were my only acquaintance during my early age.

Jinnah (*standing near the cabinet upstage*) Can I offer you both a liqueur? I have one lovely Amaretto here. A gift from a client last year. I have had a little.

Fatima I won't have any. You serve it to Dinu, *Bhaiya*.

Jinnah *pours the drink for* **Dina** *and himself. He extends the glass to* **Dina**.

Jinnah Why don't you try, Fati? You know, at one time monks used to prepare liqueur in Italy.

Fatima Okay, let them. I don't like it. Did you take a bath, *Bhaiya*?

Jinnah Yes. (*To* **Dina**.) Who informed you that I visited your *Ammi*'s grave?

Dina (*chuckles*) Neville came to know. He called me up and told me.

Jinnah Okay. Someone must have informed him then.

Dina Possibly.

Jinnah You know, Bykulla station and its adjoining areas have not changed at all. (*Pauses*.) Do you prefer high-neck coats these days?

Dina Yes, why? I always wear covered clothes and you know it well. Why do you ask that?

Jinnah (*chuckles*) Yes, I know that. Your choice of clothes is the exact opposite to your *Ammi*'s. By the way, your coat looks good . . . (*Pauses*.) Actually, you know an incident happened here in Bombay.

Dina Which incident are you referring to?

Jinnah It happened some years back. Lord Willingdon was the Governor of Bombay at that time. Once, he invited us as a couple to Raj Bhavan for dinner. Your *Ammi* accompanied me. In fact, your *Ammi* was a genuinely modern, French-speaking fashionable lady. She attended the party wearing such a bold dress that the Governor and his wife were in for a shock. *Memsahib* immediately ordered a shawl to wrap around your *Ammi*. The moment the news reached me I lost my cool. Vexed, I asked the Governor directly, why a shawl? The Governor, caught on the wrong foot, muttered that supposedly Mrs Jinnah is feeling cold. I too was a grumpy man and I shot back, 'His majesty, the Governor need not be bothered about it. If Mrs Jinnah feels cold, she will let know herself.' We got involved in a row for a brief time. Immediately after, I left the party midway with your *Ammi* in the presence of all the guests in the hall.

Dina Very good. Great.

Fatima What is so wonderful about it? Should not one follow a dress code while attending an aristocratic party like this?

Dina Why shouldn't one follow that? Surely there wasn't any at Raj Bhavan that night. And when there are no such rules, invitees can wear anything of their choice. Women especially have an exclusive right. And not just my *Ammi*, I am also congratulating my *Abbu* for having allowed his wife to wear anything of her choice in society without making any fuss.

Jinnah Come on, your *Ammi* was a young lady then. At that point in time, there was hardly any learned lady like her in the entirety of Bombay. Why would I want to curb her freedom?

Fatima Freedom? Good. (*To* **Dina**.) So why do you prefer this high-neck coat?

Dina Because, you know I was an introvert from my early age. (*Chuckles*.) The clothes I wear of course reflect my nature.

Fatima Your *Ammi*'s nature was exactly your opposite. In every aspect.

Dina Possibly. But just as a hidden craze can stay passive within an introvert, a deep depression may exist within an extrovert, *Fufi*.

Fatima I don't understand much about it, Dinu. But I can recollect that a few days after *Bhaiya*'s marriage, I started spending the weekend at your *Abbu-Ammi*'s house. And whenever I recited the Quran aloud, Ruttie used to lose her temper. Once she exclaimed that the Quran was something to be discussed and not to be chanted aloud.

Dina *bursts into laughter.* **Jinnah** *joins her.* **Fatima** *fumes.*

Fatima You all can laugh at it but I don't find it funny at all. And *Bhaiya*, to be honest, you gave indulgence to Ruttie in this regard. And which Dinu seems to think is extremely modern.

Dina *Fufi*, you could not understand *Ammi*. Perhaps you are not supposed to.

Fatima What is there to understand here? You both always overdo! I am telling you . . .

Jinnah (*interrupts* **Fatima**) You have pointed out correctly, Fati. But indulgence may not be the right word, you may say that there was a mutual indulgence.

(*To* **Dina**.) Let me share a funny incident with you. I never really visited *Masjid*s right since my childhood. I am completely ignorant about the rituals. After the proposal of 'Pakistan' was accepted at Lahore, *Maulvis* from different parts of the country started accompanying me to various programmes.

Quiet naturally, I had to visit many *Masjid*s too. So, while offering prayers they noticed that their *Quaid-e-Azam* did not know how to recite *Namaz*. Even I was clueless about how to offer prayers wearing a suit. Before this, I had never recited *Namaz* in my life ever.

Fatima You have shared this story with us before. Don't try to digress from the topic we were discussing, *Bhaiya*.

Jinnah (*did not seem to hear* **Fatima**) The same thing happened after I won the last year's election. I organized a *Dawat* at noon. There I observed that most of the leaders of the Muslim League were not having any food. It intrigued me. My secretary Chagla whispered to me, what are you doing, sir? It is the month of Ramadan. They are observing *Roza*. Everybody was utterly surprised on having received my invitation. But they could not turn it down. And here the host is completely unaware of either Ramadan or the ritual of observing *Roza*. I had never observed *Roza* in my life.

He laughs as **Dina** *joins him.* **Fatima** *still appears irritated.*

Fatima *Bhaiya*, give me a straightforward answer to a simple query. Do you feel Ruttie was justified in making her remark on the *Quran*?

Jinnah You see, Fati, we are first-generation Muslims. My *Abbu*, Punjabhai Thakkar, in his bid to protest against the injustice meted out to my *Nana*, accepted Islam as his religion. Why? Because my *Nana* was a fishmonger, a fish wholesaler.

The villagers of Kathiawar where my *Nana* used to stay were all vegetarian Hindus. Interestingly my *Nana* too was an orthodox Hindu and a pure vegetarian. Even then there were restrictions on carrying out fish business in the village. Anyone doing so was ostracized. Though my *Nana* wanted to quit the fish business to retain his community membership, he was not allowed to do so. What a peculiar *Fatwa*.

Fatima (*peevishly*) Yes, I have come to know about this. But how is it important here?

Jinnah So, leave alone reciting the Quran, we never followed any rituals nor any customs. All our brothers followed the same path. How you turned into a devout Muslim right from your childhood is still a mystery to me.

Fatima So, you mean to say Ruttie was well within her right to say what she did and I was wrong.

Jinnah I never said that, Fati.

Fatima You said so. Don't forget, *Bhaiya*, the person you were twenty-five years ago is completely different from what you are today. You cannot afford to make such comments about religion in public now.

Dina (*stops* **Fatima**) What is your problem, *Fufi*? You are picking a fight with somebody who is no more in this world.

Jinnah Fati, don't preach me. I do not want to learn from you who I was earlier and what I have become now.

Fatima *rises from her chair.* **Dina** *goes near her.*

Dina Sit, *Fufi*. Please take your seat.

Fatima *bites her lip and then sits down. Silence.*

Dina You have not changed a bit . . . Excuse me, I need to use the washroom. *Abbu*, I will have some more liqueur. I will be back soon.

She goes inside. Silence. **Fatima** *starts sobbing.*

Jinnah What happened to you? What makes you cry?

Fatima Ruttie has always misbehaved with me, *Bhaiya*, even with you.

Jinnah Okay, it's alright. We can discuss this later.

Fatima She could never tolerate me. She considered me as her enemy.

Jinnah This is not an appropriate time to talk about this, Fati.

Fatima Your daughter is exactly like her mother, *Bhaiya*. She is very stubborn and arrogant.

Jinnah She has inherited these qualities from me, not from her *Ammi*. Don't forget, Fati, she lost her mother when she was only ten. Thereafter she stayed with me till her marriage. The real truth is she was brought up by you, not me. She is your daughter more than ours.

Fatima But she does not agree with this. Whenever she contemplates a comparison between me and Ruttie, she always takes her mother's side. Even she believes, just like you, that I misbehaved with her mother.

Jinnah What she thinks is immaterial. I know it well that you never misbehaved with Ruttie.

Fatima Do you really believe this, *Bhaiya*? Do you truly think so? I am happy with that.

Jinnah Of course, I do. Fati, finally we have got Pakistan, our long-cherished dream. It will be prudent if we do not discuss our private matters anymore. You are also a political person now. How can you get so much affected by these trifling matters? (**Dina** *returns.*)

Fatima Come, take your seat.

Dina The washroom has been renovated. Right, *Fufi*?

Jinnah Yes, I did not like the tiles which Balley had fixed earlier. So, I changed those three years ago and a few things . . . Here is your Amaretto.

Pours liqueur for **Dina.** *She sips from her glass.*

Dina *Abbu*, a while ago I was thinking of a striking coincidence. (**Jinnah** *looks at* **Dina**.) You see almost all the prominent leaders of our country now are widowers – you, Gandhiji, Jawaharlal Nehru, Vallabh Bhai Patel, Maulana Abul Kalam Azad. Most of them have lost their wives.

Jinnah Yes, but so what?

Dina Nothing actually. It means most of your wives are no more, and you all do not share a healthy relationship with your children. You could not accept my marriage, Jawahar uncle could not accept his daughter's marriage as well, and I have heard that even Gandhiji is not on good terms with his son . . .

Jinnah (*interrupts*) Politics is totalitarian in itself, Mrs Wadia. This is at least true for a big country like this. You aspire to be a full-timer in politics and also wish to pay equal attention to your family – these two cannot go on simultaneously. You have to sacrifice any one of these.

Dina It's probably true. And this will burn one from within as well. But where this ultimately leads life is something that remains to be seen.

Jinnah No, the difference is that you all have unlimited time to ponder over this inflamation. But we are ultimately not left with much time in hand to even think over the agitation within. And how will life lead one and to what end is difficult to predict even a day before.

Fatima *gets up.*

Fatima It's time for you to take the medicines, *Bhaiya*.

Jinnah Ask Abul to get them.

Fatima Don't worry, I will go and bring it. Moreover, I have to instruct Gauhar about tomorrow's breakfast. I will be back soon.

She leaves the room. **Jinnah** *lights a cigarette.*

Jinnah Tell me what brings you here, Dina. Is it just to advise me not to sell the house or something else as well?

Dina (*smiles*) You read my mind well, *Abbu*, and that is why you always doubt me. You guessed it right that your daughter would not suddenly show up here after such a long gap for any trivial issue. (*She takes out a bundle of letters from her bag.*) *Ammi* handed this over to me the day before she passed away.

Jinnah What? What is this?

Dina The letters you and *Ammi* exchanged between each other. *Ammi* carefully archived all the letters after your marriage. The day before she died, she handed over these letters to me and advised me to hand them over to you. But I didn't. I kept them in my custody. Honestly speaking, initially I felt tempted to run through the letters. I read them all. Thereafter I kept those with me. I had thought of returning all to you. But somehow, it didn't materialize. As I was too young, I was scared thinking that you might take exception to it. Why I kept those letters in my possession all these days.

Jinnah Wait. You just said that your *Ammi* handed over these letters to you the day before her death to give them to me?

Dina Yes. Why?

Jinnah Where did she hand them over to you?

Dina Hotel Taj Mahal, in her suite. *Ammi* was having an acute pain of colitis when she gave the letters to me.

Jinnah Just wait, wait! You mean to say your *Ammi* did realize in advance that she was going to die the next day.

Dina (*looks at* **Jinnah** *calmly*) She knew it for sure. I think even you knew about it, *Abbu.*

Jinnah Dina!

Dina You mean to say you were unaware of the fact that *Ammi* was taking more sleeping pills than what was prescribed to her? Didn't you know, she used to keep a greater number of sedatives with her?

Jinnah I never allowed your *Ammi* to keep excess sleeping pills with her. Never.

Dina Yes, but you should have gauged much earlier that since *Ammi* was a frequent visitor at Taj from her childhood, she could easily get those procured through anybody there. Please do remember, *Abbu*, it was I who first discovered *Ammi* dead on her hotel bed that morning. Then I was only ten. After getting up from bed I went to the washroom. *Ammi* was in a jovial mood the night before. She appeared absolutely at peace. She invited me to sit beside her. She was reading a book of poetry written by Oscar Wilde. Putting the book aside, she caressed me for a long time and handed over the letters to me. She chatted with me about you for an extended period that night. She said she did not know who she loved more, you or me. You know, on earlier occasions, whenever she spoke something about you, she failed to hold back her tears. But that night when she talked about you, she did not weep even once. Her innocent face was rather glowing bright. Then she said, 'Now, you go to bed. Tomorrow early morning, your *Abbu* will surely come to take us back home.' She added, 'Once back home, we will never ever fight with each other, I know this causes an immense emotional pressure on you.' Then she said, 'Now go and sleep.'

Jinnah (*broken voice*) You . . . why did you not give me a call right then? I would have picked you up from the hotel that night itself.

Dina I did not realize, *Abbu*. I could not understand at all. I was only ten years old then. Why are you forgetting that?

Jinnah Your *Ammi* was by nature very stubborn, very obstinate. She did whatever she felt was right. But, you know, the last time she left the house after quarrelling with me, I did not mutter a word. Usually, she was the one who would barge into my room and start accusing me. After some time, I would also lose my cool, and pay her back in her same coin. Even, I would not be able to keep my patience. I was not the type to sit quietly and absorb everything. At the slightest provocation, I used to get irritated. But you know, that evening I did not utter even a word. Like a storm she barged into my room, criticized me and then finally shouted at me saying, 'I am leaving this house now and will never return.'

Dina Why didn't you stop her, *Abbu*?

Jinnah I don't know, maybe I was also exhausted. She would threaten me, fight with me and leave our house time and again. . . Dina, my love, please try and understand my condition back then. At that point in time, I was a back-bencher in politics. I became almost certain that I would no longer be able to continue with my political journey. Not only politics, I had lost all hope of being able to do my own work properly. I felt like a piece of wreckage. I smoked nearly one hundred cigarettes a day, roamed across the streets of Bombay like a crank or spent some time by the seashore. Thereafter, I used to return home to discover that my only emotional support, your mother, was practising Planchette, and cultivating the spirits. With our pet cat in one hand, she was trying to make contact with the world beyond death. We used to have fights daily, every day. At 6 o'clock in the morning, at 2 in the afternoon or even as late as 3 at night. And whenever I was alone, with a broken heart I used to tell myself, I am Mohammad Ali Jinnah, one of the most accomplished lawyers of India who has everything, including enough money to take good care of his interests and luxuries; I have all except one thing and that is peace. Perhaps it is my frenetic temperament, or my wild lunacy which springs out from a mysterious source deep inside my soul that no science can rationalize. Perhaps this has been the reason behind the tumult that has surrounded my life, this is the reason behind my ever-engulfing passionate rage.

And maybe it is in this scorching heat that my darling Ruttie, my most affectionate, the most lovable person in my life is getting singed. I could see my conjugal life getting ruined. Just imagine my dear, how awful it was. At one time, I was feeling terrible seeing your mother suffer and was blaming and cursing myself for that, and again at the same time I was unable to control my temperament whenever I was fighting with her. When she said bitter things to me, I used to give it back to her uncontrollably. Allah! Sometimes I wonder whether the heart of a person who can keep their head ice-cool in the toughest of situations is prepared in Iblis's kitchen.

Dina *Abbu*, please control yourself, don't cry. It gives me pain.

Jinnah *is seen panting. He then speaks.*

Jinnah And in politics, this half-naked fakir by that time had taken complete control over Congress. My last confidant, Motilal Nehru, also became influenced by Gandhi because of his own son. The entire middle class and working class of India, both Hindus and Muslims, were behind Gandhi and following him fanatically. And I, once the pioneer of Hindu–Muslim unity, was gradually fading away from politics. Dina, let me tell you that I gave my every bit to Congress. Despite being invited for a meeting of the Muslim League, I used to participate in the conference called by the Congress as a first priority and deliver lectures on Hindu–Muslim harmony. But the year before your mother passed away, I attended one conference held in Calcutta to discover that in the newly proposed Indian Constitution by Motilal Nehru only 27 per cent seats were kept reserved for the Muslims. I got angry.

Just because I have always spoken about Hindu–Muslim unity did not imply that Muslims will remain deprived in all aspects. I demanded 33 per cent reservations for the Muslims. Congress did not agree to my proposal in any way. In my entire political career, I had never felt slapped so hard. I returned to Bombay empty handed. There, I came to know your mother's cocaine intake had gone up. And above all, the daily feuds and unrest at home started affecting me. I felt fatigued, Dina. I was gradually feeling drained out. The same me who was once so confident about one of my hands firmly entrenched in politics and the other hand strongly clasped with your *Ammi* . . . suddenly found both my hands had been chopped off.

Dina It's alright, it's okay.

Forcibly brings energy in her voice.

But Abbu, do you remember the days when you left everything after *Ammi*'s death and we shifted to London. Oh! I still remember Heath's house at Hampstead so clearly. And the Bentley car. Bradbury used to give me a ride in that and I used to love it. As if it was built by an angel. Its interior was so quiet and soft.

Jinnah (*appears distracted*) Why did your *Ammi* pick on me to fight, I don't exactly remember now. Or perhaps I don't want to remember? She had a perception that I was harming her. She thought I was the danger incarnate in her life. As if I had deceived her by playacting a lover when she was young, I had harmed her by inviting her into this relationship and by marrying her. Since we had a huge age gap, presumably gap in mental wavelength too. Ruttie could never accept from within the alienation she faced from her own family, from her own community. At first, she had convinced herself that she would succeed in adjusting to the situation. Later on, she failed to live up to her belief. Moreover, from 1922 I got too busy in politics. I could not accompany her when she went to London with her mother. She went to Paris, but I could not go. But how I had wished to have her by my side in my political life. Once she went to the Nagpur Conference with me. But she could not quite adjust to having to meet so many people, attend boring discussions, spend hours in a small suffocating party office and listening to speeches. Probably it was justified on her part.

Fatima *returns.*

Fatima *Bhaiya*, some people from Chamanlal Association are waiting to meet you in the ground floor. They want to greet you with a bouquet of flowers.

Jinnah What? No, I can't meet anyone now. It's almost 9 o'clock at night. Why have they come so late without making any phone call?

Fatima If they were unknown to me, I would not have informed you. I would have shooed them away. Chamanlal is accompanying them. He is requesting only two minutes of your time.

Jinnah Oh, Chamanlal has come. Okay. (*Thinks for a while.*) I will go and meet them at once. Have you confirmed tomorrow's breakfast?

Fatima Yes. Gauhar informed me that you would have toast and banana for breakfast. You have to catch an early morning flight. It is better not to have anything heavy. You rather relish your lunch at Delhi tomorrow.

Jinnah (*to* **Dina**) Can you recollect Heath's house at Hampstead? It was lush green all around, isn't it?

Dina How can I forget that, *Abbu*? You had a stringent routine to follow there. We used to drink tea at the crack of dawn sitting beside your bed and had breakfast together at 9. Then the driver, Bradbury, used to turn up. You left for the council and I went to school. After returning from school in the afternoon, I used to read books and eagerly wait for you to return from the court in the evening to enjoy our dinner together.

Jinnah What about us taking a stroll together every Saturday and Sunday, from Heath to Kenwood? Can you recollect the restaurant beside Jack Straw fort? We used to have tea after a walk.

Dina How do I forget that? Oh! What a beautiful sight it was. *Abbu*, you had shared with me that Karl Marx enjoyed draught beer at the same restaurant with his daughter on their way back from the library.

Jinnah Right you are! You know, after your *Ammi*'s death I had never imagined that I would ever be able to build a house in London.

Fatima That became possible because Dinu was with you. She had carried your fortune as she came.

Dina *smiles.* **Jinnah** *lights a cigarette.*

Jinnah However, sleep eluded me every night after you went to bed and I used to contemplate a lot.

Dina Regarding what?

Jinnah About the next step of my life – whether to continue this quiet, stagnant life amidst affluence or to jump into the ruggedness of politics again after returning to my country. If at all I decide to return to my country, in what capacity should I return? Which trump card should I use next to return to mainstream politics? I used to think all this. I used to tell myself, yes, even I crave to be a leader whom millions of people would follow, exactly the way in which they follow the half-naked fakir. But how was it possible? At times your *Ammi*'s face rekindled in my memory at night. Sometimes the nightmarish frightful past would haunt me and I wouldn't even know when I used to fall deep asleep. Next morning, it was the same workaholic me, who went to the court and consulted law books. But those thoughts never spared me.

Stops, drinks water.

Fatima *Bhaiya*, you better go downstairs and meet Chamanlal at once. They have been waiting for a long time.

Jinnah Oh yes. Let me go. It went out of my mind as I was talking. You carry on, I will catch up soon. They are strange. Who comes at this hour of the night?

He leaves. **Dina** *strolls towards the window.*

Fatima Your driver has had his dinner, Dinu. He is now gossiping at Gauhar's quarter.

Dina Why do you always interrupt *Abbu* whenever he talks about *Ammi*?

Fatima What do you mean?

Dina I have noticed it since I was a child. Earlier I could not understand this but now I do understand.

Fatima You are talking nonsense.

Dina Can I ask you a question? Will you give me an honest answer?

Fatima Let me hear the question first.

Dina Why didn't you marry?

Fatima What?

Dina It is a very simple question, *Fufi.*

Fatima If I had married, who would have looked after you? Who would have taken care of your *Abbu*? You? Who would have looked after your *Abbu* after your marriage?

Dina Is it your obligation to look after *Abbu* for his entire life? Who has assigned this responsibility to you?

Fatima Who will assign me this responsibility? I myself took it on as my duty. Don't you forget, Dina Wadia, your *Abbu* was famous in the country from his early age. He is well known. Being his younger sister, I have every right to ensure that he did not spend a neglected and abandoned life after his wife passed away.

Dina You are seventeen years younger than *Abbu* and my *Ammi* was another seven years younger than you.

Fatima Yes, how does that bother you?

Dina No, nothing. Just saying. (*Pause.*) I have heard that you stayed with *Abbu* in his house, before his marriage. After *Abbu* was married, you began to stay alone. You came here at times to spend the weekend. I was very young then but I do remember, you used to reach here on Saturday morning and returned to your house on Monday morning.

Fatima Yes, my dental clinic was then running in full swing. I had to do a job to sustain myself.

Dina Yes, *Abbu* had set up your clinic after you had returned from Calcutta, earning the qualification of a dental surgeon.

Fatima Right, and I worked so hard that I gained a good reputation soon.

Dina But surprisingly, after *Ammi*'s death you closed your reputed clinic straightaway and returned to this house to stay permanently with *Abbu*.

Fatima Yes, because you were too small. Who would have taken care of you?

Dina Who had looked after me in London? You were surely not present there.

Fatima What are you trying to point at? Talk straight. Stop beating around the bush. (*Pause.*) Don't you forget, Dinu, it is me who fed you in your childhood.

Dina Yes, I know.

Fatima So? What inference are you trying to draw?

Dina That day in Bombay I ran into your friend Rana aka *Begum* Liyaquat at a party. I came to know that you were not in touch with her for a long time.

Fatima Yes, I met her on several occasions organized by the League and also at the conferences of Muslim Mahila Samity. With the work pressure increasing manifold in the past few years, who has the time to just sit and gossip. Anyway, what did Rana say?

Dina She was not in the best of her moods that day. I could not find out why. She is otherwise a modern and a very progressive woman. She is a double MSc, do you know? She used to teach economics at Gokhale School in Calcutta.

Fatima Why are you repeating the facts which I already know? Who talks about *masi* with her *ma*?[1]

---

1 A Bengali proverb which means never lecture before an expert.

Dina No, all I was trying to tell you is how erudite she actually is. She said that even till a few days ago how you guarded *Abbu* was almost unbelievable. You supposedly kept a strict vigil on *Abbu* so that no woman dared to come near to him. Is it true, *Fufi*?

Fatima I leave it up to you to decide whether you will believe the double MSc, erudite Begum Rana Liyaquat Khan or your *Fufi*.

Dina That is why I was asking you, why didn't you get married?

Fatima Now you are insulting me, Dina Wadia.

Dina No, I am not. I just want to know the facts from you.

Fatima You are not supposed to insult me like that . . .

Dina *Fufi*, I am . . .

Fatima I love my elder brother, my *Bhaiya*. I love him more than I love myself. You cannot bring disgrace to this. Your *Abbu* will be hurt if he comes to know.

Dina I wanted to know your perception of love in this case.

Fatima I know I love him, Mrs Wadia. This realization is the absolute truth for me. Love is love, what can its type be? You left happily with Neville after marriage. Have you ever thought what would happen to him if he had lived alone? Who would give him medicines? Who would have fixed his coat's sleeves when he was leaving for work? Who would oversee his meal arrangements? He is habituated to taking a bath in hot water all through the year. Who would have ensured that hot water was kept ready for him? (**Dina** *intends to say something.*)

Fatima Yes, I know. You will of course say there were so many domestic helpers, but can they give adequate care with the needed affection? This man has yearned to attain peace in his family throughout his life but failed. I am not just cooking up a story to justify but I actually couldn't manage any time to get married. I did not even feel the urge. You are right, he is my elder brother. Yes, he is seventeen years older than me. But when I was young, I looked up to him as my *Abbu*. My *Abbu* was thirty-six years older than me and he always remained busy with his own work. We, all brothers and sisters, were brought up under the supervision of our elder brother, *Bade Bhaiya*. He took all decisions regarding what food we would eat, the clothes we wore, where would we study. He was a real life hero for all our siblings. The real hero! How can I abandon this person? I did not and I will not leave him and go anywhere in the future as well. Will society decide everything? Will everything run as per society's whims and fancies? That person has taught this to us through his own life.

Pause. **Fatima** *is panting.* **Dina** *extends a glass of water to her.* **Fatima** *drinks water.*

Fatima I never abandoned him mentally, not after his marriage, not after your birth, and not even when he used to travel to London, Paris or Dublin. I know that I will be leaving with him permanently for Karachi to a new-born country the day after tomorrow. I know he is not in the pink of his health. He has not shown me his x-ray report done by Dr Patel and hidden it in the vault of his bag. *Allah Shukr*, I don't know how long he is going to survive! I wish he lives for one hundred years or that I die before him. But what if something really happens to him in between? What will be my fate in that new country? How will I survive in that newly created society? Will I get killed? All these thoughts petrify me. But I have stopped worrying. Because I know if he at any point in time tells me after a year, *Fati*, I don't feel good living here anymore, let's go to Dozakh. Gladly and ungrudgingly, I will hold his hand and leave the place with him. (*Pause.*)

Don't try to mark all kinds of love, that will not do any good to your life also. You are still young. Perhaps one day with maturity you will definitely understand the worth of my words.

Jinnah *returns with a bag in his hand. He sweeps a glance over* **Dina** *and* **Fatima**.

Jinnah What happened? What were you discussing? *Fati*, why do you have tears in your eyes?

Fatima (*wipes her eyes*) No, it's nothing. What's in your hand, *Bhaiya*?

Jinnah (*sits*) This Chamanlal was in no mood to leave. I had to call him separately to suggest that Mrs Wadia was waiting for me upstairs. Then he left. He was upset about when we would meet again.

(*Unties the string binding the bag.*) Mrs Wadia, let me tell you one thing. After your *Ammi*'s death if I had ever tasted peace in life and gained mental composure again, it was because of my Fati. Without her support, I would not have been able to sincerely focus on my goal. I was emotionally devastated, my mind was running around in the periphery, unable to return to the centre. Your *Fufi*'s diligent care helped me recover from that critical state of my mind. So, she is like my rifle, and I am the cartridge. After returning to this country, with my brittle self, that I could gather enough courage to fight the opposition, and was able to win the 'case' of 'Pakistan' within a period of just ten years, was possible only because of your Fufi's unrelenting support.

Fatima It's okay. Don't say anything else, *Bhaiya*. Now I am feeling uneasy.

Jinnah I have to accept the truth, Fati.

He holds the bag after untying the knot. Silence.

Dina Case? Yes, a case indeed. Just before leaving the room, you were saying something. Regarding devising your future strategies during the sleepless nights at London, simultaneously planning your next moves while being busy in multiple jobs. But what exactly were those plans you did not share with us. What did you envisage before returning to the country permanently, *Abbu*?

Jinnah (*smiles*) Mrs Wadia, how is it of any significance now?

Dina I am just curious. You mentioned about Gandhiji. You talked about his enormous popularity. Now you have become equally popular among the Muslim communities in this country. Despite being a staunch atheist, you changed your inclination in favour of religion. Can't it raise a curiosity in your daughter's mind, *Abbu*?

Jinnah Give up on this curiosity. I never enjoy discussing the nitty-gritty of a case after winning it, Mrs Wadia.

Dina *Ammi* was present with you at Congress's Nagpur conference. I heard from her later. I was one year old then. I came to know that Gandhiji had first proposed his non-cooperation movement at Nagpur. You opposed. You had addressed the audience wearing a three-piece suit, sewn at Savile Row.

Jinnah Yes. And the colour combination of my shoes was brown and white. It was a specially ordered pair. Before my speech, I heard sarcastic remarks from some members of the Congress about the attires your *Ammi* and I wore. Like why I did not wear *Khaddar* and so on. But I couldn't care less. I was still thinking of winning public support with my speech, because I was always far superior than the half-naked fakir in delivering speeches and making arguments.

Dina What was your main argument?

Jinnah Very simple. I argued that in such a big country a non-violent civil movement never seemed possible because it was in no way practical to control such a big population. We have to fight for independence through constitutional process, through discussions-debates and taking help of legal jurisprudence.

Dina But independence can never be achieved this way, *Abbu*. No country has been able to do this. There has to be a civil movement.

Fatima No, *Bade Bhaiya* was absolutely right. Then why did Gandhiji withdraw from the movement after the incidence of Chauri Chaura?

Jinnah Forget about the old conflicts, Fati. Those are bygones.

Dina Then what happened during your Nagpur speech?

Jinnah What else? Why should I address the half-naked fakir as Mahatma? So, when I started addressing him by his name . . .

Dina Did you address him as Mr Gandhi?

Jinnah Immediately, the crowd started shouting at me, 'Call him *Mahatma*! Call him *Mahatma*!' But why should I? During the *Khilafat* Movement, the Muslim *Maulvis* had asked me to use *Maulana* before the name of their leader Saukat Ali in my address. I refused. They got angry with me. Come on, we all are flesh and blood human. Then why unnecessarily create a *Mahatma*, or a *Maulana*? Silly attempt to personify God.

Dina You are right. But, *Abbu*, why do you address yourself as *Quaid-e-Azam* now?

Jinnah This is exactly what I used to contemplate sitting beneath a starry night sky. Does truth have no real value? Does transparency have no real significance in life? Are knowledge and rationality meaningless? Thoughts like these used to clog my mind. Does falsehood always win the world over? To counter a lie do we really need to construct another lie? These spiralling thoughts clouded my mind and the smoke from my cigarette suffused my head and lungs. But you could not realize an inch of what was going in my mind, Mrs Wadia, because in the next room, you by then were lying motionless on your bed sleeping to glory.

Dina Lies can never win, *Abbu*. The truth is the ultimate winner. Since falsehood always hops forward like a rabbit, it is ominously visible. But because the truth crawls like a turtle behind it catches our attention much later.

Jinnah I don't know. The meanings of truth and falsehood are relative to me. They change according to context.

Dina I disagree with you, *Abbu*. Absolute truth or absolute falsity can never be distorted. Anyway, so what did you decide ultimately? Which game plan did you adopt to return to your country?

Jinnah Leave it. I told you I detest dissecting the case I have already won.

Dina Please tell me.

Fatima Tell us, *Bade Bhaiya*. You never shared this even with me.

Jinnah *lights a cigar. He bends towards them and whispers.*

Jinnah If you have to win a big case you have to know that it has only one pike. Go and talk to any successful lawyer, he will confirm this. But the clue is clearly visible only after unwinding the existing knotted-thoughts. The primary challenge is to uncover the sign. Once you identify the ridge, organizing the brief is no issue at all.

Dina Well, what was your 'pike' in this case?

Jinnah (*his eyes agleam*) Very easy. I observed that two things bothered our countrymen the most. One is independence and the other is religion. So, how about blending these two and mainstreaming it? I was noticing that this crafty, half-naked fakir had actually blended them incredibly, but was presenting it behind the facade of secularism and politically neutral humanism. I was not wanting to use that mask anymore in my case. (*Chuckles.*) That's it. An outright anti-religious barrister like me had to take the side of my dad's adopted religion. It was all about winning a case. Why should common people like us be worried about how history will interpret our actions in the future? Is it making any sense now?

Silence. **Dina** *pours wine in her glass.*

Dina What is your opinion about it, *Abbu*? How will history interpret this action of yours?

Jinnah (*opens the bag*) I thank you for returning the letters to me, Mrs Wadia. Now, I wish to give you a gift as well.

Takes out a few gowns from the bag.

I have kept these dresses of your *Ammi* with me. At times, I used to have a look at them at night. (*Picks up a white gown.*) Your *Ammi* had worn this on our wedding night. And this one she had taken with her during our honeymoon in Europe. She walked with me down the street in Paris wearing this gown. She was then a few months more than eighteen years . . . I wish to present this to you.

He folds and hands them over to **Dina**. **Dina** *takes a look at the bag. She then looks at* **Jinnah**.

Dina (*receives the bag from* **Jinnah**) Aren't you feeling scared, *Abbu*?

Jinnah Why?

Dina We really can't predict how history will interpret your action. As a founder or as a traitor? As a redeemer or as a spy? As a father or as an illegitimate progenitor? There is no doubt that I am an ordinary person and so I need not take the trouble of engaging with history. But one thing is wearing me down from within *Abbu*. After a few days, this country will become independent. Felicitations ceremonies will be held, firecrackers will be lit. You will also fly across the border day after tomorrow and set your feet in your new country to receive felicitation. And just after a few days, crores of common people like me will cross the same border like orphans and destitutes. They will not take the aerial route but will cross the border on foot. One group will cross over from this side to the other side, another group will cross from that side to this part of the land. Those who will leave their homestead for good will never know where they are destined to reach. Whether they will at all reach their destination, they won't know how slippery that road will get when soaked with blood. They won't even know how they will be categorized. Refugees or infiltrators? They will only know that a handful of people in lieu of their bid to make a country independent, in their effort to create a new country, have compelled them to become landless and penniless forever. They are not just one or two in number, *Abbu*, there are crores of people. I am not talking about you. Don't you feel scared when you think about them, *Abbu*? Please answer me, *Abbu*.

Jinnah *rises from his chair. His eyes look teary.*

Jinnah You may leave now, Mrs Wadia. It is already late. I hope we did not fall short of extending our hospitality towards you.

Fatima *Bade Bhaiya*!

Jinnah Fati, if she does not leave this place right now, or if you utter a single word in this regard, I will throw you out with her as well. And you will not see me ever again in your life.

Fatima No, no. Dinu, you please go away. *Bade Bhaiya* may fall sick again. I ask you, please leave this place now.

Silence, **Dina** *gets up.*

Dina Thank you, *Abbu*. I am leaving now. We will never meet again. I am really thankful to you for presenting me with *Ammi*'s clothes. Truly unblemished was your hospitality!

About to leave.

Jinnah Dina.

Dina *stops. Looks at* **Jinnah**.

Jinnah (*softly*) I do not mind if we do not meet again. But give me your word. (**Dina** *keeps looking.*) Please do visit my new country once, at least after my *Inteqal*. To place a handful of soil on my grave. This is my only request to you. If possible, try and keep this promise for your old Grey Wolf *Abbu*. Well, nothing more, that's it. Good night, Mrs Wadia.

Dina *looks at* **Jinnah** *thoroughly. Smiles. She then leaves.* **Fatima** *looks at* **Jinnah** *and then follows* **Dina.** *Silence. Music is heard.* **Jinnah** *clutches onto the other clothes of Ruttie. His eyes well up in tears. He then picks up Ruttie's letters. He gets ready to read them, but on second thoughts puts them back. Picks up the receiver.*

Jinnah Hello, Chagla. I will be reaching Delhi tomorrow morning. You come to the airport. We will discuss everything then. No, no, I am doing fine. I am okay.

Yes, I am through with my work here. Listen, the important thing which I want to tell you is . . .

Loud music gradually makes his voice inaudible. **Jinnah** *continues speaking. Curtain falls.*

The End.

Glossary

Abbu: (lit. Urdu) Father

ADC: English aide-de-camp. A subordinate military or naval officer acting as a confidential assistant to a superior, usually to a general officer or admiral or governor

Allah Shukr: *Shukr* is an Arabic word which means gratitude. Allah Shukr means paying gratitude to Allah

Amaretto: Amaretto, which means 'a little bitter' in Italian, is an almond-flavored liqueur which, contrary to popular belief, is most often not produced from actual almonds

Ammi: (lit. Urdu) Mother

Baap-Nana's: *Baap* means Father and *Nana* means Grandfather in Hindi

Baap-Nana's home: Ancestral home

Bade Bhaiya: Elder brother

Bahen: (lit. Hindi) Sister

Baralaat: (lit. Bengali) Then viceroy of colonial India

Begum: (lit. Urdu) Begum is a Muslim honorific title for, or means of addressing, a respectable lady. Also a Muslim queen or woman of high rank and profile

Bhaiya: (lit. Hindi) Brother

Chauri Chaura: Chauri Chaura was in the Gorakhpur district of the United Province before India was freed, now in Uttar Pradesh. The Chauri Chaura movement was led by Mahatma Gandhi as a non-cooperation movement. The principle of Gandhi's movement was non-violence, but on 4 February 1922 the protestors became violent and burnt down a police station where many police personnel died

Darjeeling: Darjeeling is a city and municipality in the Eastern Himalayas in India, lying at an elevation of 2,100 metres (7,000 ft) in the northernmost region of the country. Once a summer resort for the British Raj elite, it remains the terminus of the narrow-gauge Darjeeling Himalayan Railway, or 'Toy Train', completed in 1881

Dawat: (lit. Urdu) Feast. Especially dinner for the invited guests

Dhuan: (Urdu: *Smoke*) is a collection of short stories in Urdu by Saadat Hasan Manto first published in 1941

Dozakh: (lit. Urdu) Hell

Fatwa: In Islam, a formal ruling or interpretation on a point of Islamic law given by a qualified legal scholar (known as a mufti). *Fatwas* are usually issued in response to questions from individuals or Islamic courts

Fufi: (lit. Urdu) Father's sister

Half-naked fakir: Mahatma Gandhi was first referred to as a 'half-naked fakir' by Winston Churchill. Fakir means a religious ascetic who lives on alms. Gandhi used two parts of cloth only as a part of his philosophy of austerity representing the poor Indian

Iblis: (lit. Arabic) in Islam, the personal name of the Devil, a Shayṭān, the counterpart of Satan in Christianity

Inteqal: (lit. Urdu) Death

Ji: (lit, Hindi) Means saying yes with reverence. Sometimes it is added as a suffix to somebody's name to show respect

Jihad: (lit. Arabic) Struggle or effort. In Islam, a meritorious struggle or effort

Jinnah cap: The Jinnah cap is a type of headwear specially made by him from the fur of the Qaraqul breed of sheep. This cap became famous and is now traditionally worn by men in Central Asia

Kali Shalwar: (lit. Urdu) Black trousers. A shalwar is a pair of light, loose, pleated trousers, usually tapering to a tight fit around the ankles, worn by women and men from South Asia

Khaddar: Hand-woven cloth, made from a kind of cotton or silk, specially made with the help of a spinning wheel. It was promoted by Mahatma Gandhi as *swadeshi* (self-sufficiency) for the freedom struggle of the Indian subcontinent against the colonial British

Khilafat: (lit. Turkish) The chief spiritual authority of Islam. The Khilafat movement (1919–24) was an agitation by Indian Muslims allied with Indian nationalism in the years following the First World War. Its purpose was to pressure the British government to preserve the authority of the Ottoman Sultan as Caliph of Islam following the break-up of the Ottoman Empire at the end of the war. Mahatma Gandhi supported the Khilafat movement in order to unite the people of Hindu and Muslim religion and revolt against the British Empire

Mahatma: *Mahatma* is an adaptation of the Sanskrit word *mahātman*, which literally means 'great-souled'. In India, it is used as a title of love and respect and was conferred upon Mohandas Karamchand Gandhi

Mangaldas: Mangaldas Market is in South Mumbai, a city in India. It is one of the oldest markets. It consists of small lanes inside a compound

Maulana: (lit. Urdu) A title, mostly in Central Asia and in the Indian subcontinent, preceding the name of respected Muslim religious leaders, in particular graduates of religious institutions, e.g. a madrassa

Maulvi: (lit. Urdu) A learned teacher or doctor of Islamic law – used especially in India as a form of address for a learned Muslim who ministers to the religious needs of others

Memsahib: In British India, a white foreign woman of high social status living in India especially. The wife of a British official was called Memsahib

Mera Bharat Mahan Hai: (lit. Hindi) My India is Great

Mulk Raj Anand: Mulk Raj Anand (1905–2004) was a prominent Indian author of novels, short stories and critical essays in English, who is known for his realistic and sympathetic portrayal of the poor in India

Namaz: Ritual prayers prescribed by Islam. Usually offered five times a day

Nani: (lit. Hindi) Grandmother

Nus: Short name of Nusli Wadia, Jinnah's grandson, Dina Wadia's son

Purple jamun: *Jamun* means plum. Commonly known as Java plum or Indian blackberry

Quaid-e-Azam: (lit. Urdu) *Quaid* in Urdu means leader. *Azam* in Urdu means great Quaid-e-Azam means The Great Leader

Quran: (lit. Arabic) Recitation, the sacred scripture of Islam

Raj Bhavan: Raj Bhavan is the official residence of the governor of a state in India. Therefore, in each state in India there is a Raj Bhavan

Ramadan: (lit. Arabic) Literally meaning 'the hot month', from *ramad*, meaning 'dryness'. It is celebrated as the month during which Muhammad received the initial revelations of the Quran, the holy book for Muslims. It is the ninth month of the Muslim year

Roza: (lit. Urdu) During Ramadan, many Muslims pray to Allah and fast, which is called *roza*. These fasts symbolize the devotion of these people towards the almighty. For the time period of this month Muslims let go of worldly pleasures and observe the fast along with their friends and family

Ruttie: Muhammad Ali Jinnah's wife Rattanbai Jinnah or Maryam Jinnah

Sadat Hossain Manto: A revolutionary writer, playwright and author born in undivided India (1912–55). He is best known for his stories about the partition of India, which he opposed, immediately following independence in 1947. Manto was tried for obscenity six times; thrice before 1947 in British India, and thrice after independence in 1947 in Pakistan, but was never convicted. In his short story 'Kali Shalwar' (1941) Manto tries to fictionalize the ritual of Muharram, a 'mourning practice' into the normalized 'gendered' mourning conditions of Manto's sex-workers

Sherwani: (lit. Urdu) A long coat-like garment worn in the Indian subcontinent, very similar to a Polish Zupan

Vakalatnama: (lit. Urdu) A written document that is given by a client to an advocate to appear and or plead before any court of law on behalf of him. It is also known as a memo of appearance, Vakilat Patra, VP, Power of attorney

Zindabad: (lit. Urdu) Long Live

Creusa – The Queen

Bratya Basu
March 2019

Translated by Mainak Banerjee

Female characters: 6

Male characters: 10

Country of origin: India

Original performance date: 28 July 2019, Kolkata

Characters

Xuthus *(male)*
Senior Advisor *(male)*
Ion *(male)*
Danius *(male)*
Aegyptus *(male)*
Orion *(male)*
Singer and lyre player *(male)*
Glaucus *(male)*
Patroclus *(male)*
Chronus *(male)*
Crowd
Creusa *(female)*
Duffnis *(female)*
Lachesis *(female)*
Clotho *(female)*
Atropos *(female)*
Pythia *(female)*
Group of women

Playwright's gratitude: Robert Graves, Sophocles, Rabindranath Tagore.

A palace in the city of Athens. Palace at upstage. A staircase comes down from the palace to the courtyard. Three entrances – one on the right, one on the left and one on opposite side of the palace. Crowds have gathered here. **Senior Advisor** *accompanies them. Trumpets flourish.* **King Xuthus** *comes out.*

Crowd Hail to the King! King! King!

Xuthus My adored sons and my beloved citizens. You are the gilded youth of ancient Athens. I have invited you here to share some information. Please be attentive. I insist that all the lifeless world around you – olive branches wrapped around your arms, crowns of olive leaves on your head, sweet smell of frankincense – listens to me as well. Today I want to share good news. But before I do that, hey my Senior Advisor, respected priest, do you wish to say a few words on behalf of the countless people gathered here?

Senior Advisor Hail, my King Xuthus. We know that today you had visited the temple at Delphi. When you and your admirable wife returned to the Palace of Athens passing by the bank of river Ilisus and crossing the courtyard of the temple of God Boreas, we anticipated some good news. Lord Xuthus, you are the most trusted attendant of the God of North Wind Boreas who destroyed the warship of the enemy King Xerxes when he attacked Athens, your happiness is our happiness, your glory is our glory. So, any news which makes you happy will be good news for us as well.

Xuthus Truly. This is exactly why I have come hurtling towards you with the speed of twelve colts of the chariot of God Boreas. Like the youngsters have respect for their elders and the host shows generosity towards his guests I have always been committed to serve you all. I have constantly redressed the wrongs of any unruly citizen towards a priest. Consciously my conduct has never been inequitable or distasteful to any of my bona fide citizens.

Crowd King Xuthus! King Xuthus, our King, you are virtuous and merciful in the truest sense. You have always shown great respect towards us. By all means you are devoted to us.

Xuthus But I deeply regret that I am yet to become a father. You all are aware that my wife Creusa, my royal partner, is the daughter of Erechtheus who surrendered Athens in the safe hands of Pallas, the Goddess of defence. She is a befitting imperial partner who is capable of striking a fine balance between her queenly aristocracy and innate rationality. Moreover, she is extremely sincere to me and has never ever shied away from her duties. However, being childless yet, we frequent God Boreas' place of worship with the expectation of winning his favour so that Creusa gets impregnated with our successor who will eventually save this supreme city, Athens.

Senior Advisor Yes, my Lord, we are aware of it. Despite having won the fortunate blessings of God Boreas, you remain ill-fated in this regard. The entire society thus pities you. Alas, King Xuthus, you have not enjoyed a prophecy like Zeus who secretly cared for his lover Danae's son Perseus on earth. As an elderly advisor of this city, I also pray for you regularly, and even shed tears for you.

Xuthus For this reason, my Queen Creusa has been really requesting me over the last few days to visit the temple of God Apollo in Delphi, situated on the outskirts of my holy fatherland. Today we visited Delphi largely on her persuasion. Creusa, for a reason unknown to me, has been ever reluctant to visit Delphi. But this time, because she insisted, we went there together.

Crowd Our King, you have made the right decision, you are right.

Xuthus Though Creusa did accompany me to Delphi, due to her instinctive reluctance she refused to enter the temple at the final moment. Hence, without insisting further, I alone headed towards God Apollo's temple. Towards God Apollo's place of worship.

Senior Advisor Hail, Apollo! God Apollo!

Xuthus Right you are. He is the venerable God of oracle. On my way to the temple, I passed by pasturing sheep on vast lands, an abundance of fructuous crops caught my attention as I crossed the gigantic pillars made of wax, feathers of birds and the arch gate. My journey through the horizon of opulence came to a halt when I entered the temple and finally stood in front of God Apollo's idol. I observed that somebody had just sacrificed a goat on the altar. Bloodstains were splattered across the laurel leaves and the altar had turned greyish black with blood. You know, my dear advisor, when I knelt down in front of the God like an oak tree, a priestess suddenly appeared before me.

Upstage, the Delphi temple lights up. **Xuthus** *turns towards the temple. The rest of the stage becomes dark.* **Priestess Duffnis** *appears.*

Duffnis Our God is aware of why Achatius' descendant, King Xuthus, is present here today. He is also aware that you frequented God Boreas' temple on the bank of the river Ilisus all these days. But God Apollo is not infuriated by your behaviour. Because the God of north wind Boreas once blew the sweetest wind on earth from the mountain top of Parnassus for our God Apollo. So, my God considers your God Boreas as his friend.

Xuthus People attribute to you the potential to make prophetic predictions sitting on a fernwood seat, Priestess Duffnis. This ability seems almost absent even in Gods. Will God Apollo read out any such divine message for me today? Please apprise me.

Duffnis Yes, He will. He has sent me to you to convey a message.

Xuthus What is the oracle? What is it? Am I fortunate Priestess Duffnis? Please share with me.

Duffnis Achatius' descendant King Xuthus, according to the oracle of God Apollo you will become the father of a boy. His name will be Doris.

Xuthus Hail, God Apollo! Hail, God Apollo!

Duffnis Please allow me to finish. But this will still take a long time.

Xuthus Long time? How long do we need to wait, Priestess Duffnis?

Duffnis God Apollo has not mentioned anything about the time period. Because He has another infallible commandment reserved for you.

Xuthus What is His commandment? Please tell me. Priestess Duffnis, I hope you are not unaware of the mercurial temperaments of the Kings to carry out orders issued by the Gods.

Duffnis King Xuthus, by the time you will move out of God Apollo's temple made of wax and bird's feather, it will have been evening. I know that your Queen Creusa, instead of stepping inside the temple, will be eagerly waiting for you outside.

Light on **Duffnis** *' face is seen reducing.*

Far behind, you will notice Athens having lit up with torchlights. Through the countless hanging laurels, oaks and ferns in front of the temple you will find your wife, Queen Creusa speaking to a young man. His name is Ion.

Creusa *and* **Ion** *become visible standing in front of the temple on the right side of the stage.* **Xuthus** *watches them from inside the temple.* **Duffnis** *' voice echoes and merges with the background music, 'Ion has been brought up in this temple. You may say he is a devotee of King Apollo. Not just a disciple, he is like the son of my God. So, the commandment of God Apollo is that Ion will be your elder son till Doris gets impregnated in Queen Creusa's womb. This adopted son will be your royal heir.'*

Duffnis *' voice fades away.* **Xuthus** *approaches the temple. He goes and stands in front of* **Ion** *and* **Creusa**.

Xuthus Oh man of elegance, my beautiful Ion, will you be my son?

Ion *looks at* **Xuthus**. *It becomes dark.* **Creusa** *and* **Ion** *fade away. Walking over a platform,* **Xuthus** *comes back near the crowd.*

Xuthus Honestly speaking, I have rarely come across such a gentle, handsome and wise young man. Despite his tender age, he was embodying a glowing sign of modesty instead of arrogance. Seeing him at a glance, his physical and emotional strength can be easily grasped, but his immense physical strength has never been able to curb his politeness. By the grace of the God Apollo, today I got a suitable heir to Athens. I will organize his investiture ceremony tonight. Before doing so, I request all of you to allow me to present Prince Ion before you. And I also request you all to grace the occasion of the adoption ceremony tonight with your august presence. Isn't it useless to become a King without being able to share my moment of joy with you all? Even if you fail to be present on the day of my last rite, I look forward to your presence tonight and that will make me feel specially blessed.

Crowd (*cheering*) King! Our King! King Xuthus!

Xuthus Ion, please come forward. Ion, my beloved son.

Ion *comes from behind. He stands beside* **Xuthus**. *Crowd cheers to welcome him.* **Ion** *raises his hand. Everybody falls silent.*

Ion I am a priest from the temple of God Apollo, the saviour of Delos. I am an orphan, completely unaware of any account of my birth. I am even ignorant about the identity of my parents. But my wisdom says that he who respects me, he who takes the responsibility of providing me with food and shelter for my life, he is actually my father. It is my exceptional fortune to be adopted as a son by the Great Emperor Xuthus of Athens. But this scares me too. Doesn't what we perceive as temporary pleasure always return as a cruel irony in life later? Tomorrow seems murky enclosed by a dark veil. However, if you all remain by my side and if my new father, Great Xuthus, blesses me for all future times, I will consider myself to be truly sanctified by God Apollo.

Senior Advisor Hey Ion, hey boy wonder, you appear to be a true gentleman, genuinely knowledgeable. Every word you say generates a holy grace with a benign assurance. We all wish that you bring peremptory stability, incomparable wealth and enormous fortune for us, just like your father, King Xuthus, our ultimate refuge. People pronounce our King to be naturally prudent and a natural seer. Today his decision once again proves that a King's real pride lies in giving protection to his subjects. My dear Ion, there is no pride in ruling a dead city, a desolate desert or a destroyed armory.

Crowd Right you are! Right you are! Hail, our Prince! Our hearty welcome to our Prince Ion! Though he is an orphan, he is our deserving future King.

Trumpets heard. A messenger arrives from inside.

Messenger Xuthus, your majesty, Queen Creusa has expressed her willingness to meet you immediately in her apartment.

Xuthus Fine, you may go now. I will go and meet her at the royal enclosure right now. My dear Ion, you may also go to the mansion. Make sure that your investiture ceremony is conducted without any hindrance. I swear by the lightning of Lord Zeus and his fair trial that we will definitely overcome all our delusions in the days to come.

Music is heard. **Xuthus** *goes inside.* **Ion** *moves in a different direction. Light goes off over the rest. The three Fates –* **Lachesis**, **Clotho** *and* **Atropos** *– appear on three corners of the stage. They are wearing white attire. They have spindles in their hand. They spin their wheels after every dialogue they deliver.*

Lachesis Nevertheless, man dreams. His past forbids him, yet he dreams. He knows that his dreams die collectively, like fishes lying dead on high sandy beaches, or his dreams fly in the eyes of lost sailors in the morning mist. Dreams are truly deceptive and yet, man yearns for them. What a fool he is. Dreams are a matter of past. Now it's time to caress others with hatred.

Clotho We three sisters are the Three Fates. We now cackle watching King Agamemnon taking rebirth as an eagle to avoid being born as a human being. Epeius, who created the Trojan horse in the war of Troy, wants to be reborn as a woman. Because when a man is born, he remains shackled to conspire for bloodshed and deaths throughout his life.

Atropos Why does Ajax, the Greek hero, choose the life of a lion in his next birth? Because, despite the valour shown by Ajax, society gave more recognition to Peleus' son, Achilles. Oh future, will you in the next birth return the lost pride to Ajax, the lion in disguise who roams about in the jungle amidst dust and despair? Can the future ever acknowledge the imminent blood soaked-dusty depression gripping his paws, claws and mane and show him an indelible reverence?

Three Fates Yet men approach us. Though euphoria of hatred seizes the earth, they kneel down before us. Destiny they abhor and yet again they go back to it with prayers for their prosperity.

Music becomes louder. Three Fates disappear. Stage right is illuminated. **Queen Creusa***'s room. She is sitting with her attendants at her service.* **King Xuthus** *enters.* **Creusa** *gestures. Attendants leave.*

Xuthus What's the matter, Queen? When I and my entire kingdom are busy making arrangements for the adoption ceremony at the Acropolis, when in adoration of God Dionysus actors of Athens are preparing to stage the play *Electra*, why do you keep yourself confined in your room? You know, Queen, they are preparing long masks. After the ceremony is over, the actors will light torches in the moonlit amphitheater. They will then perform the play wearing those masks.

Creusa*'s eyes flare up with rage.*

Creusa King, you are stupid; truly imprudent.

Xuthus Queen!

Creusa God Apollo had made it clear that I will give birth to your own biological child on this earth within a few days.

Xuthus Absolutely true! So, what is bothering you now?

Creusa Then why are you making this little-known orphan the inheritor of Athens' huge wealth?

Xuthus Ion? He is so courteous, really gentle and a qualified boy.

Creusa There is no dearth of such gentle and knowledgeable male descendants here in Athens. Leave aside Athens, you will find them in the entirety of Greece – from Corinth to Argos, from Thebai to Thessalie.

Xuthus True, but the oracle of God Apollo has not been showered on any of them. On my way out of the temple in Delphi, I received clear instructions from God Apollo that Ion would be my elder son till my biological child is born.

Creusa Did you hear the prophecy yourself? Or it came from priestess Duffnis! Tell me, King, don't remain silent. You tell me now.

Xuthus Yes, it was priestess Duffnis who broke the news to me.

Creusa So?

Xuthus Yes, so what?

Creusa It is well known that in all his temples spread from Laconia to Acropolis, God Apollo announces his oracles himself. People say that neither priest Duffnis nor

Aegyus are entitled to pronounce God Apollo's prophecy. They must have used coercion with an intention to deceive mankind.

Xuthus If it was true, God Apollo would have destroyed his own temple himself by now.

Creusa Fear! Fear! How long will mankind live in fear? Right after his birth man is scared of the divine, he fears for catastrophes, he is afraid of his fellow men, he fears for the conspiracies and he is also frightened of God's representatives. Why? Because after our death we have to go underground to cross the river Styx! After we enter Tartarus, the demons in the ever-dark hell-house will suck our blood. You know, King, I find God Apollo bearing a marked similarity with the gigantic dog of hell Cerberus nowadays.

Xuthus Creusa! Be silent.

Creusa As if he is always staring at us with his bloody red eyes! Go against his will and do anything, frowning he will pounce upon us and rip off our flesh. Exactly like Cerberus, the dog of hell!

Xuthus Have you gone crazy, Creusa? How can you disrespect God Apollo? You are going for an open confrontation with him!

Creusa If Oedipus' daughter Antigone, an ordinary girl, can wage a war against Menoeceus' son Creon then why can't I, Creusa, the daughter of the first King of Athens, Erechtheus, declare war against God Apollo?

Xuthus Because Apollo is a God. The wars between Clytemnestra and Electra, or between Creon and Antigone are never comparable with your war against God Apollo, Queen.

Creusa They are comparable. Of course they are. Because man creates God out of another man. Can you tell me, King, why Aphrodite, the God of heaven, fell desperately in love with the handsome youth Adonis of earth? Why did Cupid, son of Aphrodite, ignoring his mother's advice misdirect five arrows towards himself instead of the beautiful Psyche? Alas, Lord Zeus, why don't the Gods find enough Goddesses in heaven? Also, don't Goddesses find enough Gods in heaven? Why do they always come to earth and poke their noses in our decision making? Why do they interfere in our life and death and in our good and bad?

Xuthus You have become insane, Creusa. I along with my unadulterated love and fragile affection for you has made you crazy. Otherwise, how could your mortal self dare wage war against the immortals?

Creusa Listen, in no way will I allow Ion to be crowned as the Prince. It is true that when you entered the temple of Delphi in the afternoon, I did not accompany you. I have shared the reason with you earlier as well. The comfort with which I can visit God Borea's temple is completely absent while entering Apollo's temple. I am not sure why but I feel uneasy there. So, when I was taking a stroll in the courtyard of the temple that evening I also met Ion.

Lights are on over upstage. **Ion** *is seen sweeping the courtyard floor.*

Creusa At the first sight of the boy, I don't know why I felt a gush of hidden and inapt affection oozing in my heart. I asked him: (**Creusa** *moves towards* **Ion**.) Who are you, my son? How did you reach this temple?

Ion Queen of Athens, our supreme Lady, I have been here in this temple of God Apollo since my birth. It is unknown to me how I came here. I do not even know exactly who my parents are.

Creusa You are so handsome . . . you have such a beautiful voice . . . do you belong to any royal family, my dear? Are you born in the Pole Kaun family or are you the descendant of Cadmus dynasty of Thebai? I have come to know that the royal family of Pole Kaun is childless and their antecedent was also sent to exile to a remote place away from the city.

Ion I am unaware of it, noble lady Creusa. I have been residing in this temple since my childhood. Two times a day I sprinkle holy water of the river Tisius on the floors of the temple and clean it with a broom made of laurel leaves. I also shoo away Kordelius and other migratory birds who try to pollute God's *Prasada* with their sharp beaks. Priestess Duffnis provides me food for the trivial execution. I am happy with it. She loves me so much.

Creusa Everybody loves you, my dear. You have the power in your eyes to earn people's love.

Creusa *returns to* **Xuthus**. **Ion** *disappears*.

Creusa Then I saw you coming down the staircase of the temple. You unnecessarily embraced that unidentified boy. Even then I did not realize that you had such a delusion. Thereafter when you informed me that you would be adopting the boy as our son, I could not control my anger. I was thinking, did the witch Goddess Heqet recently become your lover? Or did the priestess Duffnis mix the poison of Medusa in your Prasada this evening, such that it is flashing its wings in frenzy in your head? Else, how do you make such a proposal? And even after knowing that my own son is going to be born soon!

Xuthus Creusa, my dear Queen, listen . . .

Creusa Alas, you unwise King, don't you even realize that priestess Duffnis, in connivance with someone, is pursuing you all to make this worthless servant, a mere sweeper, the legal heir to the throne of Athens? How could you become so gauche? Or is it your unending drinking bout during the celebration of Dionysus' theatre festival that has paralysed your brain? King Xuthus, I really cannot understand you now.

Xuthus What is making you feel so envious, Queen Creusa? You have so much hatred and vengeance within you. When you carry all these within you and attend the open conference of Parthenon, do you know you are going to spread the poison of Gorgon in the Acropolis and everywhere in the society?

Creusa Yes I will, because the entire world has now been transformed into Medusa of Sarpedon. There exists no Perseus around us now, who can save us from the venom exhumed by the snakes from the heads of three demon sisters. No sword of Hermes in the world can be swung hard enough to bring an end to the endless animosity, hatred and toxicity of human mind.

Xuthus Creusa . . .

Creusa King, with the strength of your love you can never win over influential hatred. You will fail to confront antipathy and conspiracy with the help of the oldest rock of Atlas named humanity. Because the human mind has itself become a dry and rigid rock like Atlas. To participate in an extensive battle against the world where connivance and wickedness are champions, you better store some amount of hatred, animosity and envy within you. Or else, despite being strong and fearless like Hercules, you will be killed surreptitiously by the lions of Kemea born out of the blood of a hundred-faced dragon.

Xuthus You have become a raving lunatic, Creusa, you have gone completely mad. I am least interested to extend this argument with you any further. I better leave now. Let me go and make arrangements for the investiture ceremony of my elder son at Acropolis. I wish you to present yourself there after sometime. I will inaugurate the programme when the moon will be right upon our heads in the sky after sometime.

Xuthus *departs.* **Creusa** *stands for some time. Her eyes turn red in anger. She claps. Servant* **Danius** *enters.*

Danius Always at your service, respected Queen.

Creusa Attendant Danius, you are pressed at my service since your childhood. And like an obedient pigeon you have carried out all my orders.

Danius I sincerely do, my Queen. I look upon you as Hera, and see King Xuthus as my Zeus. I am obliged to follow your commandment as long as I am alive.

Creusa Do you remember, Zeus converted his girlfriend Io, Inachaus' daughter, into a cow to enjoy her? Zeus' legitimate wife Hera then deployed Argus, a hundred-eyed giant, to ensure that Zeus could never go near the beautiful cow Io.

Danius Yes, I do remember, Queen Creusa. Thereafter Zeus, with the help of his son Hermes, representative of the Gods, made Argus fall asleep and killed him.

Creusa Correct you are. Even after this Hera implanted those hundred eyes of Argus in her cherished bird to prevent Zeus to go near Io. She simultaneously deployed a big fly to sting the cow continuously so that it could never settle down even for a single moment.

Danius Queen, people say that having been continuously bitten by the poisonous fly, the beautiful cow Io, daughter of Inachas, could never stand still on earth ever since.

Creusa Danius, my dear servant, you are my toxic and elegant fly. With your help, I will get Ion bitten so badly that this over ambitious orphan will be unable to rest in peace even for a moment anywhere between Crete and Sparta, or Egypt and Libya. Dear slave Danius, will you help me in expressing my savage love for him?

Danius Of course, my Queen, you have saved my life. You have provided me with food, air and life in my petty existence. I am always ready to sacrifice myself for you. I don't need to know how you are perceived by others in Athens. You are my authority, my Queen. I am ever obliged to carry out your supreme command.

Creusa Good, let's reach the Acropolis now to join the investiture ceremony of the unknown, beautiful cow Ion. Let us arrange for his last rites.

Danius *smiles. They disappear in darkness. Music is heard. The three Fates* **Lachesis**, **Clotho** *and* **Atropos** *come back on the stage. They have spindles in their hands.*

Lachesis Human past is actually like light. The more you dig deep into your memory, you will find your past emerging out of darkness like an intense bright light scattering in each of your brain cells. The gleam of the illumination is so severe that if you so wish you can observe each passing day of your previous birth. You fool, examine your past. Pay rapt attention. And learn to recognize yourself in this layout.

Clotho And the present is like dancing at dusk, soaked in contrasting light and shade. At times its glow will be visible to your eyes, at other times you will be in a dilemma when you mistake the darkness for light. The present is like a mirage in the middle of a desert that deceives a sweaty, thirsty traveller riding a camel. There is no salvation even if you take your eyes off it. You have no alternative but to follow the mirage. You thick-headed man, you have to live in it like a slithering reptile so that you can understand your unknown but inevitable future every day and every moment.

Atropos And the future is the same darkness. It's dark like Tartarus, the death house. Just imagine hell. Swimming across the black river Styx, you reach the three-way crossing, completely drenched. You know that on the road going to your right, the dangerous dog Cerberus is waiting for you. If you follow that route, it will rip you apart and eat your flesh. You then take a look at the street on your left. You expect to be safe if you by any chance can cross the river Lethe. But there you will actually face Hades, the God of death, and his wife, Queen Persephone. Once you reach there, they will get your chest torn apart and your blood sucked by the demons with gusto. So, you will want to take the path right in front of you. Following the route, you will presumably hope to reach Alicia, the heaven of hell where everlasting spring, pleasure and peace are waiting to welcome you. You idiot mankind, so thoughtless you are that you don't know the straight path will lead you to three Furies, three foster sisters of ours, the three Goddesses of vengeance, cackling at you. You feel their claws and understand them. Now try and feel these three Furies of the future – innumerous red snakes dangling from their scalp instead of hair, dog faces fixed on their human bodies, black wings of bats present instead of their arms and endless crackling whips dangling from their hands. Try and understand you nincompoop mankind, feel these.

Music is heard. Three sisters disappear. Lights are on. The entire stage is converted into the Acropolis of Athens. Centre stage, roasted mutton is on the table with a few drinks. **Ion** *and* **King Xuthus** *are seen in front of the table.* **Senior Advisor** *and a few other members standing with them.* **Xuthus** *is speaking to the priest regarding the adoption ceremony. A few beautiful women are entering to serve watermelons, dates* *and other fruits on plates to the invitees. Two Greek youths are seen stage left. They are* **Aegyptus** *and* **Orion** *and they are looking cheerful. They are laughing. They have plates in their hands.*

Aegyptus The mutton has not been marinated well in olive oil, but it tastes wonderful.

Orion You can try the rabbit Aegyptus along with boiled carrot. It is luscious.

Aegyptus Oh really? Well, let me try. Let me wet my throat with wine first. Then I will have rabbit and boiled carrot. Brother Orion, notice that Athenian girls are somehow gradually becoming barren and woody.

Orion Disgusting, they all seem to be on a controlled diet. They want to look svelte such that their waists fit between two male fingers.

Aegyptus Look, just have a look at their figures. Dry and woody build, lifeless breasts and a few coats of varnish on their skin. On taking off their clothes, they will surely resemble fried beans.

Orion (*chuckles*) Last month I went on a tour to Lacedaemon with my family. I wished to watch the Spartan Sports festival. You must have heard that Spartan girls look gorgeous but they are lanky. I somehow don't prefer such lean girls. So after leaving my son and wife to watch *Pankration*, I walked towards the bank of the river Eurotas. The Egyptian hippies had camped there. Brother Aegyptus, take my word, I was simply dumbstruck seeing the most beautiful women on earth. Those voluptuous beauties were playing harps and cellos sitting outside their tents. And all of them were bare breasted.

Aegyptus What are you saying?

Orion Besides each tent, makeshift ovens were set up. They were catching fresh mackerel and sardines from the river, frying and serving them hot. I went inside one of the tents. For only ten Drachma, I enjoyed two plates of fried fish and two hot Egyptian bodies. Uff . . . brother Aegyptus, it was like killing two birds with one stone.

Aegyptus Don't say you bought bananas, you should rather say you sold bananas.

They burst into laughter. Trumpets are heard. **Creusa** *appears.* **Danius** *follows her.* **Xuthus** *embraces* **Creusa**. *They take their seats in the middle.* **Danius** *serves a glass of drink to* **Ion**. *Others take their drinks. But when* **Ion** *is about to take a sip from his glass he cannot, because a* **Singer** *enters with a lyre in his hand. He starts a song.*

Singer (*plays the lyre and sings*)

Oh Lord Phoebus
(you) Our shelter
(you) The breeze gentler

And Colossus
You keep us well
Oh God Phoebus, you keep us well.
Oh Lord Phoebus
(you) Our fright
Santa's bite
(you) Our city's rein
Parnassus Mountain
You keep us well.
Oh Lord Phoebus
My special Lyre
And bird's tweeter
Castilian creek
And Goddess Artemis
Our terpsichore
And Parthenon of course
From night to dawn
Walking folk
You keep us well.
Oh God Phoebus.
Dweller of Greece
You keep us well
Please keep us well.

Singing ends. Everyone applauds. In the meantime, **Ion** *takes out his pet pigeon from his pocket and places it on the floor of the Acropolis. He feeds a few drops of his drink to his pet. The pigeon dies immediately after drinking it.* **Ion** *jumps up.*

Ion *Hemlock*! I have been given a drink mixed with poison. King Xuthus, you please see.

Xuthus What? What has happened?

Ion I have been offered a drink in the party. Since my childhood before taking any food or drink, I pray to God Apollo and offer a little from my share to my pet pigeon. Immediately after pecking a drop of drink that I had offered it got restless and died.

There is an uproar in the crowd.

Xuthus Who? Who handed you the drinking glass? Ion, my son, can you give me some idea about it?

Ion I am trying to recall. Yes, now I remember. (*Points towards* **Danius**.) He is the man who offered me the glass of poisonous drink.

Xuthus Danius, Danius, you . . .

Danius No. No.

Xuthus It's unbelievable. I picked you up from Thessalie at such a tender age and you grew up under my tutelage. Hey, who is around? I order my sentry to kill this unkind conspirator Danius right now.

Danius No. No, please.

Xuthus Then tell me who is behind this conspiracy? I want to know the name of the person who instructed you to mix this deadly poison in my son Ion's drink?

Danius Forgive me, Lord, I can't tell you.

Xuthus You have to tell me or else I will kill you.

He takes out a sword from a guard's belt.

Danius You may kill me, my Lord, but I will not be able to disclose the name.

Xuthus What audacity! You brute, I had picked you up from a sewerage in Thessalie. If I so wish I can cut your body into pieces and throw them back exactly from where you had been picked up.

He aims his sword towards Danius to slay him, **Queen Creusa** *comes forward.*

Creusa King, stop. Restrain yourself. Learn to appreciate your most loyal servant.

Xuthus What are you hinting at?

Creusa I mean Danius has always been the most trustworthy servant of yours. It is me, I instructed him to mix poison in the drink of that unknown street urchin, Ion.

Xuthus Creusa?

Creusa Danius mixed two drops of hot blood of Gorgon, giantess Medusa's brother, in the bottle of wine (*points towards a bottle*) kept aside for that over-ambitious vagabond. He worked on my advice, followed my mandate. King, if you really adopt this vagabond, I will immediately drink the rest of the wine from the bottle.

Silence. **Ion** *breaks the silence.*

Ion My supreme lady, Queen Creusa, why will you die? This is your kingdom, the kingdom of Lord Xuthus. And I know that you will bear the would-be King of Athens, Doris, in your womb soon. You please have the patience to wait for your own son. I take my leave now. (*To* **Xuthus**.) Oh Lord, oh my King, may this cruel world continually get a master just like you – who is perspicuous, merciful and loving towards his subjects. Now may I seek your permission to leave?

Xuthus *turns his face away. He keeps his hand on* **Ion**'*s shoulder once.* **Creusa** *comes forward.*

Creusa Yes, you leave. Leave right now. I don't want to see your face again in the palace of Athens ever. Just go away, you depraved, aspiring temple boy! Go back and resume your task of brooming at the Delphi temple.

Ion *departs. Silence.*

Creusa I am also returning to the palace, my prudent Senior Advisor.

Senior Advisor I am all ears, Queen Creusa. You may please continue.

Creusa If you feel that I have polluted and vitiated the sacred Acropolis by bringing the blood of Gorgon inside the premises, I will humbly accept whatever punishment you deem fit for me. Despite my cursed fate forcing me to do many things I have never, even for a moment, shied away from establishing my own belief and opinion. So, I am ready to do anything as an act of atonement for my misdeed. But please ensure that the punishment be administered to me alone. My holy and virtuous emperor Xuthus, my husband, should not in any manner be held responsible for any of my deeds. This is my sole plea. I am now going inside the palace.

She leaves. Trumpets beat. Music is heard. The rest all stand there astounded. Curtain falls.

Interval.

Music plays. Curtain raised. Next day. The courtyard of the Royal Palace during day time. **Xuthus**, **Senior Advisor**, **Aegyptus**, **Orion**, **Danius** *and a crowd seen. Music stops. Silence.*

Senior Advisor Emperor Xuthus, according to norms of democracy, Queen Creusa has committed a grave crime by bringing the poison of Gorgon inside Acropolis. Even you cannot deny it.

Aegyptus Absolutely correct. Besides in the premises where even taking the name of any devil is forbidden, she has carried the devil's stored blood clandestinely.

Orion Unholy and contaminated blood of Gorgon brought inside the holy temple! This is an unpardonable and punishable offence.

Senior Advisor We follow democracy in our state. Each and every rule of our city-state has been pledged with extreme faith. Creusa, our Queen, has shown utter disrespect to our devoutness. She has renounced the statute. This almost implies that she wants to renounce democracy.

Xuthus Mr. Advisor, give me a moment please. Your statement is undoubtedly logical but . . .

Aegyptus (*intercepts*) Now using your Royal power you are going to rescind the norm and impose your views on it. Am I right?

Xuthus No, Aegyptus, I have no such intention. It is well known that from the day we have accepted freedom of speech of imbeciles in democracy, the power of the Royal mandate has reduced.

Aegyptus King Xuthus, do you call me an imbecile?

Xuthus For the time being, I am unable to find an equivalent word. I would have rather been happier to call you imperviously dull.

Orion My Lord, you have said this earlier as well. Are you really of the opinion that idiots predominantly get an advantage in democracy?

Xuthus Not only do they get predominance, they are the ones who have the last laugh. But that is not the point, I was trying to be a tad rational in my point. Hey, Senior Advisor, according to norms of democracy, all including complainant–defendant, majority–minority, should be given a patient hearing. That the fundamental principle of the constitution of our city-state is based on this concept, you surely agree?

Senior Advisor Of course, I do. You give us your mandate, my Lord. You are our King. Even if your opinion goes against the views of the majority, we are still bound to accept it.

Xuthus Thank you. But since I am not aware of all the rules of the city-state and its finer details, and I am neither as eloquent nor adequately uncivilized as the majority present here, I am deploying Glaucus, an eminent citizen of Athens, to represent me in this case. Glaucus, I request you to please come inside.

Glaucus *enters with his assistant,* **Patroclus**.

Xuthus May I now request the notable citizen of Athens, debater Glaucus, to take it forward on my behalf, or rather on behalf of Queen Creusa.

Orion Well, we do not have any objection to this.

Aegyptus Glaucus, you may start.

Everybody agrees. **Glaucus** *starts to speak.*

Glaucus Our senior priest, Advisor and gentlemen present here, I hereby stand to present my argument in favour of King Xuthus and his client, Queen Creusa. But before proceeding, I would request you to reiterate the exact charges brought against the Queen.

Senior Advisor We also select Aegyptus as a representative on behalf of the people here to present our argument. Because it is practical to have a single voice to stand for the people against the King.

Orion Well, so be it.

Crowd Yes, so be it. Let Aegyptus be our face.

Glaucus Well, tell us, Aegyptus, about your complaint against our Queen. Let us all hear it.

Aegyptus Last evening, Lord Xuthus had invited us to a party organized at the Acropolis in Athens. The occasion was the investiture ceremony of the temple boy of Delphi, Ion, under the holy orders of our King. Our Queen Creusa perhaps could not accept the decision of the investiture ceremony. Going against our King's wish she therefore mixed poison in a glass of wine and offered it to Ion. Instead of having it himself, Ion offered it to his pet pigeon which died immediately after consuming it. Later we found out that the poison that was mixed with the wine was the blood of the notorious demon Gorgon. Hence, firstly, in accordance with the rules of the city-state, Gorgon's blood is completely forbidden inside the temple premises under any circumstances. Secondly, Queen Creusa wanted to organize a murder inside the temple. Though she remained unsuccessful in her attempt, her state of mind confirms that she deliberately wanted to kill an innocent person. For committing this dual crime, in accordance with the mandate given by our senior Priest of the city- state, we want Queen Creusa to be stoned to death.

Crowd So be it! So be it! Let Queen Creusa be stoned to death right now.

When the **Crowd** *falls silent, assistant* **Patroclus** *sends a signal with his hand to* **Glaucus** *to resume.*

Glaucus Well, to begin with I want to know who is the judge of this trial?

Everybody looks at one another.

What happened? Let me know. In accordance with the law of democracy of the city-state, a third party – a judge – is required to be present in a case between two parties. Who is the judge in the case here?

Pandemonium in the crowd.

Orion I propose the name of our senior Priest and our Advisor, as the judge of this trial.

Crowd (*in unison*) We second the proposal. We second the proposal.

Senior Advisor *occupies the judge's chair.*

Glaucus Okay, so be it. But then a new complication arises in this case. Plaintiff Aegyptus has already declared in his statement that, in accordance with the mandate given by the Senior Priest of the city-state the Queen be stoned to death. That is, the Senior Advisor has already passed his verdict and given his opinion, even before the trial has started. Can such a prejudiced person be qualified enough to occupy the chair of a neutral judge in this case?

Silence.

Consequently, King Xuthus remains the only eligible person to become the adjudicator. But again, his wife Creusa, the Queen, is the main accused in this case. So, he is also not neutral. But, at present none in Athens is equivalent to King Xuthus or to our Senior Advisor in seniority or in designation. No doubt, the trial of Queen Creusa cannot be conducted either by our physician Pyramus or architect Eurylochus. Hence, this trial stands flawed.

Patroclus Therefore, this trial is adjourned till a new and qualified capable judge is identified. In the interim, Queen Creusa stands acquitted.

Glaucus *and* **Patroclus** *intend to leave. A huge uproar in the crowd.* **Senior Advisor** *quietens them.*

Senior Advisor Glaucus, wait. Patroclus, do not leave.

They stop.

This is indeed true that King Xuthus is biased in favour of the accused in the first place. But according to the fourth clause of the city-state, bringing unholy blood or poison or something similar is strictly prohibited inside the holy premises. We have ourselves made this law. Therefore, whether the trial is held or not, the law holds Queen Creusa guilty.

Aegyptus So, to honour the fourth clause of the city-state, citizens of Athens want Queen Creusa to be stoned to death.

Orion Yes, let this be carried out right now.

Crowd So be it. Let her be killed.

Crowd cheers. **King Xuthus** *raises his arm. Everybody becomes quiet.* **Glaucus** *stands up.*

Glaucus Well, in that case let us dig deep into the fourth clause. According to the rules, it is not the blood of Gorgon or poison alone, any hot drink for that matter is strictly prohibited inside the temple premises. Moreover, the second subsection of clause four also states that not only drinks, any kind of animal carcass cannot be brought inside. I was not among the invitees to last night's party but many of you were present. Though King Xuthus himself abstains from any hot drinks, he had arranged plenty of meats and wines for the invitees. Most of you present here have relished the food and drinks. I have come to know that even our Senior Priest got carried away in celebrations and slugged three casks of wines all by himself. Why should only meat be restricted? Liquor of any kind is forbidden inside the temple premises. So, offering drink spiked with Gorgon's blood is second in the list of severe offences. But before that, many of you present here are already accused in the first offence. As a result, I propose to stone the Senior Advisor to death first followed by Aegyptus, Orion and other invitees one by one.

A person named **Chronus** *stands up.*

Chronus Since I am an ordinary shepherd, I never get invited to any reputable banquets. However, democracy is expected to ensure equal rights to enjoy access to any place, to any food and to any benefits. We, the poor, have always been deprived of these benefits throughout our lives. We have faced this deprivation on advice of this Senior Priest. So, this Priest should immediately be stoned to death for breaking the law of the city-state.

Many in the Crowd Yes, yes let him be stoned. Stone him.

Aegyptus Hey, have you all gone crazy? The Senior Priest is our only mediator with God Zeus. He is the one who communicates with the God on our behalf. How can you propose to kill him?

Chronus We do not want any mediator. We are capable of communicating with the God on our own.

Danius Moreover, if our senior advisor speaks to God Zeus so frequently, let us see how he makes Him come to his rescue in this situation of jeopardy.

Patroclus Especially when our Senior Priest is in real danger, God Zeus should immediately show up in this temple premises on his own will.

Aegyptus Do you think God Zeus is sitting idle that he will make his appearance in front of us because of a distress call from just anybody?

Glaucus Yes, what you have said is undeniably true, Aegyptus. The Senior Priest is a common man just like us. So, God Zeus will definitely not come here to save him. You all hear me out. If a country's law is draped in religion, at a later time, those law-makers are the first to face its flak. So, it is crucial that in our city-state we first free our state policies from politics and then free politics from religion. Else, despite having a vision, we will slowly but surely turn blind.

Aegyptus We do not want to listen to this crap. State policy without religious influence – even listening to such sceptical thoughts is a sin.

Orion We want a death sentence for Queen Creusa.

Glaucus Just imagine, Queen Creusa has admitted to her crime. But you all are saying that Queen Creusa did not carry the wine spiked with Gorgon's blood to Acropolis herself. It was Danius, her servant, who actually brought it. Servant Danius refused to disclose her name. That means had Queen Creusa not admitted her fault, Danius would have been the accused. Yet Danius is not the accused in the true sense.

Aegyptus Then let Danius be killed.

Orion Yes, so be it.

Crowd So be it. So be it.

Patroclus Wow, democracy! Great! If the real culprit is not being identified, let us label someone innocent as the culprit. Am I right?

Glaucus However, if I talk about the ill-effect of Hemlock, ultimately it is the pet pigeon of Ion who had succumbed to it. The only casualty in this case is the pigeon, which is much inferior to the human species in this world. Moreover, it was actually Ion who fed it the poisonous drink. Then Ion is the real culprit. Isn't he?

Crowd Yes, Ion is the real killer. He is the offender. Let him be killed.

Glaucus But King Xuthus was the chief organizer of the ceremony. The prohibited drinks and meat were brought to the Acropolis on his instructions. Danius took advantage of the situation and entered this holy place with the deadly Hemlock. Then, who is the main culprit?

Chronus King Xuthus. Xuthus is the main culprit. Let us kill him.

Danius Impossible. The King is never expendable. If we kill our King, the God of war, Ares, will come and kill us all.

The **Crowd** *now appears to be divided into two groups. They argue among themselves.* **Glaucus** *takes* **Aegyptus** *aside.*

Glaucus See, Aegyptus, this is how democracy functions in your city-state. Do you now realize what happens when fools take control over democracy?

Glaucus *comes forward and raises his two arms to pacify the two fighting groups. The crowd falls silent.*

It is my request to you all to rethink. Servant Danius brought Gorgon's blood in the Acropolis. Danius carried out his Queen's order. Only the pet pigeon died and became the victim of circumstances. The Acropolis which had already been vitiated because of liquor and wine cannot be further polluted because of entry of Gorgon's blood. The role of religion is not supposed to be so overt in the city-state that we have formed, and in the laws that we have enacted in democracy. This is indeed true that we are Pagans, we believe in different faiths, multiple paths and varied beliefs. Then can we really kill someone particular for some particular reason? No, we cannot. So, my appeal to you is that not only Queen Creusa, everybody should be acquitted in this case.

Aegyptus Impossible. Somebody has to be punished.

Crowd Yes. We want it. We want an enemy. We want an enemy right now.

Glaucus Well, let us nab Gorgon in that case. We request King Xuthus to give this responsibility to Aegyptus and Orion on our behalf.

Xuthus Request accepted. Aegyptus and Orion will go to capture the dangerous Gorgon right now.

Aegyptus Are we nuts! We cannot take this responsibility.

Orion Impossible, my friend Glaucus. Have you lost it completely?

Glaucus The order has been issued by the King himself. Like Perseus, you will have to cross the North Pole to reach the magic island to destroy Gorgon and his three sisters Medusa.

Orion I am leaving for my home.

Aegyptus No, we are not going anywhere. Queen Creusa has brought Gorgon's blood. Therefore, she deserves death. We want her blood.

Crowd We want blood. We want Queen Creusa's blood.

The **Crowd** *roars. Amid huge chaos* **Pythia** *suddenly appears.* **King Xuthus** *is surprised to see her.* **Xuthus** *moves towards her. Seeing an unknown person, the* **Crowd** *keeps quiet.*

Xuthus Aren't you Pythia, the senior maid of God Apollo's temple of Delphi?

Pythia Yes, my Lord. I am Pythia, servant of God Apollo's temple at Delphi. I wish to meet the Queen once.

Xuthus Why? Why do you have to meet her?

Pythia I have a requirement. I have heard that your Queen is in trouble. I have come here on God Apollo's advice to pass on a message to her.

Xuthus Message? What message?

Pythia I can convey the message only to her, my Lord. This is my God's commandment.

Queen Creusa *appears near the gate of the palace at that time.*

Pythia There she is, she is Creusa, the Queen. It has been so many years. You remain the same, my dear Queen.

Creusa Who are you? Oh, Pythia, you?

Pythia Yes, my dear Queen. It is me, Pythia. Do you recognize me?

Creusa (*cries out*) Pythia.

All curious eyes, including **King Xuthus**', *on* **Creusa**. *Light goes off. The three Fates return with spindle in their hands.*

Lachesis Man does not forget his past but loves to forget it. He wants to wipe off his sin, misdemeanour, deeds, apathy and everything from his memory. But when the past returns to the present, he perceives it as a ghost from the past. He does not actually realize that this is a warning to him so that he doesn't repeat the same mistake.

Clotho The present is like a curse personified. Man smears the rotten taste, foul smell, blood, and purge of the here and now on his body and still continues to dream. He imagines the onset of an unknown era one day when the sea will halt, the fire will extinguish and the fountain will flow in a desert. Man you do not understand that your past is responsible for creating such moments. And you are even incapable in realizing that all these moments will again lead to draught and plague on earth in the future.

Atropos Alas, we are three daughters of fate. We have to keep on rotating the spindles. The dead bodies, one corpse after the other depart, we keep rotating the spindles. As scavengers of graveyards, we enumerate the dead dreams, frozen ambitions and dead losses. Man does not realize that there is no tomorrow for him. Zeus's thunderbolt has pierced his mouth to ensure his inevitable degeneration.

Together We only count dead dreams.
Count only the frozen ambitions.
Successes and failures are all dead; they have been killed. Absolutely.

Lights are on. Room of **Queen Creusa**. **Creusa** *is sitting and* **Pythia** *is standing behind her.* **Creusa** *speaks to herself.*

Creusa They want to kill me. They want to execute the daughter of the first King of Athens, Erechthius. It was during the rule of Erechthius that Goddess Pallas was authorized as the main deity of the entirety of Greece.

Pyhtia You were three sisters, Queen Creusa.

Creusa Yes, the God of seas, Poseidon, had killed my sisters taking them away forever. I too might have been killed by him but fortunately I went to offer prayer to Delphi's temple with my mother at that time. Irate God Poseidon could not trace me thereafter.

Pythia It was God Apollo who actually saved you.

Creusa I first met you there, Pythia.

Pythia Yes, you and your mother used to visit Delphi's temple daily. I was then a young servant of the God. I had decided to dedicate my entire life for the service of God Apollo at Delphi.

Creusa Right you are. You used to oversee the temple management.

Pythia We had developed a deep liking for each other. When your mother used to offer prayer in the temple, we used to have a long chat. I used to serve you sweets made in the temple.

Creusa (*smiles*) It was perhaps the temptation of sweets that compelled me to go and sit with you.

Pythia But you were very calm by nature in your childhood.

Creusa Then my mother expired. I grew up. But . . .

Pythia But? Please continue!

Creusa The day when I reached puberty, a strange thing happened in my life.

Pythia What happened, Queen Creusa?

Creusa My puberty rituals were conducted ceremoniously at the temple of Delphi. I did not return to the palace after the ceremony was over. My father, King Erechtheus, returned to his palace with other family members. Unnoticed, I stayed back in the temple.

Pythia (*smiles*) What happened then?

Creusa I was roaming inside the temple. It was around evening. I could not find any of you nearby. Walking aimlessly, I reached right in front of God Apollo's idol. I was awestruck by the first sight of the most handsome God among the Olympians. Soaked in moonlight piercing through the door, he was wearing a crown made of laurel leaves. He held a bow in one hand and a harp in the other. His well-built naked body aroused a strange feeling inside me.

Pythia People say God Apollo is not just ever young but ever attractive too. He is the father of Greek art, my deity Apollo.

Creusa That evening became the most important eve in my life. You know, Pythia, when I was standing in front of the carved figure of God Apollo in the captivating moonlight, I could suddenly hear the wind whispering through the oak leaves around me. As if the sleeping pigeons started flapping their wings. And then . . .

Pause.

Pythia A trail of voice entered your ears. Am I right?

Creusa Oracle. It was an oracle Pythia. See, I am still getting goosebumps. Though it happened long ago, I still clearly remember every moment of it.

Pythia What did you get to hear, Queen Creusa?

Creusa It was like spellcasting. I was told to chant a mantra. Mesmerized, I chanted the mantra Pythia.

Pythia What happened after that?

Creusa (*whispers*) Just after I finished chanting the mantra, a naked youth pierced out through the statue of God Apollo and stood in front of me. I had never seen such a stunningly pretty young man in my life before. Perhaps I won't see such beauty again in my future as well. (*Pause.*) He came to me, held my hands and offered his desirous proposal of love. His incredible voice, spellbinding eyes, his heart-rending diction hypnotized me, Pythia. And then . . .

Pythia (*murmurs*) Apollo. God Apollo.

Creusa How I got back to my palace is still unknown to me. Probably late in the night, my father came to the temple in search of me with his councillors. I was supposedly leaning back on the pillar in the temple corridor with an apparently unblinking, tranquil gaze.

Pythia What happened then?

Creusa After a few days of my return to Athens, I realized that I was pregnant. I did not share the news with anybody. I had lost my mother in the meantime. I stayed alone in my room. Nobody even had an inkling. When time was ripe for me to deliver, I clandestinely slipped out of the palace and reached a mountain cave outside the city alone. When I was about to enter the cave at night, I saw . . .

Pythia (*smiles*) You saw me?

Creusa Pythia, how did you come to know that I was going to take shelter in that cave?

Pythia God Apollo sent me there.

Creusa Apollo? After I returned from the Delphi temple, he never enquired about me, Pythia, not even once. He never bothered to know what happened to me or how I would hide my pregnancy from the society. After I conceived, how many times I threw up or how many times my head spun did not affect the God of Art at all. Then I realized that Gods are exactly like human beings.

Pythia But that is not true. Else he would not have sent me to you that night. When I held you in my arms at the entrance of the cave on the mountain-top, your lips were dry, your body was trembling heavily and there was hardly any strength left in you.

Creusa I was feeling as if I was breathing my last. That night, inside the cave you had cut the umbilical cord of my newborn baby, Pythia. I was squealing in pain then . . . Ahh!

Pythia A new birth . . . a new life . . . a new possibility on earth.

Creusa Then I returned to the palace at Athens. You too left with my illegitimate son placed in a basket. After that, I met you only once, Pythia . . .

Pythia In the agricultural festival of Goddess Demeter. It was the first day of that harvesting season on earth. The village girls were dancing. You were sitting on a wooden bench in the amphitheatre and watching them dance. I went near you and sat right beside you silently.

Creusa Seeing you after so many days, I impatiently enquired about my child, Pythia. You said you knew nothing about him.

Pythia *remains silent.*

Creusa Why did you come up with such an answer? Didn't you really know about my child?

Pythia I really didn't know. That evening, after my return to the temple, priest Aegyus snatched your baby from me.

Creusa Aegyus, the principal priest of God Apollo?

Pythia Priest Aegyus then informed me that I had been discharged from all my duties at the temple. He ordered me to leave Athens immediately and join Apollo's temple at Clarus near Colophon. Next morning, I left Athens for Colophon.

Creusa But what happened to my child, where is he?

Pythia Today, Priest Aegyus has sent me two messages through a shepherd.

Creusa What are these messages?

Pythia Firstly, you are in danger. So, God Apollo had ordered me to reach Athens immediately to save you.

Creusa (*sneers*) God Apollo! Does he still remember me? Good. What is his second message, Pythia?

Pythia *remains silent.*

Tell me, Pythia.

Pythia Till today I believed your child had expired. Priestess Duffnis had once given me such a hint. But he is not dead, Queen . . .

Creusa Then, then where is he now?

Pythia He is alive. He has been brought up in the temple of Athens.

Creusa What are you saying?

Pythia Yes, my dear Queen and his name is Ion.

Creusa What!

Pythia He is at the centre of all debates and controversies today. You wanted to have him killed, Queen. He is your son, he is your Ion.

Creusa Ion!

She breaks down, then composes herself.

That is why he resembles the attractive youth I met that evening in the temple. I liked him right at the first sight. But soon after, I remembered what had happened that evening. I was reminded of God Apollo's heartless indifference towards me, his disinterest in remembering me even once. You know, Pythia, after I left the cave of the tall mountain in a huff, I never visited Delphi's temple again. I thought if God can be so cruel with mankind, then why can't human beings show their indifference towards Gods? From that day onwards I always offered my prayers to God Boreas only.

Pythia But God Apollo has never forgotten you. He has brought up your son Ion and has united you with your son in a surprising coincidence. Since you did not offer him prayers, he has taken his revenge too by pushing you so close to death.

Creusa Alas destiny! I have suffered enough. Thus, I come to know the truth. It took me to the wild past again. Ah . . . such an ill-fated person I am, rather we all are. We are always tempted to kill our progeny in the name of religion and kingdom. To be on top of power, we continue to even conspire against our offspring. We mix Gorgon's venom in our relatives' blood and we fiercely murder the divine spirit resting within us. We do it every day, every moment, relentlessly.

Pythia Queen. Queen Creusa.

Creusa Let's go, Pythia! Let's go to Delphi's temple. We will bring Ion back with me. Please don't disclose anything to King Xuthus now. I will let him know and convince him later. My husband is very good at heart. Let's go, Pythia. Let's go to the temple of God Apollo at Delphi.

Music is heard. They both go to the platform placed below on stage. Everybody is waiting there including **King Xuthus**. **Xuthus** *moves forward and holds* **Creusa***'s hands. He looks at her curiously. He probably wants to know something.* **Creusa** *maintains silence. Light goes off. The three Fates appear again spinning the spindles in their hands. They laugh but do not utter a word. Light is on. Delphi's temple of God Apollo becomes visible.* **Ion** *is singing a hymn.* **Creusa** *comes forward with a veil covering her face.*

Creusa Ion, Ion, my son.

Ion (*looks at her, then speaks*) On sacred Tysis's shore I say my prayers to God Apollo. Ion is my name,

Of unknown identity, born of an obscure womb. That's who I am. Lady, who are you?

Creusa (*uncovers the veil*) Ion, I am Queen Creusa. I have come here to take you back with me. Please come with me, Ion. Let's go back.

Ion I am not angry with you, Queen. I am truly an orphan. It was King Xuthus' wish, so I went there. I do not have any greed, Queen. So, remembering God Apollo, I am telling you,

'This quiet, unruffled hour
from the infinite sky a music drifts to my ears:

of effort without victory, sweat of work without hope – I can see the end, full of peace and emptiness.'[1]

Queen you please go back. You return to your palace. I am a poor worshipper of a temple. The temple is the best place for me. You please leave, 'let me stay with the losers, those whose hopes will be dashed'.[2]

Creusa Ion, you have to come back with me. Please don't brood over my behaviour. I am a miserable, impious woman but please don't be annoyed with me. I made a mistake. I committed a crime. But please come back with me. I can't return without you.

Ion With what right should I go there, Queen?

Creusa Right? Ion, my dear son,
'with a divine right indeed you had one day come to this lap – and by that same right return again, with glory; don't worry at all'.[3]

Come back to your own kingdom, occupy your throne. 'Take your own place on my maternal lap.'

Ion 'As if in a dream
I hear your voice, honoured lady. Look, darkness has engulfed the entire horizon, swallowed the four quarters.'[4]

Soundless Tysis! What are you saying, Queen?

Creusa Yes, dear. You are my son. You were born in my womb. Come with me, son, to take your throne.

Ion 'Throne, indeed! To one who's just refused the maternal bond are you offering, Mother, assurances of a kingdom?'[5]

It is not the throne, mother Creusa. I never yearn for the throne. I have grown up in this temple. With the calmness around and the sound of ringing bell and chirping birds, I spend a very peaceful life here.

Xuthus *enters.*

Xuthus Ion, you cannot really afford to say that. You have to go back to Athens. Goddess Pallas, the supreme deity of Athens, wants you to be present there. She says you will be the next King of Athens.

---

1 As mentioned in my translator notes, Bratya Basu has used few lines from the Karna-Kunti Samvad written by Rabindranath Tagore (1900) in this part of the play. For the full text refer, Tagore, Rabindranath. (1900). *Karna-Kunti Samvad, Kahini Kavyagrantha, Rabindra Rachanavali*, Volume 3, Calcutta: Visva Bharati Publishing House. I have used the English translation of Karna-Kunti Samvad by Ketaki Kushari Dyson (2000) here. For the full translation refer https://parabaas.com/translation/database/translations/poems/RT_Karnakunti.html

2 Refer footnote 1.

3 Refer footnote 1.

4 Refer footnote 1.

5 Refer footnote 1.

Ion But King, you will have your own child again. He will be your progeny. He should be the natural successor, the next King of Athens.

Xuthus I know that, my boy. Goddess Pallas has served her mandate on this too. My son's name will be Doris. There is still time for Doris to be born on this earth. You can enthrone Doris once he grows up and you feel that he is eligible. Your descendants will be called Ionian. The descendants of Doris will be Dorian.

Creusa God Apollo. My dear God Apollo.

Xuthus Let's go, Queen. Let all of us offer our prayers to God Apollo and then return to Athens.

They go and sit in front of God Apollo. God Apollo's idol is visible. Music is heard. Light goes off. The three Fates come back with spindles in their hands.

Lachesis Turbulent past.

Clotho Clamorous present.

Atropos Dark future.

All Three at Once Yet mankind moves on.
Gods appear.
They deliver oracles.
Our mother Nemesis chuckles.
Man believes.
Man disbelieves.
Man fights back.
Man kills.
Again, Man creates life
Provides water
Gives shelter.
Civilization progresses.
Moves on and on
Since the primitive age.

Music is heard. The **Singer** *with a lyre in his hand appears. He sings the song he sang in the first half. Curtain falls.*

The End.

Glossary

Drachma: Drachma was the ancient currency used in Greece during several periods in its history. The Greek drachma (GRD) was the basic unit of currency in Greece until 2001 when it was replaced by the euro

Hemlock: A poisonous plant, *Conium maculatum*, of the parsley family, having purple-spotted stems, finely divided leaves and umbels of small white flowers, used medicinally as a powerful sedative. An irresponsible use of the poison Hemlock disrupts the central nervous system – a small dose can cause respiratory collapse

Mantra: (Sanskrit: *manas* meaning 'mind' and *tra* meaning 'tool') A mantra is a sacred word, sound or phrase, often in Sanskrit, recited repeatedly within a wide variety of religious and spiritual traditions such as Hinduism, Buddhism and Yoga

Medusa: In Greek mythology Medusa was one of the three evil Gorgons. She represents a dangerous threat meant to deter other dangerous threats, an image of evil to repel evil. Generally described as a female face with living venomous snakes replacing her hair

Pagan: A member of a people or nation who does not practise Christianity, Judaism or Islam, especially a follower of a polytheistic religion. Early Christians often used the term to refer to non-Christians who worshiped multiple deities. Pagans worship the divine in many different forms, through feminine as well as masculine imagery and also as without gender

Pankration: Originally a sport entered into the Greek Olympic Games in 648 BC, a modern-day version of Pankration does still exist. It was an ancient Greek sports event that combined boxing and wrestling

Prasada: (Sanskrit: 'favour' or 'grace') In Hinduism, food and water offered to a deity during worship. It is believed that the deity partakes of and then returns the offering, thereby consecrating it. The offering is then distributed and eaten by the worshippers

Section Three

Intimately Political, Politically Intimate

Summaries

The Black Hole

Fifty-four-year-old Angshuman Banerjee is trying to come to terms with a self-discovery. He is gay. His comfort and confidence with 'normalcy' is shattered as he tried to come to terms with his identity. Banerjee seeks out Dr Jayanta Ghosh, a polymath. Banerjee believes Ghosh and his multi-faceted expertise will salvage him. But, as the play progresses, we realize and learn that knowledge – be it of self or of our universe – can be like a *krisnagawhbor*, a black hole, whose hunger knows no limits. One of the very few plays in recent Bengali group theatre that portrays a character going through a crisis of sexual identity, the play amplifies one character's crisis to a universal confusion emanating from our being in the information superhighway. Does knowing more absolve us or does it immerse ourselves more in the all-consuming depths of a black hole?

In *The Black Hole*, uncertainty is predominant across various planes: the uncertainty of the Heisenberg principle, the uncertainty of the status of homosexuality in India, the uncertainty of family relationships, the uncertainty of romantic relationships, the uncertainty of suicide, the uncertainty of middle-class life and achievement. The play refers to moments when black holes are created within the selves of ordinary human beings which they try their best to overcome. It is the propping up of an event horizon which gives the characters a deep desire to live. The audience or reader can very well relate to the minute fractions of pain, misery and happiness in their day to day lives. The intentionality and care given to these nuanced, complex, ambiguous topics is the defining feature of Basu's work. Each level of uncertainty has its own unique flavour and even as different emotions pop up with each level and mixture of uncertainty, the effect is a mélange that is complex and productive – offering anyone engaged in and with the play multiple roads to different flavours of the same mood.

Who?

Lily Gupta is dead, and the suspicion falls on Dr Sunil Sen, a physician who had treated Lily for her depression before she took her life. Lily Gupta's husband Srikanto Gupta suspects that an affair between his wife and the doctor is to blame for her death. An intricate family drama, a comic detective with an obsession with Indian cricket, and a penchant for mindless violence completes the narrative of this psychological thriller bordering on the absurd. All to find out the answer to the question: who did it? Was Lily Gupta's death a suicide or did someone abet it? Are there other bodies and skeletons in the closet? Does Sunil Sen's inherent misogyny have to do with how he conducts himself? Bratya Basu's 2013 *Ke* (Who?) has been characterized as a psychocomic thriller by singer-songwriter Anindya Chatterjee. The rollercoaster lives up to its reputation and is an excellent example of the Basu oeuvre that puts modern Bengali life under the microscope.

The characterization of Chatok Chattaraj, the detective hired to crack the case in the play *Who?*, ridicules the deterministic linearity of detective fiction as the playwright reminds us about the probability of uncertainty often absent in the detective genre. Chatak is a caricature of the classic pulp fiction hard-boiled detective. He has poor deductive reasoning hidden by his playful capacity to make the unreasonable sound reasonable and he has a belief in the fundamental goodness of humans. The latter can be nothing short of an unpardonable sin committed by a detective. Thus, Chatak breaks the Newtonian logic and focuses on the secrets and possibilities of human relationships to solve the mystery of who the killer is. Through the genre of a thriller and the model of pulp fiction, the playwright explores the contradictions of romance and marriage. It is by turning to the hyper-real through a high level of action performance on stage that Basu unveils the violent and aggressive alter ego of the protagonist Sunil Sen. In both *Who?* and *The Black Hole*, the playwright critiques the Newtonian dynamics of linear narrative and deterministic thinking, and uses quantum mechanics to question the normalization of social hierarchies that reinforce accepted binaries propped up by structural violence and power. He questions the notions of positivity in order to unveil the uncertainty and doubt of the human condition.

Translator's notes

Arnab Banerji

Braya Basu wrote *The Black Hole* as two long scenes. But it became quite apparent while translating the text that each half or act of the play could be easily divided up into scenes to make it even more readable to a primarily Western audience who would be encountering this material, not simply as a new play, but also as a foray into a new cultural understanding.

I also noted a small historical anomaly in the original pertaining to the Islamic rulers of Bengal being referenced by Rongon. It has been fixed. I retained the Bengali words *Dada*, *Baba* and *Ma* to emphasize the Bengaliness of the text. While Basu's concerns are undoubtedly universal, his style is idiosyncratically Bengali which makes these plays unique. I did not want to lose that flavour. It is hoped that a glossary appended to the eventual volume will help clarify some of the more quirky Bengali verbal elements of the text.

Bratya Basu teases at several elements in his short but intriguing play "Ke?," translated here as "Who?" Basu effortlessly demonstrates his eclectic command over genre and cricketing trivia while also showcasing his deep understanding of Bengali middle-class sensibility. The result is this sometimes dark, sometimes funny whodunnit thriller that is universal in appeal but sincerely glocal (globally local) in its particularities. Translating this text was somewhat easier than other Basu plays that I have worked on. And I blame the effortless prose of the original for it rather than any linguistic dexterity that I might possess. What was a bit of a challenge were the many cricketing wisdom that is happily peppered across the play especially after Chatok Chattaraj, the detective is introduced in the play. A staple information for the cricket aficionado, but non-cricket knowing readers would undoubtedly fumble at the frequency with which Basu unleashes tiny little cricket facts. I have tried to provide contextual information in the glossary for readers to follow along. I can only hope that readers have as much fun reading this play as I did rendering it in a different language.

The Black Hole

Bratya Basu
2007

Translated by Arnab Banerji

The Black Hole

Male characters: 10

Female characters: 4 Extras that are not gender specific

Country of origin: India

Original performance date: 7 September 2007, Kolkata

Characters

Angshuman *(male, fifty to fifty-five; personification of ordinary)*
Jayanta *(male, forty-five to forty-eight; sharp features)*
Jayati *(female, forty-seven to forty-eight; dignified appearance fitting of a senior college faculty)*
Rahul *(male, eighteen to twenty; good-looking)*
Mou *(female, twenty to twenty-two; looks like she appears in television soaps)*
Abhishek *(male, twenty-three to twenty-four; intellectual in appearance)*
Rongon *(male, forty to forty-five; handsome middle-aged man)*
Anindita *(female, twenty-two to twenty-three; good-looking)*
Prajit *(male, forty-eight to fifty; calm demeanour)*
Gouri *(female, forty-five to forty-six; calm demeanour)*
Alok *(male, twenty to twenty-two)*
Shubho *(male, thirty to thirty-two)*
Ratan *(male, thirty-four to thirty-five)*
Debraj *(male, fifty-five to fifty-six; aristocratic)*
Members of the theatre group *(mixed gender, mixed age but veering towards the young)*

Act One

Scene One

The curtain opens at the end of the opening score. The stage is completely dark. Therefore the scenery on stage is invisible. Only **Angshuman Banerjee***, seated in a doctor's office on stage left, is visible through the light and shade playing on the dark stage.* **Dr Jayanta Ghosh** *stands in front of him leaning on the table.*

Angshuman*'s face is visible through* **Jayanta***'s arm and body. It's a very tight composition and they are barely lit. No one speaks for a while before* **Angshuman** *breaks the silence.*

Angshuman I am – I mean – I am a gay man.

Beat.

I mean I am homosexual.

Beat.

Trust me, doctor. I wasn't like this when I was young. This has grown in me in these last few months.

Jayanta How old are you now exactly?

Angshuman Fifty-four.

Jayanta Where do you work?

Angshuman Nothing for the last two years.

Jayanta What about before that?

Angshuman I used to be a children's painting teacher. But that was under compulsion. I am actually a painter, an artist. I have a degree from the arts college. Okay, artist might be an exaggeration. I wanted to be a painter, but didn't make it.

Jayanta Hmm.

Angshuman I mean I did have a couple of exhibitions. But that didn't lead to anything. I have been working with children for the last seven to eight years. Then I lost interest in that as well.

Jayanta What did you say your name was?

Angshuman Angshuman, Angshuman Banerjee.

Jayanta Where do you live?

Angshuman Joka, near the cancer hospital.

Jayanta Who else is there in your family?

Angshuman My wife, my children – a son and a daughter. You know, the usual. My wife works.

Jayanta Where?

Angshuman In a college. She is a professor of physics.

Jayanta What about your children?

Angshuman My son went to the same college that my wife teaches at. And he studied physics as well. He just finished his Master of Science.

Jayanta What about your daughter?

Angshuman My daughter was working towards an undergraduate degree. But she left it midway and is now taking computer lessons. She is also a part of a theatre group and also occasionally appears in television soaps.

Jayanta The son is older then?

Angshuman Yes, they are two years apart.

Jayanta So, why exactly did you choose to come to me?

Angshuman Like I said, because I am a homosexual.

Jayanta So what?

Angshuman What are you saying doctor? I – I wasn't like this. I was as normal as everybody.

Jayanta Sorry!

Beat.

Angshuman Yes!

Jayanta Everyone is not normal. If they were then my profession would have been excised from medical science. And secondly, who has told you that homosexuality is abnormal? There are plenty of celebrated people the world over who are homosexuals.

Angshuman I know. But even then this feels abnormal from time to time. I don't know why. Perhaps because my surroundings inspire me to think like this? Especially when I am by myself . . .

Jayanta Do you feel guilty?

Angshuman Yes, yes. Very much so. I don't know why.

Jayanta Interesting, this doesn't happen to everyone usually.

Angshuman Maybe because this is a new thing for me.

Jayanta Maybe. But please, go on.

Angshuman I mean, how do I explain. When I am by myself this whole thing eats me from within. I think I am a pervert.

Jayanta Go on . . .

Angshuman I was very depressed for the last couple of years. And then this . . .

Jayanta Depression. Hmm, why do you think you were depressed?

Angshuman Yes. I have asked that question of myself as well. Probably because I couldn't become a successful artist.

Jayanta You mean because you didn't make a name for yourself?

Angshuman Oh yes, of course. But it is not just about fame. For the last several years I have also been realizing that I am not a very competent artist. There's a lot lacking in me. It's not surprising that I never made a name for myself.

Jayanta What do you think you lack?

Angshuman I don't think I can really explain this very well.

Jayanta Why don't you try? I will try to understand.

Angshuman Well, how do I explain? See, I – I am very mediocre. Do you understand what I am trying to say?

Jayanta *looks on without blinking.*

Angshuman I can't seem to imagine beyond a certain point. I can until a certain point but beyond that it is all hazy.

Jayanta How do you assess the extent of your imagination? And how do you assess that it is not far enough?

Angshuman I can understand. I can feel it. I have a basic sensibility after all. And of course I have read about these people. So . . .

Jayanta Which people?

Angshuman You know – Van Gogh, Gaugin, Cezanne, Matisse, or our Ramkinkar. And I have realized based on my readings . . .

Beat.

In fact, well these are greats, forget about them, even amongst my contemporaries I am worse than the most mediocre of them, forget about the ones that are well known.

Jayanta Very strange, and how exactly have you . . .

Angshuman How do I explain?

Beat.

I mean, there are doctors, right, who understand the theories of medicine very well but as soon as they enter the operating theatre, they become nervous. There are people like that, right? I am kind of like that.

Jayanta Okay, and then?

Angshuman And the moment I understood this for sure – I mean as soon as I came to an understanding with myself, I became depressed. I did not want to communicate with anybody after that.

Jayanta Did you not want to communicate? Or were you not able to communicate?

Angshuman I did not want to. I felt all my artistic lapses would be brutally exposed, like a sore wound, as soon as I would communicate with anyone. I used to imagine myself as a misfit in this world. But I have realized that I am actually unfit. Incompetent. Unstable.

Jayanta Isn't that true for a lot of creative people?

Angshuman (*slightly irritated*) That's different! That is a part of their creative expression. My incompetence is genetic.

Jayanta Genetic?

Angshuman Of course genetic. I can feel it. My father was exactly like this. He spent his entire life as a clerk for the railways. He would dream of becoming a high-ranking officer – but he was incapable of that.

Beat.

He was lazy, an idler and a cheat from within. I have inherited every last one of those qualities from him.

Jayanta Didn't you try to overcome it in spite of knowing this? Hard work can heal up any kind of shortcomings.

Angshuman I tried until I was forty-five. And then stopped – gave up. I realized this is who I am – useless, mediocre and lazy.

Jayanta Do you imagine genes are similar to fate?

Angshuman I feel it that way. Nothing is sudden and abrupt. I mean your circumstances do have a large effect on you but I can feel it in my blood that nothing is happening just like that – it is all pre-destined. My wife and son don't believe in this but I do – and I know that you will not believe in it either – you are also a student of science after all . . .

Jayanta You are right about that.

Angshuman But I understand it, you know. This mediocrity inside me – with all my bulging fat, my sweat, my lethargy – I have felt it many times. I have felt it gush out of me into a thought or in something I said or in the way that I respond to something. And I recognize it. I saw the exact same thing in my father twenty-five years ago. It's just repeating itself in me.

Jayanta I have obviously never thought of genetics in this way . . .

Angshuman I thought of sharing this with my father many, many times. But I just couldn't bring myself up to it, doctor, I just could not.

Jayanta Why not?

Angshuman He was an innocent, poor, pitiful person. An assistant clerk with the railways – the *boro babu* of the head office – you know I would call my father the *boro babu* – but I just could not share this with *boro babu*. It troubled me a lot.

Jayanta Well, you seem to be quite comfortable sharing it with me. You are, in fact, quite at ease. You don't seem to be having any trouble.

Angshuman I do have my mother's genes as well. Simple and rustic.

Jayanta Are they still around? Your parents?

Angshuman No, they are both deceased. My father passed away first. My mother left us around three years ago. She used to live with me.

Jayanta (*absent mindedly*) Hmm.

You are claiming that your sexuality was initiated by depression. It is a possibility. Sexuality can be inherited via depression.

Angshuman Who knows? I have felt it for the last seven months.

Jayanta Yes, that is what you said. Anyway, do you have a specific partner, Angshuman?

Angshuman Yes.

Jayanta Just the one.

Angshuman Yes, just the one.

Jayanta Who is it?

Beat.

Who is it?

Angshuman Let me show you a picture first.

Jayanta Something that you have painted?

Angshuman (*rummaging through his bag*) No, no. I mean a photograph. I have not painted for almost a decade now.

Jayanta Whose photo? Your partner's?

Angshuman Here.

Takes a photo out after rummaging through his bag and hands it to **Jayanta**. *Their side of the stage drowns in darkness. The back of the stage is brightly lit. The characters revealed are frozen like in a photograph.*

Living room of a middle-class household. At the centre sits **Jayati** *with a book in her hand.* **Rahul** *sits in front of her.* **Mou** *stands at the back, looking ready to head out.* **Angshuman***'s voice floats in from the dark.*

Angshuman (*cont'd*) The person in the sofa is my wife Jayati. And that's my daughter Mou. And the man in front is Rahul. Rahul Som. A student of my wife's. He is majoring in Chemistry with Physics as a secondary subject.

Jayanta Is this him?

Beat.

Beat.

Angshuman Yes, this is him. Rahul. My inspiration. The reason that my living corpse has begun dreaming of life again.

Scene Two

The people frozen in the background come alive. **Mou** *is getting ready to go out. Takes a lipstick out from her handbag and touches up her lips.* **Jayati** *is talking.*

Rahul *is taking notes.*

Jayati Is it clear, Rahul? You have got to understand this. For the last two hundred and fifty years scholars of classical mechanics held the opinion that the position and the momentum of any object could be predetermined. And therefore it was possible to predict the future location of a moving object.

Mou *Ma*, where is your purse?

Jayati And now with the evolution of quantum mechanics . . . why?

Mou (*cont'd*) I need some money.

Jayati How much?

Mou One fifty or so.

Jayati Why do you need so much all of a sudden?

Mou Uff, just give *na*.

Beat.

I have to pay back the group for three tickets. I took the tickets for the last performance. Couldn't sell three of them. Bumba's youngest uncle didn't come through at the last moment. He said he would take them but did not. I have to pay the group back today itself. Or else I won't hear the end of it from Shubho *da*.

Jayati Who is this Shubho *da* now?

Mou Why can't you remember anything? Shubho *da* is the group's secretary.

Jayati Go check your brother's room. You should be able to find money there. He was asking for money earlier. Wants to buy some books . . .

Mou Thanks, Mother!

Jayati (*to* **Rahul**) Where were we?

Scene Three

Mou *enters upstage then crosses over to come to downstage right. There is a diagonal partition here. A bed in front of the partition.* **Abhishek** *or* **Abhi** *lies on the bed. He is on his stomach reading a book. A pillow props up his chest. He has an unkempt mess of facial hair. Wears glasses. He is wearing a t-shirt and pyjama bottoms.*

Mou Hey, do you know where is Mother's purse?

Abhishek I think it's on the table – no wait –

Mou (*looks for it on the table*) Nope, not here.

They freeze. We hear **Jayanta***'s voice.*

Jayanta And this photo? Is this your son?

Angshuman Yes, his name is Abhi. Short for Abhishek.

Jayanta Is Rahul a student in the college that your wife teaches at?

Angshuman No, he goes to a different college. He comes to Jayati for private lessons.

Mou *and* **Abhi** *break out of the freeze.*

Mou Nope, not here.

Abhishek Not there? Well, then, it isn't here.

Mou Drop the humour! Please give it to me.

Abhishek (*sitting up*) Check out what this book says.

Mou Stop it, just give me the purse.

Abhishek Just listen *na*, this is about that money bag of yours.

Mou (*suspiciously*) What book is that?

Abhishek Beyond your comprehension. Rather complicated name.

Mou Uff, just say *na*.

Abhishek Connor and Robertson's *A History of Quantum Mechanics*.

Mou My foot!

Abhishek No patience to listen to anything ever! It literally talks about your purse though.

Mou What . . . What does it say?

Abhishek It says that if you know the momentum, i.e. the amount of money in the purse, then it's impossible for you to ascertain the purse's exact position or location.

Mou Cut out the nonsense bro – I am not in the mood for it.

Abhishek But let us say you somehow find out the exact location of the purse then it would be impossible for you to assess the exact momentum or the amount of money in it.

Mou Stop it please!

Abhishek I swear on Kali, trust me, that is what it says. Therefore if you are wondering if the purse must be under this pillow of mine then it is impossible for you to know how many notes are in it.

Mou Give it, give it to me now!

Abhishek And if you open the purse and find out that it is empty then you should safely assume that its momentum aka the money is right now in my pocket.

Mou Brother, dear, please, don't do this bro. Please just give me a hundred and fifty. Don't keep it all.

The stage goes dark.

Scene Four

Lights go up in the zone upstage where **Jayati** *is.*

Jayati This is known as the Uncertainty Principle. The famous physicist Heisenberg introduced this idea to us in 1927. This principle completely shattered the foundational ideas of classical mechanics and permanently changed its direction. Modern physics found an entirely new dimension. Later on Heisenberg's ideas were developed upon by . . .

Rahul What is Heisenberg's full name, madam?

Jayati Warner. Warner Carl Heisenberg. German. He won the Nobel Prize when he was only thirty-one.

Rahul *keeps taking notes as* **Jayati** *speaks.*

Jayati The knowledge of particles was revolutionized. What was deterministic became a world of probabilities. Instead of defined rules we started understanding the world through a wave of probabilities. And because it was all so uncertain, it became evident that it is impossible to know the ultimate reality of nature via science.

The stage goes dark.

Scene Five

Lights go up downstage right.

Abhishek Therefore establishing the exact location of the purse and figuring out the exact amount of money in it is an absurd proposition, Mou. You can only know the probabilities of where the purse is or how much money is in it.

Mou Trust me, if I don't clear the money today Shubho *da* is going to give me hell.

Abhishek Your growing certainty about the location of the purse makes it increasingly uncertain that you would know how much money is in it.

Mou For God's sake, bro, please don't do this, for God's sake.

Abhishek Fine – here is your purse and here is your one hundred and fifty rupees. Go on, such a duffer you are . . .

Mou (*picks up the money*) And I will continue to be that way.

Lands a playful blow on **Abhishek***'s back*

Abhishek What was that? Especially after I gave you the money.

Mou Like you said, and now I have settled it hand in hand. Every action has an equal and opposite reaction, classical physics.

Abhishek *breaks into loud laughter.* **Mou** *joins him. The door bell rings.* **Jayati** *can be heard saying, 'It is open.'* **Rongon** *enters.* **Mou** *goes out from stage right and enters from the other side. Lights go down on the downstage area.*

Scene Six

Mou *enters and runs into* **Rongon**.

Mou Bye, bye.

Rongon Oy, where are you off to?

Mou Rehearsal.

Rongon When do you get back?

Mou Nine/nine thirty. Stay until I get back.

Rongon Are you crazy? I will stay for an hour at the most and then leave. I will see you later.

Mou Okay.

She leaves.

Jayati (*showing a space on the sofa*) Have a seat, Rongon.

Rongon Are you done?

Jayati Almost. Rahul, I hope the disappearance of the cause and effect principle is clear to you now.

Rahul Yes, madam.

Jayati As is the reason why measuring x and px together is impossible.

Rahul Yes, madam.

Jayati Fine then. I will give you the note the next day, alright?

Rahul Yes, madam.

He nods a goodbye to the two of them and leaves.

Jayati Why are you standing? Have a seat. Want some tea?

Rongon Later. Where is Angshuman *da*?

Jayati Must have gone somewhere.

Rongon What about Abhi?

Jayati He is in his room. Reading something. Are you coming from the library?

Rongon Yes. Fine then, let me have a seat. Can I sit next to you?

Jayati (*with a smile*) Yes please do.

Rongon *sits. The stage goes dark. Lights on* **Angshuman** *and* **Jayanta**.

Scene Seven

Jayanta Who is he?

Beat.

Who?

Angshuman My wife's colleague. Rongon Roy. Professor of History.

Jayanta A friend of hers?

Angshuman Yes.

Jayanta A good friend?

Angshuman You could say that.

Jayanta Is he a special friend then?

Angshuman I am not entirely sure. Maybe.

Jayanta Is he married?

Angshuman No.

Jayanta Do you dislike him?

Angshuman No, no, not at all, why should I? He is a good man. He is researching something about the early days of Kolkata.

Jayanta Oh really! That's good.

The stage goes dark. Lights on **Jayati** *and* **Rongon**.

Scene Eight

Rongon Oh, the principal was wondering if you were coming in tomorrow.

Jayati Of course, why wouldn't I?

Rongon You apparently told him something about not feeling well yesterday?

Jayati Oh, yeah, because I was feeling a little feverish. This fluctuating weather. But why did you go to college on a Wednesday, our day off.

Rongon *Arey*, there was this departmental meeting about the UGC seminar we are organizing in March. So I dropped by before heading to the library.

Jayati Ah.

Rongon (*with a smirk*) The principal did pull my leg a little.

Jayati What do you mean?

Rongon (*imitating the principal*) 'Did you forget your way and end up in the college today? On your day off and on the day that JB is down with a fever?'

Jayati What did you say?

Rongon What could I have said? I just laughed a little.

Jayati You laughed it off? Why didn't you say that our common day off is a mere coincidence?

Rongon The tongues will wag even more if I offer excuses.

Jayati That is true. Uff! These people clearly have no work besides poking their nose in other people's lives.

Rongon Don't blame the nose for it all. It is seeing the head follow the ears blindly all day after all.

Jayati (*with a smile*) You are becoming smarter by the day?

Rongon Does that mean I was unsmart before?

Jayati Of course. When you first came down from Alipurduar you were a total village bum.

Rongon What? I am always and already made in Bhawanipore. Born and brought up. Alipurduar was merely my first posting.

Jayati I know and I remember. Why do you keep repeating yourself?

Rongon And the women in Alipurduar are smarter than you by legions.

Jayati Really? Anyone in particular?

Rongon I am certainly not referring to anyone specific. This is a general observation.

Jayati How does it matter even if you were being specific? You are a young professor. Women will of course fall for you.

Rongon Hardly. Some of my female students did seem to like me. But my colleagues found me unbearable.

Jayati Quite a few people like you here though.

Rongon Other than you?

Jayati Maybe.

Rongon Enough. Let us have that tea now.

Jayati I feel lazy. Wait.

Calls.

Abhi – Abhi.

Abhi *enters.*

Please fix a cup of tea for Rongon. I feel tired. I don't think the fever has subsided completely.

Abhishek Hi.

Rongon Hello.

Abhishek Does black tea work?

Rongon Just get me a tea bag.

Abhishek *Arey*, wait *na*, let me get you a killer tea.

Gets ready to leave but then turns around.

Ma, did I get any calls?

Jayati Why do you keep your cell phone off whenever you are home?

Abhishek Because I keep getting random calls. But never mind, were there any calls?

Jayati No, Anindita has not called yet. Which means she will be here on schedule.

Abhishek *offers a slightly embarrassed smile.* **Rongon** *smiles too.* **Abhishek** *turns around and exits through the partition.*

Rongon Abhi is so bright – seeing him just makes me happy.

Jayati He is waiting for Anindita.

Rongon Is she supposed to come over?

Jayati Yes.

The doorbell rings.

Ah, there she is.

Loudly.

The door is open.

Lights out. Lights go up on **Jayanta** *and* **Angshuman**.

Scene Nine

Jayanta What was the name again? Anindita?

Angshuman Ah, yes, Anindita Dam. Do you know her?

Jayanta The photo looks familiar. But I don't think so.

Angshuman She's one year junior to my son. MSc. Final year.

Jayanta Your son's girlfriend?

Angshuman Sort of.

Jayanta Are they getting married?

Angshuman That's what they say. In November.

Jayanta Wow! You have a wonderful family, mister.

Angshuman Wonderful? Sure, if you say so.

Jayanta If I say so? It is certain!

Angshuman Who knows?

Jayanta Do your genes have nothing to say about this?

Angshuman I guess not. But for the last few days, Anindita . . .

Jayanta What?

The stage goes dark.

Scene Ten

Lights come up on centre stage on **Jayati**, **Rongon**, **Abhishek** *and* **Anindita**. *Everybody except* **Abhishek** *is seated. Everyone is drinking tea.*

Jayati Ani, why have you been looking depressed over these last few days?

Anindita No, not at all.

Jayati Are you sure?

Anindita One hundred per cent, Auntie. I am fine.

Jayati Alright, off you go. Go sit and chat in Abhi's room.

Anindita Let me just finish the tea.

Rongon Anindita is becoming more glamorous by the day, isn't she, Abhi?

Anindita *offers a dry laugh.*

Rongon Why are the two of you so quiet today? No reaction from anybody? Are you all fighting? Abhi?

Abhishek Are you crazy, Rongon *da*? We don't fight amongst us friends . . .

Rongon Really?

Abhishek Yes, we split up altogether. And no one has a clue when that happens. Not even the couple.

Rongon *smiles.*

Abhishek *Ma*, you were teaching Heisenberg to Rahul, weren't you?

Jayati Yes, why?

Abhishek I overheard a few words from your lesson, that's why. Rongon *da*, do you know that Heisenberg has this very well-known book called *Physics and Philosophy*.

Jayati *Physics and Beyond*. No, no, never mind – that is his autobiography.

Abhishek Yes. Anyway, Heisenberg says in *Physics and Philosophy* that being accurate or even more specifically being perfect is against nature's will. Which means that we must make mistakes.

Jayati That does not mean that you will use Heisenberg as a shield and keep making mistake after mistake in your life.

Abhi *smiles*

I am not going to spare you, Abhi, if you have been troubling Ani.

Abhishek I will cause her pain? *Ma*, I am not Rabon. I only have one head on my shoulders.

Jayati Alright, enough. Go over to your room now. I am going to listen to Rongon's latest piece.

Abhishek 'The Concocted Creepers of Calcutta', again?

Rongon What else?

Abhishek You all are something. Ani, let's go.

Anindita Yes, let us.

Jayati Ani, is everyone okay at home?

Anindita Yes, why?

Jayati You are never so morose usually, that's why. Are you alright? Are you sad?

Anindita I am really fine. I was at the university lab until very late last night. And then had to get up early again. I guess that is why I am looking a little beat up.

Jayati Yes, maybe.

Anindita Where is Mou? At rehearsal or is she filming?

Jayati She said rehearsal on the way out.

Anindita I caught a glimpse of her on the TV the other night. She was looking so pretty.

Rongon You watch television soaps?

Anindita Not really. I was channel surfing. Suddenly Mou appeared on the screen and I kept watching. She was doing really well with her dialogue deliveries. She is really a fine actor now, Auntie. She also looked so mature.

Jayati Tell her. She will really appreciate it.

Anindita Will do. Let's go, Abhi.

Abhishek Yes. *Ma*, did *Baba* say when he was going to be back?

Jayati No, he didn't. Why?

Abhishek I think he wore my blue shirt again today. I can't find it.

Jayati Let him wear it. It's no big deal. I think he likes it.

Anindita Oh, I saw Uncle on my way over.

Jayati Where?

Anindita He was sitting in the park on the corner.

Abhishek Has *Baba* started joining the oldies in the park in the evenings?

Jayati Hey, stop joking.

Anindita No, he was actually just staring at the sky and sitting.

Rongon 'The sky smells sour'?

Abhishek My dad is not Shyamadas Banjo but rather Angshuman Banjo.

Anindita Jokes apart, you know what the strange thing was, Auntie? A couple of elderly folks approached the bench that Uncle was sitting on. And Uncle got up and left as they were about to sit down.

Abhishek And there goes my theory of his hanging out with the oldies.

Jayati Which way did he go? Towards the bus stand?

Anindita Not sure. He was talking to that student who comes to you for private lessons.

Jayati Rahul?

Anindita I guess. They stood in front of the bank near the park, talking, and then they left.

Jayati Where did they head to now?

Anindita I have no idea.

Abhishek Wow, so *Baba* chats up Rahul these days outside the park and with appointments and all.

Jayati *Arey*, this Rahul guy is also really interested in painting and art. He is not an artist himself but he apparently goes to a lot of exhibitions. And then he is also into classical music, the Dover Lane conference. He was telling me about it all one day . . .

Abhishek Wow, Rahul is quite the intellectual then.

Anindita He does look like one though.

Jayati Your father does not paint anymore. I guess he enjoys discussing art with Rahul.

Rongon Angshuman *da* has become significantly quieter than before.

Jayati True. He has always been on the quieter side though. And it is actually good if these artsy conversations with Rahul relieve him a little bit.

Abhishek Rongon *da*, Ani here is a connoisseur of classical music. She makes me listen to it as well. But it is beyond my understanding.

Anindita You don't need to specify that. Two words out of your mouth and everyone would know your standards.

Abhishek (*jokes*) How dare you?

Lights go down.

Scene Eleven

Lights rise on **Angshuman** *and* **Jayanta**.

Angshuman Anindita is a really good girl. She is intelligent and receptive. But she has been very unmindful of late. I do know the reason for that though. I overheard them talking one day from outside the door.

Jayanta Okay, why?

Angshuman Yes. She has seen me and Rahul several times, Dr Ghosh. Actually by then Rahul and I were already in a relationship. This day she was talking about was the day that Rahul, a friend of his, Tanmay, and I went to a classical music concert at the GD Birla Sabhaghar. Tanmay is also a big fan of classical music. A new young singer was singing. And Rahul was explaining the finer nuances of the ebb and flow of the ragas.

Jayanta Could you cut to the chase please without these constant embellishments?

Angshuman Please forgive me. I am a little too emotional right now.

Jayanta How did you and Rahul get to know each other? Did you not say that you had given up communicating with nearly everybody?

Angshuman Yes, I did. But Rahul . . .

Beat.

Rahul would come over around four in the afternoon for his lessons. Before Jayati would have returned from the college. And he would walk straight into my room and start browsing through my books on art.

Jayanta And you would talk to each other then?

Angshuman Jayati would never be back before five or five thirty. Initially he just hung out in my room. But then one day he just started discussing art.

Jayanta I can understand.

Angshuman I was very bored initially, Dr Ghosh, you know. But then he would raise such topics that I could not help commenting on.

Jayanta Like what?

Angshuman I am not sure you would understand. About very basic concepts and ideas surrounding art.

Jayanta Like?

Angshuman For example, he would ask me a question about something in Da Vinci's notebook and its relationship to physics. Something that I am unclear about myself. But the curiosity that emanated from his face would compel me to stay up all night and look it up.

Jayanta What kind of questions?

Angshuman *Arey*, this is something very particular to artists.

Beat.

Fine, let me try to explain. So he would say that Da Vinci has written in his notebook that the object closest to the eye in the dark shadowy part of a painting appears lightest. But why is it that the opposite appears to be true in Da Vinci's *The Last Supper*?

Jayanta Sorry, I didn't understand a word you said.

Angshuman I had warned you, this would be beyond your comprehension. This is something particular to artists.

Beat.

Or he would quote Da Vinci having said that when you look at yourself in the mirror some of the mirror's tint gets mixed in that reflection. So then . . .

Jayanta Hold on, hold on. This is rather strange. When I look into the mirror I can only see my own colour. A mirror is colourless, isn't it?

Angshuman According to Rahul, this is Da Vinci hinting at the quantum particles of light.

Jayanta Oh, okay. Anyway, so these discussions with Rahul excited you?

Angshuman Yes. I felt like this is what I have been wanting to say and wanting to hear for so long. But I had no one to discuss it with. You know, Dr Ghosh, art is complicated only as long as it is confined in books. As soon as it cascades into our lives it all becomes so simple. Dr Ghosh, I have noticed that the best things are often very, very simple – easy.

Jayanta Yeah, my wife would say the same to me.

Angshuman Why the past tense? Is she . . . I mean . . .

Jayanta No, she isn't dead. We are divorced. It's been a while.

Angshuman Oh. What about your children?

Jayanta We don't have any.

Beat.

So, your depression started getting better after Rahul entered your life.

Angshuman Absolutely. When he would come over, you cannot imagine, Dr Ghosh . . .

Scene Twelve

Lights go up on stage right. **Rahul** *is seen. He is inside the house. Inside* **Angshuman***'s room.*

Angshuman The mellow sunlight of winter afternoons was curled up in one corner of the room.

He gets up and crosses over. Lights start to fade on **Jayanta**. **Angshuman** *seems to be addressing the audience.*

You cannot imagine how my heart, all my nerves would be alert in anticipation. I have been waiting for him all morning.

When would he come with that perfectly chiselled face of his – like a bronze statue – and I would call out to him as my Dorian – my Dorian.

Rahul Who is Dorian?

Angshuman Dorian is Dorian Gray. It's a character in an Oscar Wilde novel.

Rahul Ah, yes, *The Picture of Dorian Gray*.

Angshuman You know painting underlies the main plot of that novel.

Rahul Yes that is what I have heard as well. Wasn't the novel banned?

Angshuman Yes.

Beat.

Beat.

Rahul Why?

Angshuman Homosexuality.

Rahul Was Oscar Wilde homosexual?

Angshuman That's what I know.

Rahul Okay. Why did you call me Dorian then?

Angshuman You don't know?

Beat.

Rahul No, I get it. I haven't read the novel but I can understand.

Beat.

Beat.

Did you know that Toulouse-Lautrec was a friend of Wilde's?

Angshuman Yes, but Toulouse-Lautrec was not as good looking as Dorian. He was an ugly dwarf.

Rahul But he was an extraordinary artist. You know his parents were first cousins. Rumour has it that he was born disabled because of this illegitimate relationship.

Angshuman Yes, that is what I have heard as well.

Rahul Do you think relationships can be defined as legitimate or illegitimate?

Angshuman I don't think so. A relationship is just a relationship. Why measure it on a scale of legitimacy?

Rahul I disagree.

Angshuman Really?

Rahul Yes. You know I feel guilty nowadays.

Angshuman Why? Why do you feel so?

Rahul I don't know. I think it began after I started seeing you.

Beat.

Don't you feel guilty?

Angshuman No.

Rahul I don't think you are coming clean right now.

Angshuman Yes, I am not being true.

Beat.

Rahul When do you feel it? When you remember madam? Or when you think of Abhi or Mou?

Angshuman No, no.

Rahul Then?

Angshuman (*smiles*) I feel certain that nothing can make me feel happier when I am with you. Even when we separate. Or when my hands . . .

Rahul Please stop.

Angshuman But when I am by myself . . . When the darkness of the night surrounds me like curled up cats laying out their paws, then, then a suffocating moan starts storming through my insides. I feel like . . .

Pants.

Rahul It's okay, you don't need to elaborate. You are hurting.

Angshuman Let me say it, Rahul.

Rahul No.

(*Emphasizing*). I understand. Don't you understand that I am troubled when you are in pain? Don't you?

Angshuman *looks on.*

Rahul What are you looking at?

Angshuman Nothing.

Rahul Alright, I will leave now.

Angshuman Already? Don't you have lessons today?

Rahul No. Madam asked me not to come today. She has a get-together with her colleagues. She had asked me to come and pick up a book.

Angshuman Have you taken the book?

Rahul Yeah, it was on the cupboard itself.

Angshuman So, you just came to pick up the book then?

Rahul No.

Angshuman Then?

Rahul Well, I thought I would run into you for a little bit.

Smiles.

Okay, I am off. Ta ta.

Lights start fading.

Scene Thirteen

Angshuman *turns around and slowly starts walking towards* **Jayanta** *as the lights come back on them.*

Angshuman I am not sure what you are thinking of me –

Jayanta Keep talking, I am merely listening.

Angshuman You may think that I am a pervert obsessed with physical desires.

Jayanta No, not at all.

Angshuman You may feel that way. But trust me doctor, I am not like that. You may think that these waves of emotion are washing over me because it concerns a young man. Perhaps you think that I wouldn't have had the same feelings if it were a man of my age, and maybe that is so. Or maybe I don't know . . .

Beat.

Are you listening, doctor?

Jayanta Every word. And very carefully.

Angshuman But I know this is not all about the body; those eyes, that smile, that innocent bright simplicity and the occasional brilliant sparkle of intellect and genius simply stunned me into silence, doctor. I intensely felt every moment that I am with him with all the pores in my body. I understood him with my whole being. Actually I felt a sense of compassion towards him.

Jayanta Compassion? Why?

Angshuman He is who I was thirty years ago. Exactly like me. But my spoilt genes are not in him. He was extremely sacred. Pure. It was as if a milk-white seagull had spread its wings over the azure ocean and I was standing on the shore gazing at it. Gazing at the beautiful bright flight, the gentle flapping of its wings . . .

Beat.

His hair cascading over his forehead, the gentle tremor of his nose as it glistened with sweat, his gradually closing eyes, the anticipatory tranquil wait in his barely parsed lips . . .

Beat.

Why was beauty created on earth, doctor, why?

Jayanta I think I understand you. I must confess that I am rather blunt myself. I can hardly understand these metaphors. But I think I understand. Didn't your wife suspect anything? Angshuman?

Angshuman About what?

Jayanta About this relationship?

Angshuman How would she, doctor? She is busy in her academic world and with Rongon. The other day they came back from their colleague's party . . .

Lights turn on upstage. **Jayati** *and* **Rongon** *are seen standing in a freeze.*

Angshuman Abhi and Anindita were in their room all evening. Jayati was clueless that Anindita was crying in the very next room. I could feel it from my room but those two were engaged in such an irritating conversation. Niels Bohr, Fritjof Capra's *The Tao of Physics*, atomic structure or the Black Hole Tragedy, the diary of some white woman. And I could clearly understand that these inane names – Hawking, Dirac, Fanny Parkes, Irfan Habib – these are the sources of their pleasure. Sexual pleasure.

Lights go down.

Scene Fourteen

Jayati *and* **Rongon** *start talking. The conversation resembles lovemaking.*

Jayati You know, Rongon, Hawking says that a pair of particles are continually appearing and disappearing in the universe.

Rongon Did you know that Guru Nanak had visited what is now Kolkata for missionary work, according to Nanak's biography?

Jayati But each pair has a positive and a negative particle. They destroy each other.

Rongon Nanak apparently stayed at what is now the intersection of Mahatma Gandhi Road and Chitpur Road.

Jayati But if the particles move near a black hole then the negative particles are drawn into the eternal darkness whereas the positive particles move away from it as if they were emerging from the black hole itself.

Rongon Just imagine, 1503. No one even knew the name Kolkata. The Mughals were not even in India. Delhi is under Lodi rule and Bengal is ruled by the Hussain Shahi dynasty. Job Charnock was still in his mother's womb. And Nanak in Kolkata. Isn't that hair raising?

Jayati And because the negative particles all end up in the blackhole it loses both its mass and power. Do you know what this loss is known as? Hawking Radiation. Hawking says that because of this black holes will explode in the near future. What will happen to the earth then, Rongon?

Rongon Bipradas Pipilai refers to Kolkata in his *Manasamangal*. Chand Saudagor, the merchant, enters Kolkata. He first offers his prayers in Chitpur and then again in Kalighat. Although Sukumar Sen is of the opinion that this is more of an interpolation.

Breathes heavily.

Wait a second. I am out of breath.

Jayati You get so sweaty every time.

Rongon Yeah.

Beat.

Oh, I have some good news. I mean I don't know if it is good.

Jayati What?

Rongon I think I will get the scholarship from Cambridge. They finally replied to my email yesterday.

Jayati Oh, that is good news then.

Rongon Won't you feel bad? I will be gone for nearly two years.

Jayati Why would I feel bad? This will be good for your research.

Rongon Life will change again. Perhaps you will too.

Jayati Quite possible. That is normal.

Beat.

Ask Abhi to make some tea please.

Rongon Is Abhi home?

Jayati Yes.

Rongon How do you know?

Jayati I saw Anindita's sandals outside the door.

Rongon You need a cup of tea right at this moment every time.

Beat.

Let them be. I will make you a cup.

Jayati You will find the tea bags in the kitchen.

Rongon *goes behind the partition.*

Rongon Where is Angshuman *da*?

Jayati I think he is in his room.

Loudly.

Angshuman, did Rahul take his book? Hello?

Angshuman (*from the table*) Yes, he took it.

Rongon You should have brought Angshuman *da* along today.

Comes out from behind the partition.

Rongon (*cont'd*) Somnath and all were looking for him.

Jayati I had asked him to come along. He didn't want to.

Rongon Why not?

Jayati How would I know?

Beat.

He never likes going to occasions at my colleagues' places.

Rongon I am certain you don't really insist upon it.

Jayati (*smiles*) Don't comment on things that you have no idea about.

Rongon Angshuman *da* is growing quieter by the day.

Angshuman (*addressing* **Jayati**) Jayati imagined that I would not want to find myself amongst successful people since I was a failure in life.

Beat.

Maybe she was right.

Jayati Rongon, please don't ask so many questions about Angshuman. I don't like it.

Rongon Sorry, I didn't mean it that way.

Jayati Angshuman does not consider most people in the world worth talking to. He feels suffocated amongst them.

Angshuman That is not a correct assessment. I actually feel that I would be exposed as a hollow person if I were to go in front of them.

Rongon I don't think so. Angshuman *da* does not come across as an arrogant person at all. He is quite humble on the contrary. Modest.

Jayati Could we please talk about something else?

Beat.

Did you know that Satyendranath Bose scored a hundred and ten out of one hundred in a maths test when he was in Hindu school and then during his Presidency College days he scored seventy out of sixty in an intermediate English test. Can you imagine?

Rongon Unbelievable.

Angshuman I don't remember the last time that Jayati shared something personal with me. I don't think she remembers it either. Sometimes I feel like grabbing her by the shoulders and reminding her that we are a couple – a husband and a wife. I believe she wants to do the same sometimes. It's just that she has no time to say it – that's all.

Lights go down.

Scene Fifteen

Lights come up on **Abhishek***'s room.*

Abhishek Please stop crying, Ani. Ani please.

Anindita How do I tell anything to Auntie, Abhi? What do I tell her?

Abhishek Come on, Ani. *Ma* is quite rational, I am certain she will understand.

Anindita And what about all my relatives? My father's youngest sister? I can't believe this, Abhi!

Abhishek I know. But what can you do about it?

Anindita How can *Ma* do this? That is the part I just cannot understand.

Abhishek Do you know the man?

Anindita Of course I do. He is a friend of my father's. He has some kind of a fancy job.

Abhishek Divorced?

Anindita No, a bachelor. He will not have any social issues. But my mother is going forward with this twenty-five years into her marriage.

Cries.

She has even finalized everything with the lawyer. How am I going to show my face in front of people?

Abhishek Again that same thing. What can you do if your mother will go for a divorce?

Anindita Trust me, Abhi, I know that my father is far from perfect. He has tons of issues. He is an alcoholic, a womanizer, he is corrupt – he has every conceivable fault that a man can have. But after all he is still my father. I tried talking about this with my mother. She had no response, she seems determined.

Abhishek What does your father have to say about this?

Anindita He has always wanted this. He has never thought of *Ma* as anything but a dead weight. He has never allowed her to have a job, kept her confined to the house, and now it is going to be even more convenient for him.

Abhishek Convenient?

Anindita He will now have an excuse to make all our relatives swallow their words. They always praised *Ma* while blaming my father. He has an alibi to malign *Ma* now. You know something, my father is a debauchee!

Abhishek Why are you hankering after him then? And you also seem to know that this man is a better person . . .

Anindita Who?

Abhishek I mean . . . your . . .

Anindita No, no, go on, why are you hesitating, say it, my what? My new father, right?

Breaks down.

Abhishek Ah, Ani, what are you doing? Didn't you yourself certify this person as a good man?

Ani *nods in the affirmative.*

Abhishek That's good, right? I mean a person definitely has the right to divorce and be with someone they like, right?

Anindita Absolutely. But at what age? *Ma* will turn fifty next July.

Abhishek It is a matter of personal choice. Anyone can want it at any age.

Anindita Why did they have me then? Shouldn't she think about me for once? Should she be this selfish?

Abhishek But she has been thinking about you for so long. Auntie could have left a long time ago. But she didn't. She waited for you to grow up . . .

Anindita She waited so that she would be more of a laughing stock. So that her daughter could be publicly humiliated. Actually, my parents are sadists. Both of them.

Abhishek Not at all. I am not going to buy this about Auntie at all. I have seen it with my own eyes how much she loves you.

Anindita You know what she told me over the phone this morning?

Abhishek What?

Anindita She said she was going to talk to you. So that we get married this year itself.

Abhishek Why?

Anindita Don't you get it, what if there is a problem with her daughter's would-be in-laws over the divorce? My wedding would clear the path for her.

Abhishek Just imagine how concerned Auntie is with you then.

Anindita Huh, not concerned at all! How do I tell your mom?

Abhishek Don't worry I will talk to *Ma*. Where is your mother now?

Anindita Laketown. She is staying with her youngest sister.

Beat.

I don't get it, Abhi. I just don't. Where do they have the problem. Where exactly?

Abhishek Say what you will but this is quite exciting. I am getting married in November and my mother-in-law in December. Unbelievable.

Anindita I am going to beat you to a pulp, you rascal. How can you joke about this?

Abhishek Shouldn't I joke?

Embraces **Ani.**

Abhishek Who else am I going to joke with if not with you?

Beat.

To tell you the truth, Ani, I don't know, I really don't know where do these blackholes in our souls come from. What is that depth where these waves criss-cross each other at lightning speed? Is there really no ultimate then?

Beat.

Ani, what do you think?

Anindita *embraces* **Abhishek** *back.*

Anindita I don't know, Abhi. I don't know anything.

Lights go down.

Scene Sixteen

Lights come up on **Jayanta** *and* **Angshuman**.

Jayanta Interesting.

Angshuman Why?

Jayanta Why? Yes, why indeed? I just said it. I must have thought of something so I said it.

Pours some coffee into a cup from a flask.

Here, have some coffee. This reminds me of my wife.

Angshuman Oh did she leave after having an affair as well?

Jayanta Not at all. She was not that type of a woman.

Angshuman What does that mean? What type?

Jayanta You know, romantic types. Shipra, my wife, didn't have an ounce of romance in her. She was brusk, hardcore and professional.

Angshuman Was she a doctor too?

Jayanta (*nodding in the affirmative*) Yes, a gynaecologist. One morning over breakfast she simply said I am not going to be living with you anymore. It's not working for me.

Angshuman Didn't you say something?

Jayanta What would I have said? I was in the middle of packing a bag. I had an evening flight to Delhi and then another onward flight to Belgrade to attend the World Psychiatry conference. I asked Shipra if she was having an affair. She denied it point blank. Which was the truth. She was a straight shooter. If she had had an affair, she wouldn't have kept it hidden from me.

Angshuman And then?

Jayanta Then what? I came back from Belgrade. The marriage was over. People can change in a day, Mr Angshuman – in twenty-four hours – in twenty-four minutes. May be even in twenty-four seconds.

Angshuman Did she marry anyone else?

Jayanta No, no. She went back to her house in Lansdowne. And then left for London to finish her MD. She came back a few years ago. She has a private practice in Kolkata now.

Beat.

But Anindita's mother's case is quite exceptional. Twenty- five years into a marriage she is divorcing her husband and marrying one of his friends. I mean really – I don't want to say interesting again. Because the whole situation is quite interesting. Especially you.

Angshuman Why? Why should that be?

Jayanta Isn't it interesting? A failed painter – this sudden homosexuality so late in your life, a physics-teaching wife, a history-teaching boyfriend, your son's would-be mother-in-law getting married again at fifty – if all of this together is not interesting then I don't know what interesting is.

Angshuman (*smiles*) This is true.

Jayanta Never mind. What happened after that?

Angshuman Yes, so he had seemed disturbed for some time. I had been asking him what was the matter but he never said anything. So when he came that day . . .

Lights start dimming on this zone. **Rahul** *is seen up stage as the lights go up there.*

Scene Seventeen

Angshuman Jayati hadn't returned yet. Abhi was out with Ani running some errands. Mou was the only one home. She was also on her way out. She opened the door for him.

Mou *opens the door.*

Mou Ah, Rahul, come inside, have a seat.

Rahul Are you leaving?

Mou Yes, I have a rehearsal. Where's your backpack?

Rahul Oh, I am just here to pick up a note from madam and then I will leave.

Mou Oh, okay, have a seat.

Angshuman *comes in and stands.*

Mou *Baba*, Rahul is here. Please keep him engaged. I have to leave for my rehearsals now. Prajitda will take me to task if I am not on time.

She leaves. **Angshuman** *looks at* **Rahul**.

Rahul I have actually come to see you.

Angshuman Oh, why didn't you call me for two days?

Rahul I didn't feel like it.

Angshuman *doesn't say anything.*

Rahul I want to end our relationship.

Angshuman What do you mean?

Rahul This, this is a disease. I find myself nauseating.

Angshuman I love you, Rahul.

Rahul No, you love this disease – not me.

Angshuman Trust me, no.

Rahul I don't believe you. I can feel it from the way you touch me.

Angshuman Rahul, please don't say that.

Rahul I will. You don't like what I am saying because I am telling the truth. You know very well that you are actually a pervert. You are sick.

Angshuman Rahul, please!

Rahul And you want me to be involved in this perversion of yours so that I am subject to a lifetime of taunting by people on the street yelling 'Homo'.

Angshuman That's a lie. Hold on. Rahul, are you drunk?

Rahul Yes I am. So what? That doesn't make what I am saying false. What is true remains true. You are obviously a frustrated man. Isn't that true? Tell me, isn't that true? And this frustration shows itself through this perversion of yours.

Angshuman Rahul – you loved me, Rahul.

Rahul Never. I have hated every moment of our time together. Because I had realized that you are mentally sick. Do you target all of your wife's students in this manner?

Angshuman Rahul, please!

Rahul (*breaks down*) I am younger than your son. How could you abuse me like this? How could you drag me to your bed?

Angshuman *tries to touch* **Rahul**. **Rahul** *withdraws.*

Rahul Don't touch me. You are like a disgusting cockroach.

Gets up to leave.

Rahul I am leaving. I called madam this morning and told her that I won't be taking lessons from her anymore. I am leaving for Delhi with my parents tomorrow.

Angshuman Don't do this, Rahul, please.

Rahul If you dare follow me I will come back and tell everything to your children. If that doesn't work I will let my father know. My father's friend Uncle Asit is an IPS officer in Delhi. One phone call to him and you will have the cops dragging you to the police station.

Angshuman *takes a few steps towards* **Rahul**.

Angshuman Do what you have to, Rahul. Just don't leave me please.

Rahul *withdraws hastily.*

Rahul Do not touch me, you fucking homosexual. Do not touch me.

He storms off stage. Silence. Lights start going down as **Angshuman** *turns to face the zone where* **Jayanta** *is.*

Scene Eighteen

Angshuman You know, doctor, he was doing this because he was in pain. I could understand that.

Jayanta What kind of pain?

Angshuman I don't know. That is what I was trying to understand.

Jayanta What did you do in your effort to understand the pain? Did you go off to his house?

Angshuman Yes, I did.

Jayanta Really? Oh God!

Angshuman What's there to invoke God about? I was certain that Rahul was in love with me and whatever he had said was not true.

Jayanta You knew it?

Angshuman Yes I knew. He has to love me. That's his fate. That is what his genes are saying. There is no uncertainty about it. I am certain.

Jayanta Fine. What happened then?

Angshuman Pour me some more coffee first, my throat is very dry.

The curtain comes down as **Jayanta** *begins pouring out the coffee.*

End of Act One.

Act Two

Scene One

Lights come on what was **Angshuman** *and* **Jayanta***'s zone in Act One. It is now a small rehearsal room.* **Mou** *and a young man,* **Alok***, are standing there. Behind them sit* **Shubho** *and* **Gouri***,* **Prajit***'s wife.* **Ratan** *and a few other young men are also seated around.*

Shubho Alright, I just rang the bell. Mou, start.

Mou But Prajit *da* is not here.

Gouri He will be here. He had called me. He got delayed with a meeting at work. You all start.

Mou This is not usual for Prajit *da*.

Shubho Damn it, just start! Prajit *da* will be here for sure. Don't you think he is worried? He knows an understudy is going on. Here, Alok, start please.

Mou Fine then, let us start. I am sure we are going over the fourth scene, the one with Sujoy?

Shubho What else? Alright, Alok, come on, man, let us hear you speak, brother, please don't be quiet.

Alok Shubho da, would you mind prompting me just a little bit please. I still haven't quite gotten under the skin of Sujoy.

Shubho What do you mean? We have a performance the day after tomorrow. You are new in the group and yet you landed a part. Why would you need prompting even after that? Or is being an understudy below your standards? Are you expecting a big role suitable enough for a reputed actor like yourself already?

Alok I didn't have the script, Shubho *da*.

Shubho What? Ratan, you didn't give Alok the script yesterday?

Ratan *Arey*, he's the one who refused to take it yesterday. I asked him to wait for five minutes – I will get it photocopied – but he said he didn't have the time.

Shubho You didn't have the time to grab a two-page photocopy, Alok?

Alok Not at all Shubho *da*. Actually Prajit *da* decided that I would be performing around nine thirty . . .

Shubho So what? He could have decided even at midnight. It's a two-page role.

Alok I really needed to call home. The public phone booth in front of my shared accommodation closes at ten. I asked Ratan *da* how long it would take him. Ratan *da* said it could take him an hour.

Ratan Alok, don't go around lying, man. I said five minutes, only five minutes.

Alok No, no . . .

Ratan Quit arguing, man.

Gouri Who are you bluffing, Ratan? I was there. You did say you would need an hour.

Ratan No, no, Gouri *di*, I must've said I would need thirty minutes.

Shubho This is why I do not like understudies. I had repeatedly asked Prajit *da* to not cast Montu – he will get shooting dates for his soaps and will drop everything and be off. And Montu is apparently a good actor.

Gouri Well, Montu is actually a good actor, Shubho.

Shubho Gimme a break, sister. Good actor. He can barely speak audibly, goes on stage and clowns around a bit. That doesn't make him a good actor.

Gouri You've always been jealous of him.

Shubho Don't you see his attitude? Struts around as if he is Dustin Hoffman. And when we need him the most, before this important invited performance, he abandons us. It would be something if he had a substantial role in the soaps. He is playing a servant. A servant who has an outdoor shooting schedule. A pyjama with a breastpocket!

Gouri *smiles in amusement.*

Shubho Hey, Ratan, order some tea and get the script photocopied.

Ratan Let me take care of it myself since the blame is on my shoulders . . .

Shubho Step up and don't be a namby-pamby. Fast!

Ratan *leaves.*

Mou (*to* **Alok**) Why would you have to use the phone booth in front of your mess housing? Couldn't you have used a different public phone booth?

Alok I don't have a credit arrangement with other phone booths. I have a running account with this one. I just need to pay off my dues at the end of the month.

Beat.

Actually, I didn't have a lot of money on me yesterday.

Mou Did you have to make the call yesterday? Couldn't it have waited until today?

Alok The phone lines in my neighbourhood were dead for the last three days, Mou *di*. The booth operator told me that connections have been restored as I was leaving yesterday. That's why I thought I should check in on my family since I hadn't been able to do that for a couple of days.

Mou Where exactly are you from again?

Alok *is just about to start sharing when* **Prajit** *enters in a huff.*

Prajit Sorry to everybody.

Shubho Come on in, come on in.

Prajit Shubho, can you quickly get me some tea please. Oh, and could everyone please step outside. Except Mou, Gouri and Shubho. Actually, never mind, let us step outside. The others don't need to bother unnecessarily.

Gouri What exactly is wrong? What is it? What?

Prajit Nothing.

Ratan *enters with tea and the photocopies.*

Ratan (*handing the photocopy to* **Alok**) Here is your photocopy.

Prajit What? This wasn't photocopied yesterday?

Shubho What did you think I was talking about? We have our task cut out for us.

Prajit Fine, I will listen to it all after we are done here.

Ratan *hands tea to* **Prajit** *first and then to everybody else.*

Ratan Hey, Alok, here, help me with these cups.

Alok *takes the pile of earthen cups from* **Ratan**. *Everyone takes their tea and moves to the centre of the stage. The rehearsal room goes dark.*

Scene Two

Lights on **Shubho**, **Mou**, **Gouri** *and* **Prajit**.

Shubho What's the matter?

Prajit Shubho, you must ask that Alok person to stop coming to our group from tomorrow.

Gouri But why? He seems like a good guy.

Prajit That may be. But do any of you know where he is from?

Shubho No, he keeps referring to his shared accommodation though.

Prajit Yes, but that's when he is in Kolkata. But what about otherwise?

Shubho Where?

Prajit Nandigram.

Shubho *Oy vey*. I don't think he has ever mentioned it.

Gouri So what if he is from Nandigram.

Prajit I don't want a debate, Gouri. I do theatre in my own way and that is enough for me.

Gouri This meeting that you went to, did someone say something to you there?

Prajit Not directly. But that Samanta from the trade union. He is a tool. We were discussing cricket during the tea break and he made sure I was in earshot while announcing, 'All those that protested, it is time now, they will be dealt with.'

Gouri Well, you hardly protested. You went to a couple of meetings. And that too with other theatre folks. What harm could that have done? And several others went to those as well.

Prajit There is a difference between me and the others. I am a small fry. And you know how Samanta is jealous of me. Every time we get a negative review in the press, Samanta has to buy that newspaper and tout it around the office.

Shubho In spite of that, you simply cannot throw a guy out of the group because he is from Nandigram. That is hardly a reason.

Prajit You have no idea about Samanta, Shubho. He might bring this to the notice of the neighbourhood local committee. And there you have it. Trouble.

Beat.

Fine, ask him to not show up for a couple of months then. Until all this blows over. And then he can come again.

Shubho Well, this is quite the pickle then. Where am I going to get another substitute actor? We have a performance the day after tomorrow!

Beat.

Are you sure he is from Nandigram itself? And not Khejuri?

Prajit No, Nandigram, I am certain.

Gouri Doesn't matter. Irrespective of whether he is from Nandigram or Khejuri, this guy is not politically active, what do we have to be scared of?

Shubho And besides, why should we be scared anyway?

Prajit (*forcibly*) Because we must be. If we want to survive in the civil society then we must be scared and scary. That is the norm. Please don't proselytize to me, Shubho! I have no one watching my back. No contacts, no stable support, the media barely writes two lines about our shows – we should be scared. Or else we will be wiped out. I don't know why I just couldn't keep shut back then.

Shubho If we ought to be wiped out, then so be it. But how the hell are we supposed to create theatre while living in fear?

Prajit Are you really listening to what you are saying? Are you thinking it through? You are okay with being wiped out?

Shubho There is fear everywhere. Afraid of the older brother at home, afraid of people like Samanta at work, fear of threats in the neighbourhood, and no one really knows but something to be afraid of in the theatre as well – perhaps ghosts – but fear is the constant.

Prajit What can be done? This uncertainty is a part of being alive.

Shubho (*pacing*) Damn it, where are we going to get another substitute now?

Mou (*suddenly*) What do you mean by uncertainty?

Prajit Uncertainty means uncertainty. Lack of certainty.

Shubho (*stepping up*) Prajit *da*, how about Ratan? Never mind, he can't even enunciate Ts properly. His palate goes soft on that letter.

Aghast at his own suggestion.

And oh Lord, the very first line of this character is, 'There lies the Taklamakan in front of me and Titobabu has the audacity to show off his riches – take – in front of me. I will crack open the hairless top of your skull' – a melee of Ts.

Gouri Shubho, cut out your jokes for now please.

Mou What is all this uncertainty about, Prajit *da*? You must have thought it through before you stood up to protest after those killings, didn't you?

Prajit Mou, I am from the middle class. I work, have a wife and kids, and because I want to forget this very timid existence of mine I make theatre. If tomorrow my shows stop happening, or if I stop getting prime reservations in decent auditoriums, or if I go bankrupt while bankrolling my theatre then who am I going to fall back on?

Mou But that does not mean . . .

Prajit I am not switching sides, Mou, I am merely trying to protect myself. Don't I have the right to do at least that?

Gouri Listen, I think you are overthinking this. Let Samanta report to the local committee. The local secretary Nikhil *babu*. He is a gentleman. He even likes you quite a bit.

Prajit More than likes me. He has told me himself, and publicly in the bazaar, that what I did was right. These people needed a lesson.

Mou See? You have support.

Prajit You don't know Samanta, Mou. He is very influential. Several well-placed people are amongst his acquaintances. They are like chameleons. Members of the Communist Party when in the government offices of the Writers' Building, members of the opposition when in Dharmatala, locally they are former Naxalites, businessmen for the Chamber of Commerce and darlings of the media when guzzling alcohol at the fancy soirées. I just don't understand these people.

Mou Why do you even need to understand chameleons?

Prajit When these chameleons get off their fancy foreign cars and lock eyes with me in the streets they have only one identity, that of being cobras.

Gouri They don't care about us so much, Prajit – why would they bother getting off their cars for us? Don't think about them so much.

Prajit I care about them. I do. I have to. I have quit everything, but please do not ask me to quit my theatre. I will either go mad or the version that I will evolve into will be unbearable for you.

Mou What is the point of doing theatre while crouching in fear, Prajit *da*? Isn't that being selfish in a way? Just worrying about one's own self?

Shubho Mou, please don't say these things now.

Prajit No, no, please go ahead, what did you say? Caring about one's own self only? Loving one's own self? Of course I love myself. I love myself very much. What is that to you? What kind of commitments do you have that you can question me?

Shubho Prajit *da*, I don't think she meant it that way.

Prajit (*addressing* **Mou**) Listen, I never cast my wife (*Points to* **Gouri**.) in the larger roles in our plays. I cast you. I get zero grant money, if I get meaty soap opera parts that conflict with our plays, I give those up, I don't indulge in petty politics within the group, I don't chase after the young women in our group, we never get decent performance dates in the important auditoriums – and amidst all of this, with all of this, I continue working in the theatre without picking fights, without getting petty in the name of protest, and without any connections whatsoever. And if this is loving oneself and being selfish, then yes, I am selfish.

Mou Prajit *da*, see, what I meant . . .

Prajit What is your level of commitment? You all might quit the theatre tomorrow. Or you might marry a NRI and head over to Canada the day after . . .

Mou What are you going on about?

Prajit If someone in your family has connections in the upper echelons of the pecking order then tomorrow you can turn your nose at me and discard me like a maggot crawling in the trash can . . .

Shubho Prajit *da*, please . . .

Prajit If you get a bigger role in either soaps or film then you too will quit like that Montu. But I? I will have to hunt down some like-minded, sympathetic people to perpetuate this selfishness, this reign of terror year after year, epoch after epoch, lifetime after lifetime . . .

Gouri Shut up, Prajit, enough, don't say another word.

Silence.

Beat.

Beat.

Prajit I am sorry, Mou. I am really sorry.

Smiles.

See, I am even afraid of you.

If you quit because you are upset with this outburst of mine then I will need two substitute performers for the show the day after tomorrow. That would be quite funny, wouldn't it?

Mou I am not quitting, Prajit *da*. And I didn't mind your words. At least you were able to say your piece.

Prajit Yes, true. I would have suffocated otherwise. I am sorry, Shubho. Gouri, I am sorry.

Gouri Although, Prajit, you must admit that this uncertainty that you were referring to in your diatribe is the excitement of theatre, isn't it?

Prajit Who knows? I don't understand it. Maybe I am just tired of having too much fun.

Mou I did not mean to insult you, Prajit *da*. And nor did I want to settle a personal score or address a demand when I spoke up. I merely wanted to say . . .

She gets a call on her cell phone. She takes it and steps away from the group.

Hello?

Prajit Shubho . . .

Shubho *moves towards* **Prajit**.

Prajit You don't need to worry about finding a substitute. Alok will play that part.

Shubho Are you sure?

Prajit Absolutely. Let's explore the power of our tin swords, shall we? Come on, let's head indoors. People have been waiting for too long. Come, Gouri.

Walking towards the rehearsal room.

Alok, where did Alok go? Come on, let's see where we are.

He enters the rehearsal space. **Shubho** *and* **Gouri** *talk.*

Shubho *Didi.*

Gouri What is it?

Shubho Only theatre can.

Gouri What?

Shubho Keep a person emotionally honest.

Gouri Why only theatre? There are quite a few things that can. Come, let us head indoors. Mou, come inside when you are done with the call.

Gouri *and* **Shubho** *leave.*

Mou Hello . . . Yes, I can hear you. Damn it, the signal is really spotty . . .

Lights go down.

Scene Three

Lights come up on **Jayanta** *and* **Angshuman**. *They are both standing.*

Angshuman So this call to my daughter that I was telling you about. This call came from my house itself.

Jayanta Really? Who made the call?

Angshuman Before I tell you that I need to share another episode with you.

Jayanta Go on.

Angshuman You wanted to know what exactly happened after I went to Rahul's house, right?

Jayanta Yes.

Angshuman I went to Rahul's house about a week back. I thought I will let him calm down a bit and then go see him. And so I went only to find his house locked.

Jayanta Are you serious?

Angshuman Yes. So then I went to his college. Around noon. Couldn't find him there. His classmates said that he had been absent for a few days. I went back to his neighbourhood and enquired with a neighbour of theirs. He said that they had left for Delhi. Rahul's father had been transferred. Rahul was planning on attending a college there.

Jayanta Ah.

Angshuman I cannot explain what exactly happened to me at that moment, Dr Ghosh. The whole world lost its colour for me in an instant. Each living moment started feeling poisonous. I couldn't sleep, I couldn't eat, I couldn't work – I became an insomniac within a month.

Jayanta Insomnia?

Angshuman Completely. And that was followed by a very high fever. I started raving. And in my fevered frenzy, I yelled Rahul's name. And Jayati heard that.

Jayanta She heard it?

Angshuman How could she not?

Closes his eyes to demonstrate his feverish rave and frenzy.

If I yelled 'Rahul, Rahul!' in this state wouldn't you be able to hear it?

Opens his eyes.

You heard that, right?

Jayanta Well, of course. Loud and clear.

Angshuman So did Jayati.

Jayanta And then?

Angshuman She set up an enquiry commission.

Jayanta Enquiry commission? What does that entail?

Angshuman Oh simple. She got hold of the call details for our landline from January. She analysed them to see that twenty out of the twenty-five calls made from the line were mine. And each of those calls were to Rahul's cell phone. And then she asked me. And I came out with the truth.

Jayanta Your wife, in spite of being an educated woman, in the truest sense of the word, could harass you like this? Strange!

Angshuman I asked her the same question. She said she just wanted to know the truth.

Jayanta Well, yeah, that is quite possible. Anyway, after that . . .

Angshuman And then she knit her brows together.

Lights come up on **Jayati** *upstage.*

Angshuman She started getting dark circles, became irritable, distracted, losing interest in food, you know everything that a deceived person tends to go through.

Jayanta Hmm.

Angshuman Actually she had to keep all of it bottled up. A young woman would have had an emotional outburst – and then this concerned a young boy. A nubile young boy. And she couldn't yell at me either – our children were within earshot. And they are not young. They understand these things.

Abhishek *joins her mother upstage.*

Jayanta Yeah, that is true. But perforce . . .

Angshuman Perforce a strange conversation took place between mother and son. It really was very strange.

Jayanta Like what?

Lights go down on **Angshuman** *and* **Jayanta**.

Scene Four

Jayati Abhi, please dial Rongon's number for me.

Abhishek Could you please tell me what is happening with you for these past few days?

Jayati Nothing. Just get him on the phone.

Abhishek *Ma*, you are hiding something from me . . .

Jayati What would I be hiding? What are you insinuating?

Abhishek You are different. Do you know what Hawking has to say about this?

Opens a book.

Hawking says, if the life events of a person enter into a blackhole then what lies ahead for the person is an event horizon.

Jayati Stop acting smart, Abhi.

Abhishek And then that person can see through to the end of time through their life.

Jayati Alright, that's it. One more bad joke from you and you will be slapped across your face.

Abhishek *Ma*, just tell me what is bothering you already. Are you worried about *Baba*? But *Baba* has been doing well for the past couple of days. Touch wood.

Jayati Nothing. I am fine. Would you go check to see if your father had his afternoon medicine on time. And then call Rongon. Meanwhile, give me your cell phone. I will call Mou.

Abhishek *hands over his cell phone and walks inside.* **Jayati** *dials the number.*

Jayati Hello, Mou? Do you hear me? Damn it, network problem. Hello, Mou? Mou? Hello?

Lights go down.

Scene Five

Lights go up on **Angshuman** *and* **Jayanta**

Angshuman And this is that call to my daughter from earlier?

Jayanta Did your wife set up a meeting at home?

Angshuman Almost.

Jayanta And what was the agenda of the meeting?

Angshuman Well, she tried telling but could not really. Except when Rongon came over the next day . . .

Lights go down on the two.

Scene Six

Lights come up on **Rongon** *and* **Jayati**.

Rongon Why were you calling me so many times? I would have come anyway.

Jayati Sorry. But I actually . . .

Rongon What is it? Any problem?

Jayati Problem? Yes, it is a kind of a problem.

Rongon What?

Jayati Rongon, are you a friend of mine?

Rongon What do you mean? Why this question all of a sudden?

Jayati Please answer me first.

Rongon Of course. Of course I am your friend. What is going on?

Jayati Please be honest with me. Our relationship. How much of it is friendship and how much of it is . . .

Beat.

Rongon What – romantic?

Jayati Something like that.

Rongon What has got into you all of a sudden?

Jayati Please just tell me.

Rongon So, I don't quite understand romance and romantic feelings. I used to, up to a certain age, but I really can't grasp these feelings any more. See that's the reason that I didn't even get married – but yes, if you think of romance as a very intense camaraderie then our relationship is somewhat romantic.

Jayati No, listen, Rongon.

Rongon But, honestly, I do not want to kill our friendship by calling it romantic and what not. I have seen as soon as we invoke all this romance and all that's when we start talking about rights et al.

Jayati (*impatient*) Fine, I get it. No more explanation needed. I didn't ask you to come here for a lecture on romance and friendship.

Rongon Alright? I really don't know what you are talking about.

Jayati Let me explain.

Beat.

Ok, why didn't you get married?

Rongon I don't understand your line of questioning.

Jayati Answer me.

Rongon I didn't. Just didn't. Didn't get the time to. So many others didn't either. Nietzsche didn't, Schopenhauer didn't, Kant did not marry either.

Jayati God damn it – can you stop lecturing! Why do you always have to theorize theorize and then glorify yourself?

Rongon What is it, Jayati? Why are you yelling at me after having dragged me all the way here?

Jayati No, listen, sorry. I am sorry.

Beat.

Rongon, please don't be angry. I hope you can understand that I am very restless.

Rongon And that is what I am trying to get to the bottom of. Why, Jayati, why?

Jayati Let me explain.

Rongon Yes, please.

Jayati Why didn't you get married?

Rongon Uff. I simply didn't get the time to marry, Jayati. I got too busy with my research and didn't get the time.

Jayati Fine. Are you gay?

Rongon What?

Jayati Are you a homosexual?

Rongon Come on, Jayati.

Jayati No, please answer me.

Rongon No, not at all. I am heterosexual. Absolutely 100 per cent heterosexual.

Jayati Really?

Rongon You should know that.

Beat.

But why are you asking me this?

Beat.

I think I know. Is it because I was discussing the history of homosexuality the other day in the staff room? But you listened to all of it. In fact, you praised me for it. You said that this theory of mine on alternative sexuality is really unique. Didn't you say that?

Jayati Theory, theory and theory! Theory and life are separate, Rongon. Absolutely different. Showering praises after listening to something pleasing to the ears and standing face to face with life – they are hell and heaven different.

Rongon I can't agree with you on that. Theory emerges out of life. Folks who observe life are historians and folks who theorize are theoreticians. And artists are the ones who bring the two into conversation.

Jayati Artists? Well, may be. Rongon, are you a bisexual?

Rongon I am going to get going now.

Jayati Rongon, please.

Rongon Enough is enough. I have a lot of work at home. I was in the middle of responding to my emails when your incessant calls dragged me here.

Jayati Rongon, are you Angshuman's . . .

Beat.

Rongon What?

Mou *and* **Alok** *enter.*

Mou *Ma,* this is Alok. He is a member of our group. He lives in a shared accommodation which has a curfew at ten. We have a performance tomorrow. We need to rehearse pretty late tonight. After that, he is going to crash in Abhi's room. I have already told Abhi about it. Alok, this is my mother, and this is the great Rongon *da*.

Alok Hello.

Mou Come, let us go to Abhi's room.

Mou *and* **Alok** *take a few steps forward. Lights dim on* **Jayati**.

Mou What do you eat for dinner usually? Rice or chapati?

Alok I will eat whatever you all are having.

Mou Why are you always so formal with me?

Alok You are older than me, that's why.

Mou Not at all. I am certain we are of the same age. What year were you born in? 1982?

Alok No, 1977.

Mou I am younger. Please call me Mou from now on and quit being so formal.

Alok As you say, Mou *di*.

Mou Again?

Lights go down.

Scene Seven

Lights come up on stage right. **Angshuman** *and* **Jayanta**.

Jayanta Was Jayati able to share what had happened with Rongon?

Angshuman *nods in the affirmative.*

Jayanta Was she able to?

Angshuman Yes.

Jayanta How did Rongon react?

Angshuman I am not sure. He must have come up with some kind of a theory. But Rongon was the first person to suggest consulting a psychiatrist. Although I was thinking about doing that for a while myself. Rongon had suggested someone else's name to Jayati but I had read about you in the papers . . .

Jayanta I get it. But did Rongon speak with you directly?

Angshuman No he didn't. He would have I suppose but Rahul's letter beat him to it.

Jayanta A letter arrived?

Angshuman Yup, arrived from Delhi. In my name. And it landed straight into Jayati's hands.

Jayanta Oh, wow! What did the letter say?

Angshuman I have it with me. Let me show it to you.

Reaches into his bag to look for the letter. Lights go down.

Scene Eight

Rahul *appears downstage left.*

Rahul My name is Rahul. Rahul Som. I could have emailed you. But I don't know your email ID and I don't want you to know mine. I learnt that you had gone over to my house in Kolkata, and then to my college. And I can somewhat imagine your mental state after everything that you have been through. And therefore this letter.

Jayanta (*he reads the letter by himself*) 'You know I am in Delhi now and here is where I will be. Please forget me. Please don't do anything crazy. You know why I went to your house drunk that evening, because otherwise I would not have been able to tell you those things. But why did I say those things? Why did I move to Delhi? You must be dying for answers, no? And that is justified. I know you didn't understand and I don't think you are supposed to understand. Only a handful of us friends get it.'

Rahul Actually I am a homosexual. I realized this when I was fairly young. Everyone in my home is aware of this as well. My body is that of a man, but my soul isn't. I have been like this since childhood and I have somehow reconciled with it. I pity those that do not understand me from within. Anyway, that's a different story. Let's get back to the point. You, me and that friend who had joined us when we went to the Birla Sabaghar for that concert, that friend, Tanmay, is a long-term partner of mine. You never suspected anything because you cannot even think like this.

Jayati (*lights come up on her centre stage; she is reading the letter as well*) 'Besides that, this whole thing is still very hush hush in Kolkata. But it isn't that way in Delhi. People here are far more open. We have community organizations, publications and NGOs here. Overall, I have a space here. Tanmay does not agree with me. He thinks that our city is just as open. But I think he is wrong. And that is why I have decided that I am going to do everything in my power to bring him over here – to me.'

Jayanta 'But your case is different. I provoked you, led you on, you naturally had no idea about me, and we fell into each other's arms. I realize now that it was probably your solitude that drove you into my arms.'

Rahul But I do not find myself drawn to you at all. I belong to someone else. And therefore I cannot keep doing this to you. It's wrong. Whatever and how much I did was temporary, it was just like a trip. Maybe I will have to face the consequences of my actions down the road. Maybe at your age. Maybe that is when my life will also be shrouded by an obvious solitude. Detached from society and my surroundings, may be I will have to live like a fugitive animal in a cave, in a home, or in a hermitage. May be that is my fate.

Jayati (*keeps reading;* **Angshuman** *is now seated in front of her*) 'But why should you choose this life for yourself? Madam, Abhi da, Mou – I feel a strange pain waft through me every time I remember their faces. And their faces allowed me to muster the courage to say the things I told you that day. And I am truly apologetic to you for saying those things. Please forgive me. Be well and please forget me. Completely. Yours truly, Rahul.'

Rahul *and* **Jayanta** *exit as the lights gradually shift to reveal only* **Jayati** *and* **Angshuman** *seated facing each other.*

Scene Nine

Jayati

Beat.

Beat.

You?

Beat.

How could you?

Throws the letter to **Angshuman**.

Jayati What are you actually?

Angshuman *reads the letter.*

Jayati Oh yes, read, read your letter. Why don't you read it aloud? Huh? Should I ask Abhi and Mou to join us? Do you want to read it to them? Disgusting!

Beat.

Angshuman, how could you do this?

Loudly.

How could you?

Stops.

Beat.

Sorry. I didn't want to scream. They – they didn't hear anything. Why are you looking at me like that? What? What do you want to say? That I am interfering in your personal terrain? Angshuman, this is no personal matter! You are perverted, yes, you are a total pervert – from your head to toe!

Silence descends on stage.

Beat.

Beat.

Angshuman (*takes a deep breath*) Rahul, my Rahul.

Jayati What?

Angshuman I want to see Rahul. Just once. I am in pain, Jayati. I am pining over him, Jayati. Rahul, my Rahul.

Jayati (*beside herself with anger*) FUCK OFF! To hell with your pining and your solitude. You sick man. Are you not ashamed of yourself?

Calls out.

Abhi, can you come here please.

Angshuman Please call Rahul once, Jayati. Just bring him to me one last time.

Jayati Oh, so it means that you don't even care if your children find out? Does this mean that you will be able to continue with this perversion knowing that they know it all?

Beat.

You are not a human anymore, Angshuman, you are an animal.

Angshuman *nearly prostrates to* **Jayati**, *holding her hands.*

Angshuman I want to see Rahul, Jayati. Please bring him to me once, please.

Jayati *shakes him off and leaves.*

Angshuman Rahul, oh, Rahul, my Rahul. Why did you hurt me so much? Why? I am missing you constantly, Rahul. I am missing you terribly. I really just want to see you once, Rahul. Please come to me one last time. Oh Rahul, my dearest Rahul!

The musical score envelops the stage. Lights go down.

Scene Ten

Lights go up on **Abhishek***'s room. It is afternoon.* **Abhishek** *and* **Alok** *are in the room.* **Mou** *stands to the side. She is pacing back and forth while reading a script.*

Abhishek What time is your show this evening?

Alok 6.30.

Abhishek Madhusudan?

Alok Yes.

Picking up **Abhi***'s phone.*

Alok Is this your cell phone?

Abhishek Yes. So that part is yours now, right?

Alok Yes, I am a permanent member of the group now.

Beat.

This is a Samsung, isn't it?

Abhishek Yes.

Beat.

What time are you all leaving then?

Alok Around three. At least that is what Mou said. Abhi *da*, which credit card do you use?

Abhishek Are you crazy? I don't have any credit cards. Is everyone okay at home?

Alok Yes. I called them this morning. *Ma* is feeling much better now. And so is *Baba*.

Abhishek And, er, what about your sister?

Alok Not really. She still has that mental issue. But she should be getting better. This time she actually spoke with me for a while.

Beat.

You still haven't bought a car either, have you?

Abhishek Are you crazy? I have to land a job first. Why?

Alok No, just like that.

Abhishek Were you ever into politics?

Alok No, never. I was always interested in music. I used to watch a lot of *jatras*, the travelling plays. Several top-tier operas still make a stop near my neighbourhood. I have wanted to be an actor since childhood. I am really fortunate to have landed this job in Kolkata.

Abhishek You sing as well, don't you?

Alok A little bit. I used to sing in my neighbourhood. Just this other day, there was a cultural event in the neighbourhood. The organizers had asked me to sing for them. But I didn't get time off from work and so had to cancel on them.

Beat.

What colour car do you want to get, Abhi *da*? Blue or maroon?

Abhishek Hold your horses. Do not count your chickens before they hatch. But why do you keep asking about cars?

Mou *gets a call on her cell phone.*

Mou Prajit *da*, yes, hello. Yeah, we will be there for sure. Don't worry. Alok is here in our house. I will take him with me and we will be on time.

Hangs up.

Mou Alok, where is the prop bag?

Alok In the living room.

Mou Come, come, we have to leave. Wait, let me grab my costumes.

She leaves.

Abhishek Yes, what were we talking about? Ah yes, cars, why were you asking about cars?

Alok I really like cars, Abhi *da*. Like them a lot. What do you think, Abhi *da*, if we turn over our lands to the government then we should be able to afford cars, etc. like you folks, right?

Abhishek I have no idea. You are asking the wrong person.

Mou *comes back. She has a bag slung across her shoulder.*

Mou Let's go, Alok.

Abhishek *Ma* mentions buying a used car from time to time. Mou, did you get a call from *Ma*?

Mou No. Alok, did you take the tea set?

Abhishek It's Friday today. She doesn't have the late class today.

Mou What about the vase and the ashtray?

Alok Everything has been accounted for. Don't worry about anything.

Abhishek *Baba* has also not been at home since the morning. No idea where he went.

Mou I have the comb and the mirror in my bag – why are you worrying for no reason? They must've gone somewhere. They will be back. They didn't have lunch, right?

Abhishek No, they didn't. Something has been bothering *Baba* for the last few days.

Mou Nothing has happened. He is like that. Quiet. Something has been bothering, *Ma*.

Abhishek What? Maybe. Maybe that is what it is.

Anindita *enters.*

Mou Look who is here? Stop sitting here at home and worrying about nothing. Ani, have a seat, I have to take off, I have a show today. I will see you later. Come, Alok, let us be off.

Mou *and* **Alok** *take a few steps to the centre of the stage. Lights go down on* **Abhishek** *and* **Anindita**.

Mou I hope you didn't mind?

Alok About what?

Mou When *Dada* asked you about your sister. I know you don't like talking about her.

Alok Nah, nothing like that. And besides your brother enquired out of the goodness of his heart. He cares about me.

Mou True, he does care about you. But even then, your face assumes this strange shape whenever your sister is mentioned.

Alok (*looks at her*) If you were raped in front of your brother then his face would also look like mine.

Beat.

Beat.

Abhi *da* is a good person, Mou. I know he didn't ask me about my sister to make fun of me or to provoke me. Let's go.

Alok *leaves followed by* **Mou**. *Lights go down.*

Scene Eleven

Lights come up on **Abhishek***'s room.*

Abhishek You are early.

Anindita Abhi, that man came to the university today.

Abhishek Who?

Anindita Come on. Who else could it be?

Abhishek What are you saying? Really?

Anindita Why are you becoming so slow? This is why we are never compatible?

Abhishek How could we be? According to Hawking's proposition, you dwell in the real time-space and I am in the realm of the imaginary time-space. How would these two be compatible?

Anindita Alright, forget your Hawking. Listen to what happened.

Abhishek Yes, go ahead.

Anindita I got a call on my cell exactly at 12.08. He says, I will call you once I get to the gates.

Abhishek And you went down to meet him?

Anindita What else could I do? He said he was standing at the bottom of the steps.

Abhishek What did he have to say?

Anindita I wasn't paying too much attention at first. My ears were ringing. I asked him if my mother was here. He said . . .

Debraj *appears stage left. It seems as if he is addressing* **Anindita**.

Debraj No, your mother is not here. She is not even aware that I am here to see you. Actually, I was compelled to come here, Ani. Please do not mind. And I came here all the more because of your mother. Ani, your mother is not well. Not at all. And it is from worrying about you.

Anindita (*addressing* **Abhishek**) At first I thought the asshole was here to act all namby-pamby.

Debraj Ani, you might not agree to this but your mother has suffered a lot throughout her life. A lot. You might even say that everyone suffers in life. And you are probably right. But just think for a second, Ani, one day your mother decided that she had had enough. That she was not going to suffer anymore. She was going to change everything. Change herself as well as her life.

Anindita (*addressing* **Abhishek**) So far so good.

Debraj Don't think that she suddenly said this to herself today. She thought about this ten years ago. And I know about that. But your mother could not take any steps back then because you were young. She didn't want you to be affected in any way. Because your mother was aware that if she were to take a decision like this ten years ago then your whole life would have been shattered.

Anindita (*addressing* **Abhishek**) Just think about it, this dude has been waiting on my mom for ten years.

Debraj She is able to do this today. Because you are almost settled in life. You are done with your master's this year. You can now pursue a doctorate, take your GRE and head abroad, or simply settle down to a married life. You have several options ahead of you. In fact, you can pursue all three options at the same time as well. Overall, you turned out to be exactly the way your mother wanted you to be.

Anindita (*addressing* **Abhishek**) I was almost on the verge of saying, why are you singing all these hymns to me – but I couldn't bring myself to it.

Debraj But she is still in pain, Ani. Because she realizes that you are in pain. And that is why her insides are crying. And I can see it clearly. You are like a daughter to me. I am requesting you. Please try and understand your mother a bit. Please see her, for a moment, not just as your mother but also as a human being.

Anindita (*addressing* **Abhishek**) And this brought tears to my eyes.

Debraj I know that you will be happy in your life. I have heard about Abhishek from your mother. But, Ani, let us also find some happiness in the twilight of our lives. We have both been through a lot in our lives. We have suffered a lot. But we will not be happy if we see tears in your eyes. Just think about it once, Ani, just think about it once.

Anindita (*addressing* **Abhishek**) And here the gentleman took a handkerchief out.

Debraj *follows the actions that* **Anindita** *narrates.*

Anindita And then wiped his tears. And then just walked away with a steady gait.

Lights go down on stage left and steadies itself again on **Abhishek** *and* **Anindita**.

Anindita And instead of going back to the lab I headed straight to you.

Abhishek How do you feel?

Anindita I have always maintained that this person is a gentleman, dignified, polite and sober. At least he is significantly better than my father.

Abhishek Well, seems like your heart has softened a bit.

Ani *smiles.*

Abhishek You should have called him back with a melodramatic, '*Babaaaa*, please don't go!'

Anindita Okay, this isn't funny.

Beat.

And you know, I felt this pall of sadness come over me during the bus ride over here.

Abhishek Thinking about your mother?

Anindita No, thinking about me.

Abhishek What? Why?

Anindita This guy really loves my mother. And has loved her for a while now.

Abhishek Isn't that a good thing? Why would that make you feel bad?

Anindita Not that. I was feeling bad thinking about us. Abhi, do you think we will be able to continue loving each other this deeply at that age? Can we?

The score envelops the stage as the lights go down.

Scene Twelve

Lights come up on stage right to reveal **Dr Jayanta Ghosh**. **Dr Ghosh** *addresses the audience.*

Jayanta I was under a lot of work-related pressure for these last few days. And amidst all of that I had almost forgotten about this queer person – Angshuman,

Angshuman Banerjee. I remembered him when I chanced upon a featured article on homosexuality in a medical journal. I began wondering why had he not shown up for a few days now? I know that I am not supposed to be encumbered by such thoughts professionally, but I couldn't help wondering nevertheless. After waiting for a few more days, I rang his house.

Lights go down as a phone is heard ringing.

Scene Thirteen

Lights come up on **Angshuman***'s house. The living room. The phone continues ringing.* **Rongon** *picks it up.*

Jayati *is next to him.*

Rongon Hello? Who is it? Oh, hold on.

(*To* **Jayati**.) Someone by the name of Dr Jayanta Ghosh is on the line. Wants to talk to Angshuman da.

Jayati Hello – no, he is unwell. He is lying down. Who are you? Oh, yes, I will let him know.

Angshuman *enters the room.*

Jayati Actually, he is here. Here, let me put him on.

(*To* **Angshuman**.) There's a call for you. Someone by the name of Dr Ghosh.

Angshuman Hello, oh yes, yes, I have missed our sessions for the last few days. I have not been feeling particularly well. Yes, I will be there soon. Thank you, Dr Ghosh.

Hangs up.

Jayati Who is this? A relative of Rahul? Have you gone after him now? To get hold of Rahul's address?

Rongon Jayati!

Jayati How deep will you drag us down, eh? Aren't you worried about your family at all? Will you never start thinking beyond yourself?

Rongon Jayati. Jayati please. Angshuman *da*, please go back to your room.

Jayati No, he is not going to go back inside. He will be here.

Rongon I was going to say . . .

Jayati Please take your leave, Rongon. Let us please talk for a little bit.

Rongon *casts a strange look at* **Jayati**.

Jayati Sorry, I am saying this as a friend. Please . . .

Rongon *leaves.* **Jayati** *moves closer to* **Angshuman**.

Jayati What has happened to you?

Grabs his shoulders.

Why do you sit by yourself quietly in your room all day? Why? How did you become this way? How? How did the two of us become so different? When did all of this happen? I had no idea – absolutely no idea.

Breaks down while holding **Angshuman** *but then gathers herself.*

Jayati Let us take a trip together, Angshuman. Like in our younger days. Let us go to Deoghar. Just the two of us. Will you come? What happened? Why aren't you talking? Hey, what happened? Angshuman, hey, Angshuman, what happened?

Angshuman Just bring me Rahul, Jayati. Please have a little pity on me. Just Rahul. I swear to you that I will not stay in touch with him after that. I just want to see him once. Just once.

Jayati *breaks down again.* **Abhishek** *enters from the outside.*

Abhishek What is going on? The door is wide open. Oh sorry, were you talking? *Ma*, is everything all right, any problem?

Jayati *gets up, wipes her tears, and leaves without a word.*

Abhishek *Baba*, what happened to *Ma*? *Baba*? Why has *Ma* been agitated for the last few days?

Angshuman *stares on.*

Abhishek Oh, I forgot to give you your morning pill. I am certain you must not have taken it.

Goes up to the cabinet next to the sofa. Picks up the medicine from there and a glass of water from the table.

Abhishek Here, take it. *Baba*, can I ask you something? Why don't you start painting again, *Baba*? I think *Ma* will feel better again if you do that.

Angshuman What about me?

Abhishek What?

Angshuman Will I get better then?

Abhishek (*smiles*) I think so for sure.

Angshuman *gets up and takes a few steps forward.*

Angshuman I don't think so.

Abhishek Why? Why don't you try it for a bit?

Angshuman Somethings are not worth trying, Abhi.

Beat.

Did you go out to buy cigarettes?

Abhishek Yes.

Angshuman Why aren't you having one in front of me? Have one.

Abhishek No.

Angshuman Why? Out of respect for me?

Beat.

Meaningless, this too is meaningless. I am not a very respectable person.

Abhishek *lowers his head.*

Angshuman Do you find me disgusting?

Abhishek (*with conviction*) Absolutely not.

Angshuman Are you certain?

Abhishek I am absolutely certain.

Angshuman I found him disgusting.

Abhishek Who?

Angshuman My father.

Abhishek I don't think so. I think you like imagining it that way. I think you really loved Grandfather.

Angshuman True I loved him very much. And that is exactly why I found him just as disgusting.

Abhishek These two things are one and the same for you?

Angshuman They are the same. Exactly the same.

Abhishek In that case, I am disgusted with you.

Angshuman I knew it.

Abhishek No, didn't you just say that love and disgust mean the same to you.

Angshuman I am confused. I have confused it all.

Beat.

Abhi – you must understand that when someone commits a murder or when someone destroys a relationship they do it out of extreme passion, right? Or say when someone commits suicide? At those very moments those people want to grab this mundane routine life by its neck and give it a good shakedown, isn't it? What do you think?

Beat.

Beat.

You are just like my mother. You understand it all but don't respond.

Abhishek I don't think I understand it, *Baba*. I pretend to understand. Come, let's go to my room.

Angshuman Why?

Abhishek Come, let us talk like we used to when I was younger.

Angshuman Will you like talking to me?

Abhishek Yes. Do you remember how you would explain what lines were, the different kinds of colours and how Rembrandt would see colors when looking at alphabets, and the resulting hue after mixing green and white, do you remember?

Angshuman No, not really. I seem to have forgotten it.

Abhishek I remember. You know, *Baba*, I realize that I have learnt to appreciate physics from you.

Angshuman Yeah, right. Quit bluffing.

They both take a few steps.

Abhishek No, seriously. The first line of my autobiography, written after I become very famous thanks to having conducted some path-breaking research, would be, like Heisenberg, that I am who I am because of my father. Yes, my father.

Angshuman Stop it. What a joke? What did I ever do . . .

Abhishek *keeps talking.* **Angshuman** *keeps protesting. The score overtakes their conversation. Lights go down.*

Scene Fourteen

The sound of applauding hands pierce the darkness on stage. Lights come up on stage left. The rehearsal room. **Prajit**, **Gouri**, **Mou**, **Alok** *and a few others.*

Prajit Fantastic. Fantastic improvement, Alok. Brilliant. I had no idea that one could improve as fast as you did. Congrats, Alok, congrats.

Alok *seeks* **Prajit***'s blessings.*

Prajit Keep up the good work. I wish you all the very best.

Alok Prajit *da*, this achievement of mine is your handiwork.

Prajit Huh, you are too kind.

Alok I am being honest Prajit *da*. No one would have recognized or praised me if you hadn't placed your hand on my shoulder. And there is one other person that I would like to split the credits and praises with.

Prajit Who is that? Mou, for sure?

Alok Yes, Prajit *da*. The way she rehearsed with me day and night over these last few days . . .

Mou Stop, that is enough.

Gouri Well, he is telling the truth, Mou. Why are you stopping him?

Prajit Exactly. Let him say his piece. We have forgotten the art of publicly acknowledging our gratitude.

Alok You are absolutely right, Prajit *da*. I want to acknowledge in public that I am grateful to Mou.

Prajit This is really exciting. I feel like our group is about to do something really phenomenal. Finally we will able to show our mettle to the theatre community. Finally. And we will do it!

People gather together in celebration. **Shubho** *enters. He is quieter than usual. He enters slowly.*

Gouri What is wrong, Shubho?

Prajit Shubho, what is wrong? Why do you look so pale?

Mou I am certain that he has some kind of a practical joke up his sleeve again.

Prajit No, I think this is serious. He looks different. Shubho, what happened?

Shubho I will . . .

Beat.

I am quitting theatre Prajit *da*.

Gouri What?

Shubho You know how my older brother has to bear the burden of the entire family since my father's passing. But it is becoming too much for him. There are so many mouths to feed in the house. Our mother, his wife, two children, and then there is me, a total nincompoop good for nothing non-contributing sponge. In spite of this my brother has done a lot. But I don't think he can anymore.

Ratan What exactly has happened, Shubho? Please just tell us.

Shubho My older brother has found a job for me at a hotel in Kalimpong. I will be the manager. The hotel is owned by a friend of his. He has just taken over the lease. They will pay me five thousand rupees a month. I make nothing from the theatre. And I am not getting any younger. I must take this opportunity, Prajit *da*. I absolutely must.

Gouri What if we can find an alternative arrangement?

Shubho Tell me what arrangement? Prajit *da* did get me a role in a television soap. I couldn't make it. Montu and I had started together. He made it – but I – I could not make that work, Gouri *di*. Everyone says that I am a bad actor. I had a hard time believing people earlier, but now I do. Prajit *da* says that I am a very good worker. But I know that I perform the duties of the group secretary because I cannot act. And to be honest, I do not dream of becoming an actor. I just wanted to be associated with the theatre in any way possible. But I could not, Prajit *da*. I just really could not.

Beat.

Beat.

Beat.

Prajit I will be helpless without you, Shubho.

Shubho What can I do, tell me? And moreover, people like Alok are with the group now. I am certain that they can manage. Please don't be upset with me, Prajit *da*. I beg you, please just don't be upset with me.

Prajit *takes off his glasses and moves to one side of the stage. Everyone is quiet; the silence is interrupted intermittently with some murmurs from* **Shubho**. **Mou** *clears her throat as she readies herself to speak.*

Mou Er, I would like to say something. It's probably not right for me to say it this way but I must anyway. Could I ask my brother to help in any way? He might be able to arrange something.

Gouri Why not? Please, absolutely, please ask him. That would be wonderful.

Prajit What kind of an arrangement? Isn't he himself quite young? What can he possibly do?

Mou True, he is rather young. But he has a few friends that care about him quite a bit. In fact, just last week he was mentioning a friend of his who has the connections to help someone land a small sales job. In fact, he had asked me if I knew someone. I had obviously said no at the moment.

Shubho What kind of a job? My English is not the best . . .

Prajit Hey, keep quiet. We will all help you. Please ask your brother, Mou.

Beat.

Wow, this is quite wonderful. And such a young person.

Mou Yes, my brother is very mature for his age, Prajit *da*. And he is very responsible. I will mention this to him right away, as soon as I get home. And if he puts his head and heart behind it, I am sure that he will be able to make something work.

Scene Fifteen

Lights come up on **Abhishek***'s room.* **Abhishek** *is lying on his stomach in his bed reading a book.*

Gouri Your brother does look like he is a very serious type.

Abhishek *gets a call on his cell phone. He sits up to receive it.*

Abhishek Hello, sorry, I couldn't hear the phone. It was in silent mode.

Mou Yeah, he is very serious from within. But he masks that with a jovial exterior and with his incessant jokes.

Abhishek (*Still on the phone; smiles*) Why are you worrying *Ma*? I just peeked into his room a moment ago. *Baba* was busy writing something. Nope – you don't need to worry about nothing, *mataji*.

Mou He jokes around quite a bit with our mother though.

Abhishek Mom, why are you worrying? Cause others to worry but don't worry yourself is the mantra to live by mater! Can you imagine *Ma*, *Baba* is sitting at his desk and writing! Now, that has been a rare sight recently! This is bigger than the Big Bang itself.

Mou And he is genuinely concerned about everybody. Ask Alok, if you don't trust me, Shubho *da*.

Abhishek Why are you worrying, *Ma*? Take your time. Yes, I have given him his medicine. *Baba* held the glass like a ten-year-old kid and sipped his medicine down.

Mou My father, you know, Prajit *da*, is a firm believer in the theory of genetics. *Baba* has several childish quirks like this. And my brother jokes that while my father is curious about the mysteries of life, he is a firm believer in the art of living.

Abhishek 'Life is here, as is death, Mother.' Nothing to worry about. *Ma*, *Baba* is fine. Please stop acting like a child. Focus instead on ensuring that the fishmonger slices that precious Hilsa properly.

Mou But he never gets into an argument with *Baba*. Never. In fact when *Baba* says something, he listens to it very carefully. Actually my father is rather calm and quiet. But he really gets upset with petty verbal arguments. And my brother understands that. All his fights are always with my mother.

Abhishek There's no convincing you now, is there? Seriously, I can't deal with all this mushy love of you two. Oops. Alright, sorry, sorry, very sorry, Mother. Please don't be upset. Alright fine, I will go check on him one more time.

Abhishek *goes inside and the lights go down on his room.*

Mou Recently, *Ma* has been constantly worrying over *Baba*. Possibly for nothing.

Beat.

Prajit *da*, all of you must come over one day. Let me introduce you to my parents. I think you will like them. My father barely speaks though. But you know, Gouri *di*, my father is very different from most people.

Beat.

Why don't you all come over tomorrow or the day after? And by the way, my father is an artist. He used to be really good back in the day. But he does not paint or draw at all nowadays. And I don't really know why that is.

Scene Sixteen

Mou *gets a call on her cell phone.*

Mou Speak of the devil. It's my brother. The dude will have a long life.

Abhishek *appears on stage. The score begins to envelope the stage.*

Abhishek Mou, where are you? Come back home right now.

Mou What is going on? What happened?

Abhishek Please just get back home and I will explain everything. Mou, my darling, just come back home as fast as possible.

Mou (*hangs up*) I need to head home immediately, Prajit *da*. I think something must have happened.

Alok What happened? Come, let me go with you.

Mou No, thank you. I will let you folks know if I need anything.

Shubho One of us at least should go with you.

Mou I will be fine for now, Shubho *da*. I promise I will call if I need something. Prajit *da*, I will be off.

Lights go down on the rehearsal room.

Scene Seventeen

Mou *runs across the stage to* **Abhishek**. *The two of them rush inside. We hear* **Mou** *screaming after a little while puncturing the score to a silence. A little later* **Jayati** *comes on stage. She goes and sits on the sofa. Silent. Still. Lifeless. A single beam of light surrounds her.* **Dr Jayanta Ghosh** *appears downstage right.* **Angshuman** *appears on the opposite side of the stage. The light on* **Jayati** *goes out as* **Angshuman** *starts speaking.*

Angshuman Dr Ghosh, I am certain that you remember me. I am Angshuman. Dr Ghosh, I am about to commit suicide. I am going to learn about the ultimate truth. At this moment I have a bowl of ice-cold water and a blade in my hand.

He lifts his hands to show these objects.

I am going to slit my right wrist gently with this blade before immersing it in this bowl of ice cold water. Warm, black blood is going to spurt out of the wound. The blood will start cooling as it flows into the icy water. And gradually my beating heart will start cooling down as well.

Beat.

Dr Ghosh, please do not be upset with me. This was inevitable. A person who has always believed in love and beauty but could never experience either would want to take at least one last decision in their life that gives them a sense of control, isn't it? Wouldn't such a person want to make one last attempt at being completely in control of their lives? This decision is mine, Dr Ghosh. Mine alone. And life won't be able to escape me this time. It is my turn to win.

And this is what was to happen, Doctor. I had told you when we first met that I do not understand uncertainties. The things that torment us, make us cry in private, things that pierce through our bodies and souls, things that we confuse as uncertainties are actually pre-destined.

And therefore these uncertainties are all pre-ordained. Definite. This is exactly what was to happen, Dr Ghosh. Exactly this.

Angshuman *recedes into the darkness.* **Dr Jayanta Ghosh** *continues reading.*

Jayanta 'You know, Doctor, my son had once shared an anecdote from the autobiography of the physicist Heisenberg. Apparently, Heisenberg had spent an entire night giving mathematical form to the main principles of quantum mechanics. That is when he discovered his legendary Uncertainty Principle. And at daybreak he ascended to the top of a cliff adjacent to the North Sea. And there he witnessed the sunrise. The millennia-old phenomenon that appears new every day. At that moment, Heisenberg writes, his whole being was filled with a divine happiness. He was able to witness and experience the crux of all earthly beauties at that moment.

Beat.

You know, I think Heisenberg intimately understood the rhythmic crashing waves of the North Sea, the peak of that sloping palisade and the impenetrably peaceful existence of the Heligoland archipelago around it at that moment.

Heisenberg was no doubt aware that at that very moment someone somewhere in the world must have been cursing, having an argument or even torturing someone. But Heisenberg, basking in the glory of the discovery that he had made, chose to accept this moment and its truth as ultimate and definitive. This in spite of the fact that the sage man stood diametrically opposite to the ideas of certainty with his research findings – his principles of Uncertainty.

Beat.

I am a simple person, a nobody. I don't understand Heisenberg, neither do I understand his theories. But in spite of that, I want to defy his work on uncertainty by taking this obvious, drastic and certain action. Let this be the mark of my obeisance to the great man.'

Jayanta *recedes into the darkness as the sound of crashing waves surrounds the stage.*

Scene Eighteen

The musical score entwines itself with the sound of the waves. We see **Jayati** *clearly now.* **Rahul** *stands in front of her. When the lights become brighter, he goes and sits at* **Jayati***'s feet.* **Jayati** *touches his head.*

Jayanta *leads the ensemble on stage. We see* **Abhishek**, **Anindita**, **Mou**, **Rongon** *and the rest.* **Jayanta** *walks up to the centre. The rest cluster around* **Jayati**. *The score has faded out by now.* **Rongon** *takes a few steps to address* **Jayanta**.

Rongon What will happen, Dr Ghosh? Will he survive?

Jayanta *takes a few more steps forward.*

Jayanta (*with a smile*) The whole thing is uncertain.

He exits. As soon as he finishes talking the whole stage sinks into a shadowy frieze. The blackhole motif at the rear of the stage grows bright and clear.

End of Play.

Glossary

Boro babu: senior clerk in a government office. The adjective *boro* means big, which in this context can be a marker of both age and designation

Na: in this context it represents a nagging insistence rather than 'no,' its usual translation

Ma: mother

Baba: father

Da: a typical Bengali honorific. It's expanded form is *dada*, which means 'older brother.' But it's very common to use the single 'da' after the names of people to signify the same thing. For eg. Shubho *da* means 'older brother Shubho'

Arey: figure of speech in Bengali without an equivalent expression in English. In this present context, it is a stand-in for because

'The sky smells sour'?: a line from the Bengali absurdist poet Sukumar Roy

Dover Lane conference: a three-night Indian classical music program held in the southern part of the city of Kolkata. It is a prestigious concert series which first began in 1952

GD Birla Sabhaghar: a well-known performance venue in South Kolkata

Ragas: melodic framework in classical music similar to that of the melodic mode. The word literally means 'coloring' or 'lining'

Mataji: literally, honored mother. Abhishek is using this form of address here as a joke

Hilsa: a very sought-after fish in Eastern India related to the herring family. It is known for its oily and tender flesh. It is mostly harvested during the monsoon months

'The dude will have a long life': a popular adage in Bengali to mark the coincidence of a person's appearance or, more recently, a call/text from a person while they were being discussed in their absence

Who?

Bratya Basu

2013

Translated by Arnab Banerji

Female characters: 5

Male characters: 9

Country of origin: India

Original performance date: 27 February 2014, Kolkata

Characters

Gurard Sunil *(male, thirties)*
Srikanto *(male, thirties, similar to Sunil in build and height)*
Lily *(female, early thirties, petite)*
Arun *(male forties)*
Bula *(female, mid thirties)*
Rabi *(male thirties, well put together)*
Manoj *(male late thirties, quietly distinct)*
Kurchi *(female thirties, attractive)*
Gonjona *(female late twenties to early thirties)*
Pittu *(male, fifties)*
Chotok *(male late fifties to early sixties, quirky)*
Keka *(female, thirties)*
Police Orderly *(male)*
Security *(male)*

Act One

Scene One

The sound of a doorbell pierces the score. The curtain opens. It is daytime. Our scene takes place in Baruipur, a suburb of Kolkata. A wooden cot is seen downstage left. **Dr Sunil Sen** *lies curled up on it.*

He is asleep. His face is covered with the morning newspaper. A cat sleeps next to his cot. By the time the curtain opens completely, we only hear the incessant doorbell. **Dr Sen** *wakes up. He is in his mid-thirties. He is wearing glasses, has an unkempt beard, and is wearing a shirt and trousers. He rubs the sleep off his eyes while walking to the wings to open the door. A man steps inside. Aged around forty. He is wearing jeans and a t-shirt. He has a bag slung on his shoulder and a cricket bat in his hand. Silence. The two look at each other.*

Sunil Who are you?

The other person keeps looking on.

Ahem, you are . . .

The Man Are you Sunil Sen? Doctor? Clinic in Baranogor?

Sunil Yes indeed. And you?

The Man I am Srikanto. Srikanto Gupta.

Sunil I am not sure that I . . .

Srikanto You don't recognize me, do you?

Sunil No, not really. Sorry.

Srikanto How about Lily Gupta? Sounds familiar?

Sunil No.

Srikanto Your patient. And you don't know her?

Sunil I see a lot of patients in my clinic. I cannot possibly remember or know everybody by name, can I? And besides that I haven't been going to the clinic for the last few days. What did you say the patient's name was? Lily? How are the two of you related?

Beat.

Beat.

Srikanto Wife. She was my wife.

Sunil What do you mean 'was' your wife?

Srikanto Lily committed suicide the day before yesterday. On the sixth. She took thirty sleeping pills at once. The neighbours found her, dead, the next morning, in our bed.

He abruptly punches **Sunil** *in the stomach.* **Sunil** *folds over in pain and lets out a cry of pain.*

Srikanto You are refusing to acknowledge your own lover, brother? How can you pretend to not know the woman who is lying dead in the morgue because of you?

Sunil What are you going on about? What is this?

Srikanto *sets down the cricket bat and grabs* **Sunil** *by the collar.*

Srikanto Lily Gupta, age thirty-three years, do you know her? Tell me now.

Sunil I am, I am going to call the police.

Srikanto Forget the cops, call for the military too. I am not going to leave you. Tell me now whether you know her or not?

Sunil Listen, brother, I think you are mistaken. I have not been practising for the last three months. This house is not mine. It belongs to my sister. I am merely staying here. I live in Salt Lake.

Srikanto Near Sraboni. In the FC Block. Two-storeyed house. You and your wife live there. Your wife runs a clothing boutique.

You are having some problems with your wife. Which is why you are staying here in Baruipur. For the last six or seven months now. This house does not belong to your sister, it is your brother-in-law or her husband's. Arun Dasgupta. A very affluent businessman. This garden house in Baruipur is where he hosts his booze parties. But he has allowed you to be put up here.

Beat.

What did you think? I just showed up without having done my due diligence on you? I know everything that there is to know about you. A quick click on my mouse and everything will come outpouring. Lily told me everything.

Sunil Listen, please listen to me. Everything that you claim to know about me might be true but I honestly don't know this Lily Gupta person.

Beat.

Fine, just help me out a bit, okay. Could you describe your wife to me a little bit?

Srikanto *lets go of* **Sunil**'*s collar and breaks down in tears.*

Srikanto Oh Lily, my darling Lily. My sweetheart. She was so pretty. Fair and thin. Suffered a little from tension and anxiety, but still . . . Oh Lily, oh my little Lily flower, I will never be able to see you again, oh my little flower. Oh my Lily.

Sunil (*in a soft voice*) Could you tell me where did you all live?

Srikanto (*still heaving*) North Calcutta. We had an apartment there. She was by herself that day. I had left town for work the previous day. I rushed back on receiving this news. The press has even printed her news today under the byline, 'Housewife commits suicide.' How the hell would the asshole papers know about the swine for whom she committed suicide. Why did she do this?

Sunil What do you mean? Why?

Srikanto Why? Did you think that I did not know that Lily was pregnant when she killed herself? Do you think I don't know who the father of that child is?

Sunil What are you saying, brother? Nonsense.

Srikanto You bastard! I know everything. And what you don't know is that I have been back in the city for almost a fortnight now. Lily did not tell you about it. She was afraid that you would get scared. She understood you after all. She knew that you were actually a chicken.

Beat.

We argued over you the other day. And she accepted that the child in her womb is yours. I threw things around in anger. And then left the city the following morning for work. I got the news halfway during my travel and rushed back to find that all was over.

Breaks down crying.

Sunil So, you vandalized your own house and then left the next day? Where were you going to?

Srikanto (*crying*) I was going to our main office. Indore. I am the Chief Sales Executive of our company.

Sunil (*suddenly recalling something*) Indore? Oh wait . . . wait . . . do you live in Paikpara?

Srikanto Yes. You already know everything. Why are you pretending to be innocent brother? Yes, Paikpara. An eight-hundred square-foot apartment. Just the two of us lived there.

He moves to the stage right while saying these words. He eventually vanishes into the darkness. **Sunil** *keeps speaking.*

Sunil Right. This must have been six months ago. This woman came to my clinic.

Lily Gupta *is seen on stage.*

Sunil It must have been around eight or eight thirty in the evening. That day she was my last patient. She looked a little melancholic. And she was talking about her husband to me.

Lights go up on downstage right. It is a doctor's chamber. **Lily Gupta** *sits on a chair.* **Sunil** *has walked over while speaking the previous line. And by the time he is finished, he is seated across from her like a doctor would.*

Lily Doctor, please save me from this chronic depression. I cannot take this anymore. Last I heard that he was in Indore.

Sunil What do mean he was in Indore?

Lily He works in the sales department of a multinational company. He has to travel all around the country on account of that. There are times when he is not home for almost a month. But this time around he has been untraceable for almost a year.

Sunil What do you mean? Have you tried calling him?

Lily He doesn't use a cell phone. I called his work yesterday. Their response was very strange.

Sunil What did they say?

Lily They said that your husband is not a permanent staff of ours. He works on the basis of commission. And therefore we cannot share any news of him with you.

Sunil Alright. But why are you here? Shouldn't you have gone to the police?

Lily I will. But I am feeling very depressed, Dr Sen. I don't get it. Did he lie to me?

Sunil Oh, everyone lies a little bit. That is no big deal. The big deal is the direction that the lie forces your life into.

Beat.

Do you suffer from chronic depression or is it something that has been triggered by the news or no news of your husband?

Lily I think I have always had a dour demeanour. My father would even joke with me about it. But things have taken a serious turn for the worst since learning this about my husband. How am I going to survive by myself in this world, Doctor?

Beat.

Tell me how, darling Sonu!

The stage goes dark. **Srikanto** *roars from the other side. Lights go up on* **Srikanto**.

Srikanto She didn't know about my promotion. It is company policy to not divulge any details about any of us to outsiders. I have been shuttling between Indore, Baroda and Ahmedabad constantly for the last nine months. Sixteen-hour work days. I haven't had the time to even call home. And this was not the first time that this had happened. I had planned on taking a long break to go home. And as per plan I got back home a fortnight ago.

Beat.

And I noticed and felt a change in her since getting back. When I asked her about it she got angry. Started misbehaving. And then, after a couple of days, one night she admitted that she was pregnant. And that she was in love with someone else . . .

Lily *steps in front of* **Srikanto**.

Srikanto Who is he? Tell me? Why aren't you telling me? Tell me the truth? Who is that jackass?

Lily I won't tell you, Srikanto. You have never paid any heed to my feelings, to me . . . you have always considered me to be a laughing stock.

Srikanto An old flame always appears villainous when the heart is swayed by new love. People turn a blind eye to everything, even when confronted directly with a wrongdoing. But as soon as a new love appears in the horizon then the blind suddenly gain sight and the dumb starts speaking. I understand it all. Just come out clearly and admit that you are in love. Bloody sadness, depression. All selfish, namby-pamby excuses. Who's the guy? Tell me, who's your chevalier?

Lily Whoever he might be. He is far more sensible and sensitive than you. And most importantly, he gets me.

Srikanto So basically he butters you up. I understand all this 'getting you, understanding you' crap. Why don't you simply say, he is massaging your ego. Softly, and sweetly, he is pouring all the lard on you. And you know that everyone can be buttery smooth. As long as you don't have to deal with the household, the spouse, everyone has a reservoir of butter to pour on somebody. Seldom do they realize that as soon as you start living together – it becomes a race to reduce your partner to the role of a domestic help.

Shakes **Lily***'s chin.*

Srikanto Oh my lovely flower, the blossom of my garden. It's all flowery before the wedding and foolery afterwards.

Lily Only a dirty-minded boor would have such an uncultured perspective on everything. You have been ill-mannered and uncivilized all your life. The way you look at the world itself is dirty.

Srikanto Oh, that's what you have always told me. What is new about that?

Beat.

What is the name of this brand new, gentlemanly cock anyway? The one who has been crowing every morning for my wife from my rooftop itself? Tell me, what is his name?

He grabs **Lily** *by the neck.* **Lily** *is somehow able to respond through the attack.*

Lily Dr Sunil Sen. My private physician.

Sunil *is heard screaming through the darkness on his side of the stage.* **Lily** *drifts into the darkness.*

Lights come on as **Lily** *exits.*

Sunil It's a lie. It's an absolute lie. I saw her only that one time. And I remember that day particularly well because I haven't been back to the clinic since then.

Srikanto *steps forward. He is in tears.*

Srikanto Yeah right, you have been going around with my wife for the last six months! You have been sleeping with her in my own house! Doctor! Doctor indeed! Some fucking doctor you are. Neglecting your duties to go around with my wife.

Sunil I will file a lawsuit. I will file a suit of defamation against you.

Srikanto Son of a field rat! Tsk, man, what kind of a man are you? You took advantage of my being busy with work? Hard workers like me, daily wage earners, we have to work non-stop disregarding our physical comforts. And in spite of being a professional yourself, you took advantage of the situation and burrowed your way into my home like a petty rat? And the burrow you dug compelled my wife to swallow thirty sleeping pills? Huh?

Sunil Hey, wait, wait. Did your wife leave a suicide note behind?

Srikanto *pauses for a second.*

Srikanto No, why?

Sunil So what is your basis for making these baseless nonsensical accusations against me?

Srikanto Nonsensical? Do you know what Lily told me just two days before she died?

Sunil What?

Srikanto Lily wasn't meeting you for a few days since my return because she was scared of me. She would just stay at home. One evening I woke up from my siesta to find out that Lily wasn't at home. She returned after eight o'clock looking very depressed and with a sullen expression. She said that you have not been picking up her calls. She also said that when you met her earlier that day you misbehaved with her and turned her away.

Lights go down on **Sunil** *and* **Srikanto**. *We see* **Lily** *on stage right.*

Lily I am feeling nauseous, Srikanto. My whole body is nauseated. What am I supposed to do now? What?

Beat.

Sunil behaved very badly today, Srikanto. He is very disturbed. His wife hasn't agreed to their divorce yet. That woman is also having an affair. Sunil left their Salt Lake home after he came to know about it. But that woman is still refusing a divorce. And you are being a giant jackass on top of that. I am falling sick again, Srikanto. Sick. I need to sleep. I am going to sleep. Where are my medicines? My medicines?

She exits stage right. Lights go up on **Sunil** *and* **Srikanto**. *The music underscoring the previous action stops. Silence.*

Srikanto You are right. You are absolutely right that I won't be able to prove that Lily killed herself because of you. Just like if I were to murder you here in this empty garden house, no one will be able to prove that I am the murderer. Well, except that cat there but then the poor animal is of no use as a witness.

Sunil What?

Srikanto Yes, I can kill you just now.

Picks up the cricket bat.

It will take me just five seconds to land this on your skull. And trust me, I will do just that unless . . .

Sunil Unless?

Srikanto I don't want anything from you, Dr Sen. I don't want money, I don't even want to kill you. I want you to report to your local police station within the next seven days and make a deposition. I just want to learn the truth, Dr Sen, just the truth. I know Lily suffered from chronic depression. It is quite possible that you are not directly responsible for her death. But that does not mean you get to deny her role and presence in your life. You will confess publicly at the police station that you had an affair with Lily Gupta from Paikpara. The same woman who committed suicide by swallowing thirty sleeping pills two days ago. And you will also accept responsibility for it. Because she was carrying your child.
Just tell the truth. That is all I want.

Sunil But, but, but . . . this is all a lie. I have only seen your wife that one time.

Srikanto Seven days, Dr Sen. Seven days only. And the countdown begins now.

He shoves **Sunil**. **Sunil** *loses his balance and stumbles onto the floor.* **Srikanto** *exits.* **Sunil** *sits expressionless for a while. Then he picks up his cell phone from the bed. He is seen dialling a number as the score floats in.*

Sunil Hello, hello is it you, Bula? Bula, can you please get Arun and come over immediately to this place? Please, Bula, this is an emergency. Right now. Hello?

The stage darkens. Lights come up after a bit. We see **Arun**, **Sunil***'s brother-in-law on stage. He has a book in his hand.* **Sunil** *stands facing him. There is a small bandage on his forehead.* **Bula**, **Sunil***'s sister, is pacing back and forth across the room.*

Beat.

Bula And this person was also aware of the fact that this place is not your home? That you have only been staying here for the last six months or so?

Sunil Not just that. He knows every last detail about me and about Kurchi too. Gave me a whole presentation of it.

Bula Hmm. Got it.

Beat.

You can come clean about it, there is no truth in these claims, right?

Sunil What do you mean?

Bula I mean you didn't really have any relationship with this Lily Gupta person, right?

Sunil What are you insinuating?

Bula You have been staying over here for about six months. And you have stopped going to the clinic for about five months, right?

Sunil Yes. So what?

Bula No, that's what I am wondering about.

Sunil *Arey*, what are you wondering about?

Bula Why did you go out every day in the evening in spite of having stopped going to the clinic? Every day!

Sunil What? How many times have I been out? Maybe seven times tops. For about an hour or hour and a half. I drove myself at the most to the South City Mall to run a few errands and pick up a few things. The cook you had appointed would come every evening at eight. Why don't you ask her if I am being truthful or not.

Bula Hmph.

Sunil Why are you interrogating me when I am telling you repeatedly that the affair is a lie?

Arun It's not that, Sunil. I am actually thinking about this man. Can we be certain that he was not affiliated with any intelligence agency, like RAW maybe?

Bula Oh shut it, will you? Look, you know that I have never been a big fan of your wife. Kurchi has never behaved well towards us. In fact she hardly considered Arun to be human. She sure learned the art of arrogance well from you if not anything else. But . . .

Sunil But what? Why did you stop, Bula? Go on. Remind me that I am no cherub either. That I would have one too many patient consultations every day leaving no personal time. Not having a work–life balance is my cardinal sin, isn't it?

Bula Oh, stop bluffing, okay? Personal time, work–life balance? One too many consultations? Huh. Everyone knows that it was Kurchi's boutique that kept the lights on in your house. You may have been a good student but you flopped as a doctor and your medical career barely went anywhere. We all know that your clinic and your car are also paid for by my sister-in-law.

Sunil A wife can buy her husband a car for sure.

Bula Of course she can. Who has said anything about that? But I just want to remind you that you never behaved well towards Kurchi.

Sunil Brass tacks, get down to specifics? How did I misbehave?

Bula Oh, I can read off an entire list. Do you have a specific instance in mind that you would want to be reminded of?

Arun Oh cut it out you two. We are already in the middle of something. I literally ran out of the office after hearing from Sunil. And on top of that the two of you have to get on with the same old dispute . . .

Beat.

Could it be that this guy was affiliated with the CBI?

Bula Shut up now. Kurchi wanted you to make something out of your life. By yourself. So that people would take pride in you. But you never really wanted to do much with your life.

Sunil That is quite alright, isn't it? It is not necessary that everyone must achieve everything in life. Everybody doesn't win in this game. In fact, most people turn out to be losers. But that does not mean that these losers are discarded from the world.

Bula True, some people win and some lose. But everyone has to take the field. You were never even interested to take to the field.

Sunil I have always been an introvert. Shaky and hesitant. And you know that. I find most people stupid, gross, cruel and dumb. What can I do?

Bula And that there is your pride. That is your superego. This thought process itself is wrong. Not all of your fingers are of the same size. But that does not mean you chop off your entire hand. You have to learn to adjust. And you have been distancing yourself from your surroundings ever since your college days. You have literally done one good thing in your entire life. And that is convincing Kurchi to fall in love and marry you.

Sunil Wow! You are suddenly quite the supporter of Kurchi I see. Who can say that there were at least two years when the two of you would turn away from each other should your paths cross accidentally.

Beat.

Look, Bula, just because I am holed up in your house does not give you the right to insult me like this. One can have problems in their personal lives. And Arun, if this random person had not threatened me out of the blue I would not have called for you people in the middle of a work day. You all should remember that if something untoward were to happen to me while I was living in this house the two of you would be the first people to get implicated.

Arun That is exactly what I am thinking about.

Beat.

Could it be that this person belonged to some kind of a secret society? The 'Four Quartets' or the 'Black Rose'?

Bula Are you serious? Stop it please! Your brain has rotted from incessantly reading those stupid hard boiled detective fiction.

Bula *snatches the book he is reading.*

Bula What the hell is this?

Arun It is a brand new book. Picked it up from Janbajar just yesterday. *The Hungry Ogres*.

Bula *throws the book away.* **Arun** *picks it up most nonchalantly and resumes reading.*

Bula (*addressing* **Sunil**) What are you going to do now? Have you told your 'wife' about it?

Sunil Kurchi? Are you crazy? Just like you she will immediately assume that I actually had a secret affair with this Lily Gupta.

Bula So what, let her think. She herself is living together with that family friend of yours. What is his name? Manoj something?

Sunil Manoj Haldar. Well, it is Kurchi's house after all. She can do as she pleases. She has her own right.

Bula What do you mean? She is not officially divorced yet. There are still laws in this country, aren't there? She is even going on trips apparently. Didn't they go to Ladakh or some place recently?

Sunil Sikkim.

Bula What she has been doing is a crime in the eyes of the law. She cannot live with this other guy. At least not until your divorce is finalized.

Sunil When the laws of the heart have been broken, what can the laws of the society do?

Beat.

Bula, I think I will reach out to Rabi once. Actually I will visit him either tomorrow or the day after.

Bula Rabi as in that man who works in the police?

Sunil Yes, he works for the IB.

Arun Sunil, could this man be a dragon in disguise?

Bula *glowers at* **Arun**. **Arun** *stops short of pursuing his train of thought.*

Arun I was wondering, Sunil, if you would be open to consulting with Chotok Chattaraj first before involving Rabi in this matter.

Sunil Who is that?

Arun Oh, he is a private investigator. I have only met him once. But he is simply awesome! Would you like to meet him?

Sunil Sure, if you insist. But let me talk to Rabi first.

Arun You can't imagine how excellent Chotok Chattaraj is. We should definitely visit him.

Bula God damn it! Will you please stop? All nonsensical stuff. So this Rabi, he is not a fan of you either, right? He took Kurchi's side when the two of you were having that falling out, isn't it?

Sunil *looks at* **Bula**. *Lights go down. The score picks up punctuated by* **Sunil***'s voice.*

Sunil Yes, that is correct. But Rabi has a weakness for me as well. After all we are college pals. Rabi felt that I am a nincompoop whereas Kurchi is very dynamic. That's up to him. He can think as he pleases. But I am confident that Rabi won't turn me down if I go and share this pickle that I am in.

Lights come back on. **Rabi***'s office is seen downstage centre.* **Rabi** *and* **Sunil** *sit facing each other.*

The score dies down gradually. **Rabi** *is writing something. He raises his head to look at* **Sunil**.

Rabi What did you say his name was, Srikanto Gupta?

Sunil Yes.

Rabi From Paikpara.

Sunil That's what he said.

Rabi Do you have his exact address?

Sunil How would I? I don't even know the guy.

Rabi And what about his dead wife?

Sunil I only met her that one time. In my clinic.

Rabi Your clinic? Oh, you mean the clinic that Kurchi paid for and the one that you used to take naps in?

Sunil Yes, that one.

Beat.

Rabi, won't you help me?

Rabi I will have to think about it. Helping you and depositing a post-dated cheque at a failing bank are identical endeavours.

Beat.

But I agree with you on one thing. You didn't have any relationship with this woman. There is no way. You don't have the kind of balls that one would need for anything romantic. I still can't imagine how you convinced Kurchi to date you.

But at least both of you were younger, so somehow something must have happened, a confusion. But now? An affair, that too by hiding it from your wife, and you? Yeah, no, I cannot imagine that.

Sunil That is exactly my point. But Srikanto Gupta is not saying that. He is insinuating that I have been going around with his wife for the last three months . . . and much more than just going around.

Rabi Hmm. And this woman, this Srikanto Gupta's wife, what does she look like?

Sunil Good-looking. I really don't remember very well. I have literally seen her only once.

Rabi But you at least remember that she was good-looking. That is good. At least you aren't completely sheepish yet. Are you absolutely sure that you have only seen that Lily Gupta once and in your clinic?

Sunil Come on, Rabi. What are you implying?

Rabi Fine, fine. So this Srikanto Gupta, what does he look like? How old do you think he is?

Sunil He is probably a little older than us. Looks raffish, like a thug. His sight inspires fear. And those eyes, *oy vey*.

Rabi (*laughs uproariously*) You castrated skittish asshole. Fine, let me look into it. How is Kurchi?

Sunil She is fine. I haven't spoken to her for the last few days. But I will be speaking with her today.

Rabi What do you mean? Are you guys meeting?

Sunil Yes, I have asked her to meet me at the Salt Lake CCD. We need to give our divorce a final legal shape. It's getting dragged out too much.

Rabi Why a CCD? Why can't you go home?

Sunil Nah, that's okay.

Rabi Why? Because you will run into that Manoj Haldar, isn't it? You know, Sunil, sometimes I feel like thrashing you hard. You asshole, why can't you get drunk, go over to Salt Lake and create a fucking scene?

That Manoj Haldar – a bloody paints salesman, beholden to bloody Kejriwal – three tight slaps under his ear and he will run away shitting his pants. Are you a human or a bloody earthworm?

Sunil Both.

Beat.

Rabi, you know that I don't drink. It doesn't really suit me. And the mere thought of yelling at someone sends shivers down my spine and my extremities retracting into my body. And besides that, didn't you just applaud Kurchi for her decision? Didn't you say that her marrying me was a mistake because our temperaments are so different?

Rabi *Arey,* I said all of that because I was upset with you. I was hoping that you would get angry and react to my accusations. You know, behave like a real man. And instead you are being fucking cordial.

Mockingly.

'Kurchi has every right to pursue another relationship. I have never lived up to her expectations.' Fucking sissy. I should kick you in the arse.

Beat.

Besides, I always detested this effeminate side of yours. I always thought of you as a mean person. Small-minded. I always felt that a large-hearted woman like Kurchi was unsuitable for a small-minded man like you. You should not have gotten married. Kurchi would sweat in the kitchen to feed you before dashing off to run her boutique. I have seen this with my own eyes. Fuck, Keka has never even poured me a glass of water all my life. And you bloody son of a pig – you fucking asshole.

Beat; drinks water.

Beat.

Wanna come over for dinner tonight? Keka and the kids have gone to her brother's house for the night. I have the apartment to myself. Let me treat you to some fine lobster and Black Label whisky. Come on over anytime after nine.

Sunil I can't make it tonight, sorry. And as I said, I don't drink and I am rather awful as a companion. You wouldn't be able to bear me! You will begin cussing me two drinks in. Also, brother, that was not me being courteous. I heard Manoj and Kurchi's conversations every night while lying in bed. Kurchi would stay up all night to talk with Manoj. All night long. I knew everything. Kurchi really wanted me to leave her house.

The stage goes dark as the score floats in. The interiors of a Café Coffee Day aka CCD are seen downstage right. **Sunil** *and* **Kurchi** *sit facing each other. Two cups of coffee sit in front of them.*

Sunil Where is Manoj?

Kurchi He is outside. Smoking a cigarette.

Sunil Hmm. He could've sat here. There are quite a few empty seats around.

Kurchi It's all right. Tell me.

Sunil Has Manoj stopped his photography?

Kurchi No he hasn't. Why do you ask?

Sunil Oh, I was scrolling through Facebook. Didn't see any new photos by him on your profile.

Kurchi Could be. I mustn't have noticed. What did you want to talk about that required us to meet?

Sunil Yeah, I wanted to discuss some things . . .

Suddenly stops short.

Manoj seems to have gained some weight, hasn't he?

Kurchi Please call Manoj over if you want to talk about him. He is right there. I am going to leave in that case.

Sunil No, no, please, have a seat.

Kurchi *sits down.*

Sunil Sorry. I – actually I don't know where and how to start. Anyway, Kurchi do you know someone called Srikanto Gupta.

Kurchi (*surprised*) No, who is he?

Sunil No one. Are you sure you don't know him? No one by this name has been in touch with you?

Kurchi No, not at all. I don't think so. What has happened?

Sunil No, nothing.

Kurchi Srikanto Gupta? No – I don't know that name. Tell me, what did you want to talk about?

Manoj *comes in from outside.*

Manoj Sorry to disturb you, Kurchi, your phone . . .

He hands **Kurchi** *her cell phone.*

Kurchi Hello? Oh, Payel, yes, tell me.

She gets up. **Sunil** *looks at* **Manoj**. *Offers a weak smile.*

Sunil How are you, Manoj?

Manoj Good.

Beat.

Sunil Don't you want to know how I am?

Manoj *doesn't speak.*

Sunil I am well. I am fine.

Beat.

Beat.

You both went to Sikkim recently on a tour?

Manoj (*looking away*) Yes.

Sunil Very nice. South Sikkim?

Manoj Yes.

Sunil Did you spot a good bloom? Or did you bird watch?

Manoj Well, we found some decent orchids, that's it. No interesting birds. The same as last time.

Sunil Very good, very good.

Manoj What do you mean very good? I just said nothing really interesting. But yes, we had some really clear weather.

Sunil Clear blue skies. Very good, wonderful.

Kurchi *comes back and hands the cell phone back to* **Manoj**.

Kurchi Payel. She wants to change her college and asked for my suggestion.

Sunil Payel?

Kurchi Manoj's sister. Cousin. Manoj, I will be done shortly. Please wait. And don't give me the phone if I get any other calls.

Manoj *pulls a shawl from a bag.*

Manoj Okay. Please wrap this shawl around you. It's pretty chilly inside. And the seasons are changing. You don't want to catch a cold now.

Kurchi (*smiling*) Thanks.

Manoj *wraps the shawl around* **Kurchi** *before leaving.*

Kurchi Yes, please go ahead.

Sunil (*clearing his throat*) I think we need to give our case a final legal shape now.

Kurchi Fine. I have no opposition. How would you want things settled?

Sunil However you want.

Kurchi I have decided that I am going to transfer our joint account at Axis Bank in your name.

Sunil Isn't that the account associated with your boutique? Why would you give that to me?

Kurchi That's where I have most of my savings, Sunil. Please keep it. I think you should be set for life with it.

Sunil Doing me a favour.

Kurchi No, you will need it. And besides that, the Baranogor clinic will be in your name as well. If you ever feel like it, resume a diligent practice. I think you can.

Sunil You have been saying this to me for the last ten years, Kurchi. Did anything happen? And a decade ago I was stronger, sharper and had warm blood coasting through my veins. I don't get enthused any more!

Kurchi And that is the problem, Sunil. I have been constantly telling you to not sit idly at home. Stay focused. Concentrate on your work. There are good people in the world too. Not everyone is a slob, or stupid, or crass.

Sunil You would continue that someone who constantly thinks of others as stupid is actually stupid themselves. You would say, why was I so arrogant? What was the source of that?

Kurchi No, it wasn't arrogance, not ego, but rather your inferiority complex. Or some kind of a lethargy. Actually you are very averse to hard work, Sunil. And from a young age too.

Sunil What can I do? I feel very sleepy. If I didn't like someone then I would fall asleep right in front of them after a mere ten minutes. I would fall asleep even in my medical school classes, if I did not like the teacher or their teaching. Otherwise I would have performed even better in that final semester.

Kurchi You are not professional at all, you know. Not at all. You had an opportunity to teach at a private medical college, but you quit after only a year on the pretext that your colleagues incessantly discussed their stock portfolios. I got you a column in a medical journal and you lasted three months. It was too boring for your taste. I got you a private clinic.

You would head over there at noon after lunch. And return late in the evening. Six months into the practice I went over to see that you had bolted the doors from inside and were enjoying a nap. I would have never believed that a person can wake up at ten thirty and go off to sleep again at one if I hadn't met you.

Sunil Let it be. It is all over anyway. What would you get from complaining about me?

Beat.

Kurchi, I do not need your Axis Bank account. I am going to sign that over to you. Instead give me the insurance papers and our Public Provident Fund, the PPF accounts. I had made some deposits to that account at some point. And I will write the clinic over to you as well.

Kurchi (*in a dull voice*) What am I going to do with the clinic?

Sunil Give it to Manoj.

Kurchi He won't need it. He has enough to not need anyone's help. You know that.

Sunil Oh yes. Haldar and Kejriwal. One of the largest paint companies in Eastern India. A reticent successful bachelor with the looks of a Jitendra and a Tom Cruise – unbelievable combination, no?

Kurchi Stop it. Stop ridiculing.

Sunil Sorry.

Beat.

Beat.

Kurchi Sunil, don't you want to start afresh? Can't you discover a motivated self? Can't you inspire yourself, challenge yourself to transform your surroundings? To completely transform it all with your willpower? Can't you?

Sunil What is the point of telling myself any of this? You won't be with me anymore.

Kurchi I don't know.

Sunil Oh you do, you know it very well.

Kurchi You can never tell what can happen, right?

Sunil No, you cannot. But I don't think I can ever change this habit of solitude that I have got used to. I am too used to this shrivelled-up existence.

Kurchi I know. You have always been like that. Tell me that you don't need me anymore. You haven't needed me for some time now. Accept that. Tell me, do you need me?

Beat.

Beat.

Sunil (*shaking his head*) No, I don't need you.

Kurchi (*her face tightens*) I am leaving. You will get everything that you are asking for. But not immediately. After some time.

Sunil Meaning?

Kurchi I need a little more time. I will let you know when it is time.

Sunil I thought we just settled everything.

Kurchi That is what you think. I don't.

Sunil That's strange. Kurchi, listen. What the hell?

Kurchi *stops him short. Waves to* **Manoj**. **Manoj** *steps inside.*

Manoj Let's go.

They get up to leave.

Sunil Manoj, do you know someone called Srikanto Gupta?

Manoj No, who is he?

Sunil Nobody. I got the name as a reference. Never mind, carry on.

Lights go down. **Sunil** *can be heard calling for a cup of coffee. The score wafts in. Lights go up on* **Sunil***'s room. A cell phone ring is heard.* **Sunil** *enters. He has a bag in his hand.*

Sunil Uff, where did I leave my phone this time?

Fishes out the phone after rummaging through his pockets.

Hello, hello, yes, Kurchi, tell me.

Kurchi *is seen stage right.*

Kurchi Hello, Sunil, can you hear me, Sunil?

Sunil Yes, I can hear you, tell me.

Kurchi Have you heard? Sunil, hello?

Sunil What? Hello, Kurchi, tell me? What?

Kurchi Someone tried killing Rabi by breaking into his flat this evening. He was struck on the head with an iron rod. He has been admitted to a nursing home. He is senseless. The doctors are saying that he is in a critical condition. Hello, Sunil, hello.

Sunil *cannot speak anymore, he disconnects. Because* **Srikanto Gupta** *has entered his room. He is holding the cricket bat in his left hand. He seems to be chewing on something and has a smile on his face. Music accompanies his entrance.*

Srikanto You must have heard by now? Here, I hit him with this. Strange man! He didn't have any security at the entrance to his building. Possibly because he was a cop. Over-confident. The door was wide open. I went straight upstairs.

Stops chewing for a second.

Oh, this, this is the food that your cook made for you. Fried eggplants and rotis. When I was climbing into the house through the bedroom windows she was rolling out the rotis.

She did not notice me at all. She left about thirty minutes ago. I got hungry waiting for you which is when I decided to help myself to these two rotis and fried eggplants. Don't worry, there's extras for you too, I checked.

Stops chewing again.

You have five more days, Dr Sen. Only five days. And I hope you have realized after today that I am not just joking with you. Wait, let me go rinse my mouth.

Goes inside. Leaves the cricket bat behind. The sound of a running tap. **Sunil** *is visibly shaken. He picks up the bat very slowly.* **Srikanto** *enters. He laughs.*

Srikanto *Arey*, what are you doing? Put that down, put that down!

The bat falls out of **Sunil***'s hand.* **Srikanto** *steps forward and picks it up.*

Srikanto It's heavy, isn't it? Very heavy. One would immediately be in the care of the messenger of death if you can land a diagonal blow to the back of the head. That Rabi fellow was hardy – solid. I think he works out everyday. I had to hit him twice. Don't worry, he won't survive. Dr Sen, you lost one of your influential cats. But I didn't have a choice you see. He was sending a steady stream of cops to my house. I knew he would. When you left his office this afternoon I was at the pan kiosk across the street. My back was turned away from you, that's why you probably missed me.

Beat.

Beat.

So then, five more days, right, Dr Sen? The inspector in charge of the Baruipur Police Station is waiting for you. I will be satisfied as soon as you submit the confession. Bye!

He turns to leave. Then stops and comes back.

Oh, here. A gift for you. I almost forgot.

He hands the bag over, picks up the bat and leaves. **Sunil** *is still shaken. He opens the bag very slowly. His hands soak in blood. He shakes the bag.*

We see the decapatitated head of the cat mentioned at the start of the play before the rest of the hapless animal falls out of the bag. **Sunil** *screams. His scream leads into the score before the overture takes over. Curtain.*

End of Act One.

Act Two

Scene One

Curtain up after the opening score to reveal a room in the upstage centre of the stage. It is the office of the detective **Chotok Chattaraj**. **Kurchi** *and* **Bula** *are seated.* **Arun** *enters.*

Arun Manoj didn't want to come inside.

Kurchi It's fine. Let him be outside.

Bula What good is going to come of this meeting anyway?

Arun If something were to be done it will only be done here. There is no point of going to the police. It will only set tongues wagging – a scandal. This is a better approach.

Bula Are you certain that this person is any good?

Arun You cannot even imagine. Just meet him once.

Kurchi What is his name? Chotok Chattaraj?

Arun Yes. Chotok Chattaraj. A private investigator. And not just a detective, he knows astrology and Feng Shui. He is an expert in cricket. He has apparently written a new book on cricket – *The Influence of Danguli and Roshkosh on Recent World Cricket.* Roshkosh, do you remember? We would play it in school. The more powerful the fist the harder the whack. Uff, you would get a serious sore arm after a round of playing.

But, anyway, the point is, the man knows a lot of things. Just like that detective fiction writer Swapan Kumar.

Apparently he used the alias Sri Bhrigu to practise astrology as well. And just like that guy Chotok Chattaraj is also a genius.

Bula How do you know him?

Arun A friend of mine told me about him. After he solved the mystery behind his grandmother's death. The police had ruled it as a murder.

And they had pinned the blame on my friend, the grandson. Chotok Chattaraj investigated to reveal that it was actually a suicide. Apparently the old hag had guzzled fifty-seven lyangra mangoes on the occasion of Ambubachi leading her bowels to explode into a fatal diarrhoea. The case of the granny made me a fan. You all know how much I love reading detective stories. I came down a few days ago to meet the man. A detective in real life! Not the Robert Blake of fiction, can you even imagine?

Gonjona Ganguly, *personal secretary to* **Chotok Chattaraj**, *enters. She has a notebook in her hand.*

Gonjona Hello, I am Gonjona Ganguly. I am private investigator Chotok Chattaraj's secretary. Do you folks have an appointment with Mr. Chattaraj?

Arun Yes, we do.

Gonjona (*opens her notebook*) 11 a.m. on the 21st – Mr Sen and Mr Dasgupta. Are you Mr Dasgupta?

Arun Yes. Mr Sen is on his way. Er, Ms Ganguly, how did you guess that I am Dasgupta?

Gonjona I didn't. Sir made the observation.

Arun What did he say?

Gonjona I went and told him that only one of the men have shown up thus far. He heard that and said that it must be Dasgupta.

Arun Oh wow, is that so? Was Mr Chattaraj observing us through that loophole?

Gonjona No, he is actually . . .

Arun In his laboratory? Examining twenty different kinds of tobacco?

Gonjona No, he is watching cricket. The Australia vs New Zealand series. He is going to be here soon.

Arun Madam, has he ever chased after trawler pirates on the Ganges with a submarine?

Bula What are you doing? Stop it!

Compounder **Pittu**, **Chattaraj***'s assistant enters.*

Pittu Gonjona, please go inside. I will take over.

Gonjona *leaves.*

Arun You are?

Pittu Compounder Pittu, assistant to Detective Chotok Chattaraj.

Arun Compounder?

Pittu Yes. Sherlock Holmes had a doctor and Chotok Chattaraj has a compounder. Pittu Compounder. Mr Chattaraj had started a homeopathic dispensary early in his career. I was his compounder there. And that is where I acquired the name Pittu the compounder.

Arun Wow! Wow!

Pittu For your information, Chotok Chattaraj is a conservative classical investigator. I should let you know at the get-go that he does not accept any trivial cases. By trivial I mean lacking intrigue. Mr Chattaraj is even willing to consider frivolous cases involving squash thefts and cattle pilfering. But cases like following a spouse on behalf of the other, tapping their cell phones, spying on a suspected third wheel by enduring mosquito bites outside their house, etc. is below Mr Chattaraj's dignity. Our agency hopes that you have not brought a frivolous case with any of the above characteristics involving the very intimate enmity between a couple to us.

Arun Not at all. We are here with an old school bloody whodunnit case.

Pittu Good. The agency would also like to request that you do not waste Mr Chotok Chattaraj's precious time with any mentally unstable clients, or as we say in layman's terms, a crazy person or a nut job. It is important that we make all of this clear in light of the rate at which the number of crazy people are multiplying all around us.

Arun Our case is perfectly normal. No Kanke, no Lumbini. A regular intriguing case. The agency can be assured that none of us bite.

Pittu Good. The agency can now summon Chotok Chattaraj.

He takes a flute out from his pocket and blows into it. The lights dim. **Detective Chotok Chattaraj** *enters from behind the stage and walks down. He is wearing a yellow tracksuit and sunglasses.* **Pittu** *stops playing the flute.* **Chotok** *looks at the rest of the group on stage.*

Chotok Where is Mr Sen?

Arun He is on his way.

Chotok You will be four when he arrives. Good, good, four of you. All four at the same time. You know, Pittu, there come certain times when due to some inexplicable mystery four people rise a cut above the rest in their respective milieus. Take Bengali literature for example: Bibhuti, Manik, Tarashankar and Satinath. Or Bengali theatre: Shombhu, Bijan, Utpal and Ajitesh. Or classical music: Faiyaz Khan, Abdul Karim Khan, Enayet Khan and Nissar Hussain Khan. But, Pittu, do you know when was the last time a group of four – a quad – left their mark not just regionally but globally as well?

Pittu No doctor I do not know? Who would they be?

Arun Can I? Byomkesh, Kiriti, Hukakashi and Robert Blake.

Chotok Incorrect! Hukakashi precedes them by quite a few years. And none of these are international names anyway. The last internationally renowned Indian quad were Bishen Singh Bedi, Erapalli Prasanna, Bhagwat Chandrasekhar and Srinivasraghavan Venkatraghavan.

Just like classical music, the Japanese and the Bermuda Triangle, spin bowling is a mysterious treasure. And the spinner . . .

Beat.

What do you think of their case, compounder? Is it a leg break or a googly?

Pittu We have just tossed the coin, Doctor. About to take the field after initial pleasantries.

Chotok (*shakes hands with* **Arun**) And you are the vice-captain! Where is the captain then?

Kurchi *had been on the phone in the interim. She hangs up.*

Kurchi Arun, Sunil is here.

Arun Ah, the captain is here!

Sunil *enters supporting himself on* **Manoj**. *He looks particularly devastated.*

Arun And here, here is our captain, Sunil Sen.

Chotok (*after shaking hands*) And what about him?

Sunil (*pointing at* **Manoj**) He is my wife's husband.

Chotok What?

Arun Never mind that. I have a question: are you able to tell a lot of things about people by simply looking at them, like a detective?

Chotok (*smiles*) Sure. Some things.

Beat.

For example . . .

Looks at **Manoj** *carefully.*

Chotok You are an only child. Your family owns a brickyard. You recently came down with a fever. You are a hapless alcoholic.

And you have a mastiff for a pet. This much for now. Am I right?

Everyone is taken aback. **Manoj** *stumbles.* **Arun** *supports him from falling down.*

Arun (*barely controlling his excitement*) That was just BRILLIANT. Just BRILLIANT, how did you know all that?

Manoj Yes, seriously, how did you work all of that out?

Chotok (*smiles*) Gopal Basu was struggling with Bhagwat Chandrasekhar's leg breaks during a Moin-ud-daula Trophy game. At the end of an over he went over to his partner Gundappa Vishwanath and asked him what his strategy to play the spinner should be. An indifferent Vishwanath offered a stoic solution, 'Why, just carve him away with square cuts.'

Beat.

The magic loses its sheen when the trick is revealed. But we are detectives so we have to explain our deductions. And therefore I shall explain.

(*To* **Manoj**.) I can see a photo of your parents peeking from your shirt pocket. Why would anyone travel with a photo of their parents in their shirt pocket unless they were an only child, right? There is an old slightly red and brown stain on your shoes. Tell-tale signs of a brickyard. I see the outlines of a Crocin tablet next to the photo of your parents. I deduced that you must be recovering from a fever. But you want to be cautious and therefore you are carrying meds with you. Alcoholic, because your lips are moist. Drunks usually have that situation. There's a scar from a dog bite on your right leg just above the ankle. It's not a very deep scar though. The nature of the bite and the shape of the teeth tells me that your pet must be a mastiff. So, what do you think?

Manoj Marvellous!

Pittu The fiery Shoaib Akhtar looks rather hapless right now. His body language tells us that right now he is thinking just like his predecessors Wasim Akram, Imran Khan and Waqar Younis did when Sachin Tendulkar played his first Test match in Faisalabad: Get the petite fellow first or he will get all of us. There is only God in cricket and his name is Sachin Ramesh Tendulkar.

Manoj Indeed.

(*Addressing* **Chotok**.) It is now time for you to hang up your boots.

Chotok What do you mean?

Manoj Is it my turn now?

Takes out the photo from his pocket.

Alright, so these are the spiritual guides to our family and his wife. Srimat Swami Dipankar. We are three brothers and two sisters. All of us are well settled in life. Secondly, yes, my father ran a business, but an insurance company, not a brickyard. This reddish stain in my shoes is from the construction site right next to this place. I was walking around the construction area. I must have kicked up some brick dust.

Takes the supposed medicine out from his pocket.

This is not a Crocin tablet. Rather an amulet that has been handed down in my family. It is supposed to be very lucky and that is why I keep it with me all the time. I had several cups of tea because I got bored waiting for Sunil. That is why my lips look moist. Not only do I not drink but I also dislike it with a passion. And this scar above my ankle is rather old. As a kid I took a stumble at the Chandpal Ghat of the Hooghly and bruised myself. The scar never went away.

Beat.

Beat.

Beat.

Kurchi, I will be outside waiting for you folks to be done.

He leaves. Silence descends for a little bit before **Pittu** *pierces it.*

Pittu There was a top spin from Abdul Qadir which fooled even the master batsman David Gower. By the time he figured the delivery out he had already lost his middle stump.

Bula Ei, you, please shut up.

Kurchi Really disgusting! Where have you brought us to?

Bula (*addressing* **Arun**) Why do you have to pull off these random shenanigans? You have lost your marbles reading those trashy novels all day long. Otherwise who would drag us to meet such a clown.

Arun It's not that at all. Actually Sunil eventually agreed to meet with him. And so I thought, why not, let us.

Pittu *takes the flute out from his pocket and plays a tune on it.* **Chotok** *is sitting down, exasperated.* **Pittu** *walks over to him and puts his head on his shoulder.*

They both seem to be on the verge of tears.

Sunil Wait . . .

Beat.

Beat.

I . . . I want . . . I want to share my troubles with this person.

Pittu *stops playing the flute.*

Kurchi What? Come on Sunil. Come, let's go.

Sunil No. I like this. I really like everything going on here. After a while. And above all, I get the feeling that this person makes mistakes. But he also knows how to own up to mistakes. And not in a pretentious way, sincerely owning up. How many of us are able to do that? I absolutely want to share my case with you.

Chotok *gets up from his stupor. Gheorghe Zamfir's 'The Lonely Shepherd' wafts in as the score envelopes the moment.*

Chotok You are absolutely right, brother. Owning up to one's mistakes. And not as a fake gesture, not to make someone else seem small, not to serve some kind of self-interest or not even for cheap popularity. Just a good old confession. First to one's own self and then to the world – how many people can do that? How many people are able to humbly point out their mistake? Even at your own expense? Gundappa Vishwanath was able to. Courtney Walsh was able to. You know, Mike Brearley says that he remembers Sunny Gavaskar admonishing himself even after hitting a six with a straight bat. Because he was still getting set which required watching the ball and taking it slow. Why would he take such a risky shot then? Because now his concentration was compromised.

Brearley had said that he had never seen anything like this and he was sure he wouldn't ever see anything similar in the future either. Zahir Abbas had done the same for Azharuddin. Azhar was going through a bad time then. The fine player who had begun his Test career with three consecutive centuries in his first three games got benched for the Karachi game. He made it to the playing eleven at the very last moment when Raman Lamba was ruled out with a fractured finger on the morning of the game. Zahir Abbas then called Azharuddin over and asked him to change the style of his grip. That was the root of his problem. Azhar paid heed and scored a ton in the very next game – his first overseas century for India.

Beat.

This, this realization of one's mistake, owning up to it, or listening to and making changes based on someone else pointing out a mistake is a rare quality, right? How many people are able to do that? Dr Sen, I want to know all about your case. I have advanced in years, my guesswork is not as sharp as it used to be. I mostly spend my days dwelling in the past and obsessing over cricket. I am gradually becoming an expert at crushing and containing all my emotions and feelings inside myself. But I still am the investigator Chotok Chattaraj. On behalf of all those people who make mistakes on the basis of a conviction, and even those whose greed, jealousy, betrayal, revenge and solitude ultimately amount to an immodest child's play thanks to some divine touch, I can tell that you seem like someone who has gradually learnt the art of being quiet. You have been able to adjudicate that it is better to destroy yourself rather than someone else. You have learnt to step outside of yourself and evaluate yourself honestly and completely. I salute you and humbly accept your case irrespective of wherever it takes us with it.

Beat.

Waits for **Pittu***; then says.*

Chotok *Arey*, applaud now. Do I have to tell you even that?

Pittu *applauds. 'The Lonely Shepherd' increases in volume. Lights go down. When the lights come back on we see* **Kurchi** *and* **Bula** *seated opposite each other at a CCD, coffee in front of them.*

Kurchi Bula, I know you don't really like me and that you really love your brother. But what he did to me eventually is not right. It's not like that he physically or verbally assaulted me, neither did he cheat on me, but is that all? Your brother does not understand the meaning of an actual relationship, Bula.

Bula It's not always possible to understand time. In fact that can only intensify problems, rather than solve them.

Beat.

It's not that I dislike you, Kurchi. But I get annoyed at times with your pointless arrogance.

Smiles.

It would be strange if you thought women are the worst enemy of women.

Kurchi Please don't misunderstand me, Bula. I like you as well. But Sunil's issues are very psychological and deep rooted. You cannot see them from the outside. At all. He is a split personality.

Bula Possibly, I don't deny that.

Kurchi For example, he could never accept the fact that I am likable or that people are readily attracted to me.

Bula (*smiles*) You mean he was always jealous of your so-called popularity.

Kurchi Not just that, he also understood that people don't particularly like him. And that made him a very complex kind of a person. It is not easy to handle him, Bula.

Bula There is complexity in every one's lives. But they are very different from each other. Every one is happy and unhappy too. In their own ways. Anyway, forget all that. Drink your coffee.

Kurchi Is Sunil visiting that investigator Chotok Chattaraj even today?

Bula Yes. This would be their fifth seating in three days.

Kurchi The man is useless. He won't be able to do anything. We must go to the cops. Did that Srikanto Gupta visit him again?

Bula No. And I don't think he's going to come back again. Arun has hired this gigantic security guard for the Baruipur house on the advice of Chotok Chattaraj. I don't think Srikanto Gupta will dare to be in the vicinity of the house.

Smiles.

Sunil was always a coward and he's become a complete earthworm now.

Kurchi (*hesitatingly*) Bula, you haven't seen this Lily Gupta, right?

Bula No, not at all, are you crazy?

Beat.

Do you think that my brother actually had a relationship with this Lily Gupta? Do you think Srikanto Gupta's accusation is correct?

Kurchi Who knows? I am indifferent to it.

Almost an aside.

I am certain that this Lily Gupta was very ordinary. Sunil's choice after all.

Bula Yes, one can ascertain my brother's choices easily by looking at you.

Kurchi (*angry*) Don't be ridiculous. How can you compare me with that Lily Gupta? Whatever little Sunil has accomplished today is because of me. Anyone else would have abandoned it all and left years ago.

Bula I mean eventually you are leaving him as well. You couldn't stay with him after all. And for Manoj Haldar, eh? So, where is this Manoj today?

Kurchi Oh, they are at the hospital. Rabi is being released today. Sunil is going as well. Manoj will head to the airport from there. He has some work in Delhi.

Beat.

Is Sunil travelling with his security in tow?

Bula He did for a few days. Now he is driving by himself again. But the security is posted round the clock outside the house.

Beat.

When are you finalizing your divorce, Kurchi?

Kurchi (*smiles*) Let's see. I will let you know.

Bula Yes, let me know.

Beat.

I just wanted to share an observation of mine.

Kurchi What is it?

Bula Most people would assume from the outside that you keep Manoj on a short leash. I get the impression based on my conversations with him that Manoj is quite dominating although he presents himself as a docile person to the outside world. Am I wrong?

Kurchi (*serious*) Manoj is a good person. He gives me a lot of time. And he also listens to me. The main difference between Manoj and Sunil is that Manoj is very obedient. These days I feel like that is even more important than romance in a relationship. I hope you feel the same way too.

Bula Hmm.

Beat.

I am of the opinion that women are much better humans than men, isn't that right?

Kurchi I am of the same opinion. But a bad woman is far worse than the worst man.

Bula Maybe so.

Beat.

Irrespective of opinions to the contrary I like to think of my brother as a good man. And I am not saying that just because he is my brother. He is . . . he is misunderstood by many.

Kurchi (*smiles*) You are among those that misunderstand him too, Bula.

Bula *smiles as the score envelops the stage and looks at* **Kurchi**. *Lights go down.*

Lights go up on stage left. **Chotok***'s office.* **Chotok**, **Pittu** *and* **Sunil** *are seen.*

Sunil Mr Chattaraj, I am ready for the divorce. But in spite of everything being final, Kurchi wants to avoid any discussion on the divorce. I don't know why.

Chotok Well, this means that she still possesses you. She may not love you but she still wants to possess you.

Sunil But this, this is a kind of incivility, right? Trying to retain control over everything.

Chotok Yes, indeed. But that is human nature. Humans tend to value each other like this even while insulting or neglecting them.

Sunil But this is not right. Not right at all. Not the right mentality. When everything is said and done then we should take a clear decision. Otherwise the other person is just being taken along for a ride. Not right at all.

Chotok Hmm. Anyway, so, she will marry Manoj after the divorce. What will you do? Have you thought about that?

Sunil I don't know. I haven't thought about it. I am sure I will do something. Or maybe I won't. Will just live my days. I mean that is not very easy now, is it? Just living through the days? Not everyone's cup of tea.

Chotok No, it isn't. And I will ask Kurchi to finalize the divorce with you as well. But please remember one thing, Dr Sen. You will be by yourself after the divorce. Completely alone. And Srikanto Gupta and his henchmen will hound you for the rest of your life. In the same way that Roy Gilchrist and Wes Hall hounded Pankaj Roy in that infamous Eden Test match of 1958. And you must know that Gilchrist's beamers were delivered at a menacing pace of ninety miles per hour. And they never hit the ground, full toss. And their target: Pankaj Roy's bespectacled face. Isn't Srikanto Gupta like that Gilchrist? For whom be it cricket or life, it is all a murderous plot. A brutal perverted attack.

Sunil (*stands up*) I am . . . I am not feeling well. I will take your leave now, Mr Chattaraj.

Chotok And where are you headed to now?

Sunil Hospital. To visit my friend, the cop. The one assaulted by Srikanto Gupta with that iron mace behind his head. He miraculously survived the attack. They will release him today.

Chotok Hmm. Okay, go. I went and visited Rabi yesterday as well. But he doesn't remember anything about the assault. Anyway, in spite of several requests you are not letting the security accompany you, Dr Sen. This is not right. I hope you know that even the great Sunny Gavaskar started using a skull cap towards the end of his career. Bear this in mind.

Sunil Mr Chattaraj, I do not understand cricket. But I understand this much that if someone is not willing to play and wants to forfeit the game then that wish should be respected.

Unfortunately, my wife does not seem to understand that. I feel insecure from the inside, Mr Chattaraj. What good is then all this external security for me?

He leaves. **Chotok** *sits contemplating.*

Chotok Compounder?

Pittu Doctor?

Chotok Get me that guy on the phone in half an hour, will you please?

Pittu Which guy? That . . . Arun?

Chotok No, no, the husband of Sunil's wife, Manoj Haldar.

The stage goes dark and the score wafts in. Lights go up on centre stage. A hospital bed. **Rabi** *sits on it with a bandage covering his head. He looks rested and recovered.* **Manoj** *and* **Arun** *are on either side of the bed. A* **Police Orderly** *stands to one side.* **Rabi***'s wife* **Keka** *stands on the other side from the* **Orderly**.

Rabi Ah . . . urgh . . .

Arun They are releasing you tomorrow itself. Two days before schedule. You are fit now.

Rabi Yes, but the pain is still there. Here, that's where he hit me.

Arun What were you doing when the assault happened?

Rabi Oh, I had just settled down for my diurnal?

Arun Diurnal?

Rabi *Arey*, whisky. Had just put two cubes of ice and poured the soda into the glass. My wife wasn't home. The cook was frying up some mango fish in the kitchen. And I was listening to music – Pankaj Udhaas singing Chitthi Ayee Hain, gazal on my music system. And then I heard a noise . . .

Sunil *slowly enters* **Rabi***'s hospital room.*

Rabi I think my security person downstairs had left to get smokes. The blow landed on the back of my head even before I had had the time to look behind me. I don't remember anything afterwards.

Keka I came back running from my parents' home that night itself. I can't tell you how I've spent these last few days. He wouldn't have survived. I prayed to Ma Tara every single day. We had visited Tarapith just last month to offer *puja*. He refused to listen to me and didn't fast until the *puja* like I asked him to.

Rabi Stop it please! You have been whining about the same thing constantly. And she has been at it ever since I regained consciousness. I swear even Srikanto Gupta's mace is better than this whining. *Arey*, Sunil, how are you doing, my man?

Sunil I am fine. But your police still hasn't been able to apprehend Srikanto Gupta.

Rabi He will be caught. Don't worry. Where will he escape to?

Keka Mr Bijoy visited this morning. And he said that they are conducting an extensive manhunt. Combing every inch. They got a tip that apparently he was seen in Beleghata last evening. He escaped before the police could get there.

Rabi I need to look through Lily Gupta's post mortem report. But first let me get released and then we will see. Thank you for visiting, Mr Arun and all of you. Manoj, when are you back from Delhi?

Manoj I will be back tomorrow. I am only going for a day.

Rabi Hey, Sunil, come here.

Sunil *comes close to* **Rabi**. **Rabi** *whispers something into his ears.* **Manoj** *gets a call and steps aside to attend to it.* **Arun** *and* **Keka** *step forward.*

Arun I will lend you this book, *The Hungry Ogres*, it's the fifth title on the Detective Chamanlal series. There is a similar attempt to murder case in the novel. But the highlight has to be this hair-raising fight between Chamanlal and Khokkos, as in the villain, on top of the Eiffel Tower. You would love it.

Keka *offers a thrilled greeting.* **Manoj** *comes back after finishing his call.* **Rabi** *speaks while laughing out loud.*

Rabi Jackass, and this is why I think you are a castrated sheepish asshole.

The stage goes dark. **Sunil** *enters his Baruipur residence and turns on the lights. We see* **Srikanto Gupta** *seated on a chair.* **Sunil***'s* **Security Guard** *can be seen further upstage. He lies in a bloodied heap.* **Sunil***'s bag falls from his hand in fear.*

Srikanto Good evening, Dr Sen. Come on in. I was waiting for you. What are you looking at? Oh, your security? There he is. I don't think he will make it. I mean what kind of security is this anyway? This tin soldier. One blow behind the head and the man was reduced to a plank.

Beat.

Beat.

Today is the eighth day. Yesterday was the seventh day, a week. I had planned on visiting you yesterday but then I learnt about the raid on my friend Bulton's house in Beleghata. I figured that the police dogs must be going around sniffing the hair around my arse. But my name is Srikanto Gupta – if I decide to find you, then find you I will.

Sunil *tries to escape.* **Srikanto** *lunges after him. The two tumble together into a heap.*

Srikanto There is nothing to worry about, Dr Sen. I won't kill you. I will chase after you all your life.

I will stick to you forever until you go to the local police station and confess the truth. I went after your friend Rabi and now your security. And now I am going to kill that bloody sleuth you have hired, Chotok Chattaraj. But before that . . .

Sunil What?

Srikanto Operation Kurchi . . .

Sunil What?

Srikanto Why should only my wife die, Dr Sen? While your wife gets to wear make-up, wear sunglasses and enjoy the sights around Lachun, Lachen, Yumthang? Go bird watching? Star gazing? Take their fancy ride for weekend trips to Garpanchakot and Galudi?

While I sit hear tearing at my pubes? While my wife burns on a pyre in the Kashipur crematorium your wife gets to visit Rangpur in Darjeeling to click photos with her new paramour! Photography! How dare she? I will reduce your wife to a photograph in a photo album today, Dr Sen. A mere photograph.

Sunil No.

Srikanto It's just you and me and me and you. Everyone else is a bastard. Bloody sons of whores, you will play divorced to the outside world and keep doing these coochie-cooing on the inside, eh? Fuckers! It's me or that Kurchi Sen today!

He leaves **Sunil** *and gets up.* **Sunil** *sits panting.*

Srikanto The news will reach you tomorrow morning. That half wife of yours . . . dead! Her playing half a Sen while living as half a Haldar will soon be over. And if you don't go the local police station and confess by tomorrow then I will fuck up that gunky-eyed sister of yours and that fubsy husband of hers. Where, where is your fucking cell phone?

He grabs **Sunil***'s cell phone from his pocket.*

Srikanto Ah here it is. Here, and turned off. I am not gonna let you call for the cops as soon as I leave here.

He kicks **Sunil***, picks up the bat and then leaves.* **Sunil** *sits in a stupor for a little bit. And then somehow gets up and stumbles off the stage. The stage goes dark before the score wafts back in.*

Gradually a song takes over the score. It is a Bengali mystical song, 'Tomar ghore bosot kore koyjane, mon jano na . . .,' which roughly translates to, 'You don't know the people who live within you.' Lights go up ever so slightly on stage. We see **Kurchi***'s Salt Lake home. She is listening to the song and humming while running a comb through her hair. We figure out that the music is playing over the radio. She gets a call.*

Kurchi *picks it up.*

Kurchi Hello, yes, tell me. Have you had your dinner? Good, I hope you had a stew? Good. Ah, Manoj, I keep telling you to not have greasy stuff like tadka dal, especially after eating a light stew. Your cholesterol is bound to escalate if you have so much oil after boiled green papayas!

Beat.

Mr Prakash was not upset about this Delhi trip, right? No, I mean, you asked for his permission for this trip, I hope.

Yes, yes, I know, you don't do anything without his approval. Oh, his and mine approval, isn't that right? Okay, I am going to let you go now, yes, bye.

Hangs up and then gets a start.

Who is it? Who's there? Oh, a cat!

She settles down again. And then resumes humming the tune. After a bit, she is about to turn around when **Srikanto Gupta** *creeps up from behind her and grabs her by the neck. She struggles to break free for a bit before someone else sneaks up from behind* **Srikanto** *and grabs him from behind. This person overcomes* **Srikanto** *and pushes him down on the floor.*

We see it is **Chotok***. He is holding a gun in his hand.*

Chotok Hands up, put your hands up. Get up, madam.

Kurchi Who is this?

Pittu *enters.*

Pittu Out! Out! And out! And we have been denied the chance to witness a fine century today.

Chotok Is it Srikanto Gupta? Or . . .

Pulls the mask off **Srikanto***'s face.*

Chotok Dr Sunil Sen.

It is **Sunil Sen**. *He has a completely different demeanour. Ferocious. He pants. It might be apropos to mention here that for the sake of the drama,* **Sunil** *enters this scene dressed and made up to look like* **Srikanto**.

Chotok Ah, It is like a Dr Jekyll and Mr Hyde. Sunil and Srikant are the one and the same.

He deliberately pronounces Srikant and not **Srikanto** *to emphasize the cricketing pun.*

Like Merchant and Mushtaq. Or Mankad and Roy. These are opening batting pairs. Starting the innings together. To get into more detail, Ravi and Shastri are the same, as are Arun and Lal, and Manoj and Prabhakar. Partners. But a lot of people often can't recognize their partners. Sunil is lucky, he could.

(*Addressing* **Kurchi**.) Madam, Manoj did not go to Delhi today. Upon my suggestion he has been waiting behind the wall opposite your house. And enjoying mosquito bites of course.

Pittu Although being eaten alive by mosquitoes opposite one's own house is no problem at all, especially since this is no trivial matter.

Chotok Rabi and I were near at hand. Manoj called me around twenty past eleven to inform us that the eagle had landed. I knew that Srikanto Gupta would appear today. Because Dr Sen knew that Manoj would be out of town with work. Which is why I coaxed the doctors into releasing Rabi two days ahead of schedule. I visited him in the hospital the day before he was released and explained everything to him. And then the two of us came up with this plan. Dr Sen left home to kill his wife in the car that his wife had given him. Around half past ten. Of course he didn't forget to knock his security guard unconscious before he left. His plan was to kill his wife, go back home and lie unconscious there. He had hoped that the following morning Arun and the others would call the cops or visit him when they found his phone switched off.

Arun *and* **Bula** *enter.* **Chotok** *gestures at them to sit.* **Rabi** *walks up to* **Sunil**.

Rabi You, you, you, how could you, Sunil? You tried killing me?

Sunil *doesn't speak.*

Chotok You must have always been really insolent towards him. And besides, he was convinced that not only did you support Kurchi madam during their divorce but you were also really pleased over it.

Sunil *keeps looking at* **Rabi**.

Chotok He must have heard from you that you would be by yourself that night. Dr Sen has been to your house a million times. He knows the interiors by heart. And he entered through the main entrance. Your security wasn't present downstairs.

Arun How did you figure all of this out?

Chotok (*smiles*) My guesswork might be wrong, Mr Arun, but my philosophical powers can't be mistaken.

Bula What do you mean?

Chotok Meaning, I might be a mixed-up, shaky and random detective but I am first and foremost a philosopher. A failed philosopher but a philosopher nonetheless. I get duped because of my assumption, because of my belief that humans are programmed to be good. I repeatedly place my faith in this ideal and get deceived. But nevertheless this conviction of mine refuses to leave my being and the way I perceive the world around me.

Beat.

Beat.

Don't think for a second that Sunil Sen shared his case with me because he was impressed with my vulnerability. He smugly assumed that I was a nincompoop, kind of like Bhagwat Chandrasekhar with the bat, highest score zero. But he didn't realize that I was basically the all-rounder Victor Trumper, who had once sent a ball soaring past the stands to shatter the windows of a neighbourhood shop. I had my doubts about the existence of this Srikanto Gupta during our very first appointment. I started looking into the matter. And I learnt that Srikanto Gupta was among the twenty-five fatalities of a bus accident between Indore and Baroda three days before Lily Gupta went into Dr Sen's clinic. The man had been missing for four years prior to this. In fact, Srikanto had married a Gujarati woman. Of course, Lily Gupta could never accept any of this. She suffered from chronic depression, which was exacerbated when she learnt about her husband's death.
And she went to Dr Sen's clinic and shared all this with her physician. Isn't that right, Dr Sen?

Sunil *nods in the affirmative before speaking. He sounds tired.*

Sunil She said that they do not have any family anywhere. Her husband had been missing for a few years and she had just heard a rumour that he might be dead. I asked her to go to the police. She said that the cops had told her a couple of years ago that her husband was missing and there was very little that they could do to help. They had basically given up. And then she requested sleeping pills. I gave her the name but did not write her a prescription.

Chotok Of course he didn't write her a prescription. Because he had already started picturing Srikanto Gupta. He figured out that Srikanto was going to make his debut very soon. As significant a start as Kapil Dev Nikhanj's debut was for Indian cricket.

Srikanto *arrives at the corner of the stage adapting the stance of a cricket bowler. And then* **Sunil** *and* **Srikanto** *start dancing together. The dance of the alter ego. When the dance stops* **Bula** *walks up to* **Sunil**. **Srikanto** *freezes.*

Bula How could you, brother, how could you kill my cat? My dear darling cat, why did you have to kill it?

Sunil *looks at* **Bula** *and then claps his hand.* **Srikanto** *breaks out of the freeze and walks next to* **Bula** *while talking. Everyone slips into the darkness. Only* **Chotok** *is seen with* **Sunil** *and* **Srikanto**.

Srikanto Because I fucking wanted to. So what? I wanted to kill you too. But could not. After all you are my own sister. But if the right opportunity presented itself, I would have killed you too. And that real pussy of yours, your sheepish coward husband.

Sits down.

Fucker, you stay in your husband's house and live off of him, just eat and sleep all day, you don't work but take fucking pride in flaunting your status, flirting with other young men and obsess over your self-interests. And your spineless jack ass of a husband understands everything but turns a blind eye to it all by burying himself behind a pile of cheap detective fiction. I may have failed but someone will come and set your funeral pyres alight. Mark my words.

Stops. **Bula** *and* **Arun** *leave.*

Srikanto I was certain that Rabi was dead. I had hit him squarely behind his head. The bastard has been taunting me since our college days. The sheer joy of swinging the iron rod towards his skull. An indescribable feeling! Oh, unimaginable thrill! But I learnt from Kurchi – Rabi didn't die. Anger coasted through my body, burning every inch of my being. I saw Bula's darling cat roaming in front of my eyes – I picked up the kitchen knife and . . .

Beat.

Silence. **Srikanto** *stops.* **Sunil** *starts speaking. It's just the two of them who remain on stage along with* **Chotok**.

Sunil You know, Mr Chattaraj, I have always been very cowardly and introverted. Right from my boyhood days. I realized fairly early on that I don't quite fit in with my surroundings. And consequently my surroundings were being antagonistic beyond words towards me. I felt like I had no choice but to begin disliking everything and everyone around me. I was compelled to find everything around me repugnant. I was becoming violent inside. Busybodies, fools, arrogance and liars angered me. I wanted to thrash them but couldn't. My instinctive familial sense of decency prevented me from doing that. And, of course, my cowardice. I cannot tolerate loud voices since my childhood. They make my ears ring. I have always been wary of loud verbal outbursts. And amidst all this I met Kurchi. Kurchi was a wonderful woman, Mr Chattaraj, very different from most women. She has done a lot for me. But it must have been difficult for her to accept me. Accept my nature. Because I had already begun withdrawing myself from my surroundings. Perhaps from Kurchi and myself as well. Our relationship died gradually. Very well. I wasn't actually opposed to it. Manoj and Kurchi fell in love with each other. Which was great. I wasn't opposed to that either. I left her Salt Lake residence. Bula's husband Arun had a garden house near their home in Baruipur, started living there while looking for paid accommodation options. In the meantime Kurchi and Manoj moved in together in her house.

Very well. I asked Kurchi for a divorce. But Kurchi said . . .

Kurchi *appears downstage left.* **Sunil** *walks over to her.*

Kurchi What is the need for a divorce? Why don't you be the way you are and let me be the way I am? I don't feel enthused to pursue a divorce and all the fuss that it would entail, Sunil.

Sunil So, you won't give me a divorce then?

Kurchi You won't be able to be without me for long, Sunil.

Lights go down. **Kurchi** *leaves.* **Srikanto** *speaks when the lights come back on.*

Srikanto You get the plan, right? What a scheme, eh? She is keeping the path back to me open on one side, while living it up with Manoj on the other. And that poor fucker doesn't even know that sooner or later Kurchi is going to kick him to the curb and go off with a Fahrukh or a Nayek. But one can never tell how any of these will end and so keep Sunil at hand as a last fucking resort. Especially if there is trouble at an older age. And it is quite possible that these men like Manoj are knowingly setting foot in the trap. You have no idea, Mr Chattaraj, the depths that men can sink to for lust. And what is funny is that they try to pass this off as love.

Smiles.

Men are rapists? Yes. Molesters? Yes. But they start their sexual misadventures by getting their own asses fucked.

He comes and sits next to **Srikanto**.

Sunil Kurchi refused me a divorce. And the same day Lily Gupta came to my clinic and told me about the possible death of her husband Srikanto Gupta and her depression. She asked for sleeping pills. I gave her the name but did not give her a formal prescription. And then waited to see the news of her suicide in the papers. Srikanto Gupta came to my house the day the papers broke the news.

Sunil *talks to* **Srikanto**. **Srikanto** *responds in a machine-like monotone.*

Sunil Mr Gupta, you will listen to every word of mine, right?

Srikanto Yes, sir, I will.

Sunil You will kill my friend Rabi, right? You will not say no to it?

Srikanto I won't refuse. I will kill him.

Sunil And Kurchi after that?

Srikanto Yes.

Sunil Bula and Arun next?

Srikanto Yes, sir.

Sunil You don't need to kill Manoj. Congratulate him on my behalf. Just box his ears a couple of times and kick him in the arse. And you would do that, right?

Srikanto Yes, sir.

The score floats in. Everyone leaves the stage. Only **Chotok, Srikanto** *and* **Sunil** *remain.*

Chotok Are you a misogynist, Dr Sen, woman hater?

Sunil (*smiles*) A misogynist? Like Nietzsche? You know this word is Greek, right, Mr Chattaraj? Woman hater. *Misos* is hate. And *gunē* is woman. Incidentally, the word *gunē* is also the source for gynaecology.

Laughs.

Beat.

If women can be misandrists, men haters, then why can't men be misogynists? All laws, all social advantages are geared towards women, and if a man were to be polite, courteous and introverted then those become his weak points, right? The law turns a blind eye to women who are actual victims of abuse.

And women who are just as corrupt, nefarious, fake and power hungry like men take advantage of the situation. They sell their misandry to survive and thrive in this society.

Srikanto Fuckers, men are womanizers! And what about women? Aren't they meneaters? And so be it. No one has said no to being one. But then why the holier than thou attitude? Why all this fuckery with 'heart' and 'soul'?

Sunil Oh, Srikanto, take your leave now. We will need you later.

Srikanto *leaves.* **Sunil** *remains alone on stage with* **Chotok**.

Sunil Excuse his language. He is a little rough. I hope you will not mind his overuse of expletives.

Chotok (*smiles*) You know I was having this strange feeling while listening to you and Srikanto speak. I was wondering if the institution of marriage will continue to remain relevant fifty or sixty years from now. I mean it perhaps will. In some village around Kolkata, or in a remote corner of Tamil Nadu or in some parts of North India, Maharashtra, or perhaps in Gujarat. But I was wondering what would happen if this institution lost its relevance? Absolutely nothing! I mean, look at me, I never got married – did anything really change in my life? Not at all. Your Srikanto would perhaps suspect that Pittu and I were gay and in a relationship. And society may have even awarded him with laurels for this unique theory of his but I know what I am, right? And then it struck me that even Sachin had to hang up his boots. But that didn't stop cricket, right? Maybe a new Sachin will burst into the scene, or a new Dravid, or a Sourav, someone more relevant today. You know, Dr Sen, I breathed a sigh of relief that not everyone in the world has begun thinking like you. No, not just like you or Srikanto but not even like Kurchi or Bula and Arun and Rabi. There are other people in the world too.

And we are fortunate that there are other people. Otherwise can you imagine the kind of mess we would be constantly surrounded by? Just think about it for a second. And this is my philosophy, Dr Sen, just this.

Sunil *gets up. He is in handcuffs. He walks up to* **Chotok**.

Sunil I reject you. I hate this self-deceiving, fake and made-up philosophy of yours. I hate your arrogant complacence just as much as I hate your boastful bossing. You, and not just you but all of you, are afflicted like me. It's just that you all are too blunt, dim and rugged to understand your afflictions – that is what separates us.

He is about to leave but stops when **Kurchi** *appears.* **Kurchi** *looks at him.* **Sunil** *looks at her and recites . . .*

Sunil 'I could leave, and I could go in any direction I please, but why should I? Why should I go into the bad time by myself?'

He leaves. **Kurchi** *follows him out.*

Chotok You are right, Dr Sen, and that is our good fortune. It is our good luck indeed. But you are unfortunate enough that you never realized that Kurchi madam loved no one but you in the end.

Beat.

Compounder . . .

Pittu *enters.*

Pittu Doctor?

Chotok Did we win the series or lose it?

Pittu Why don't you say?

Chotok 1966. West Indies' tour of India. Conrad Hunt was batting in the opening rubber of the series in Bombay. Facing the mysterious Bhagwat Chandrasekhar. Hunt's partner and the captain of the side, Garfield Sobers, had asked Hunt to fend off Chandrasekhar while he took care of Durrani and Nadkarni. Hunt eventually scored a century in that epic battle between bat and ball. But Hunt later admitted to having lost to Chandrasekhar. But why? Hunt explained that a West Indian needing more than six hours to score a mere hundred and one runs was similar to defeat.

Beat.

No one wins, Pittu, and no one loses. Only cricket wins as does life.

Beat.

Come, let's go.

They both get ready to leave. **Srikanto Gupta** *stands in their way. He is holding the same cricket bat that he has been wielding during the play. The score wafts in.*

Srikanto I failed this time. But I will have the last laugh in the next game. I absolutely will.

He freezes. The other actors come on stage. The score increases in volume. Curtain.

End of Play.

Glossary

Salt Lake: neighborhood in North Eastern Kolkata, its name derives from the marshland that was reclaimed beginning in the 1950s to create this area. It has for several decades now been one of the swankiest neighborhoods in Kolkata

CCD: Café Coffee Day, one of the largest coffee chains in India

Lyangra: a variety of mango

Ambubachi: an annual Hindu festival celebrating fertility

Compounder: physician's assistant with the requisite skill of combining and preparing tailor made medications. Seen almost exclusively in homoeopathic clinics in India nowadays

Leg Break: cricketing term used to describe a special pitching type used by slower spin bowlers. Simply put, a leg break pitch turns away from a right-handed batter (hitter) and into a left-handed batter after pitching onto the field

Googly: cricketing term used to describe a special pitching type used by slower spin bowlers. In this delivery the ball is made to behave in the opposite way of the description above to confuse the batter

Moin-ud-Daula Trophy: Moin-ud-Dowlah Gold Cup Tournament is a first-class domestic cricket tournament held in the southern Indian city of Hyderabad since 1930–31

Gopal Basu (1947–2018): former cricketer. Represented Bengal in Indian domestic cricket

Bhagwat Chandrasekhar (1945–): former Indian cricketer

Bishen Singh Bedi (1946–): former Indian cricketer

Erapallai Prasanna (1940–): former Indian cricketer

Srinivasraghavan Venkatraghavan (1945–): former Indian cricketer. He also worked as an umpire after his retirement from international cricket

Shoaib Akhtar (1975–): former Pakistani cricketer

Wasim Akram (1966–): former Pakistani cricketer

Waqar Younis (1971–): former Pakistani cricketer

Sachin Tendulkar (1973–): former Indian cricketer. The most successful batter in the history of the game in terms of runs scored. Arguably the finest batter to have ever played the game

Test match: the longest format of cricket. Played over five (5) days with five hundred forty regulation pitches allowed on each day

Abdul Qadir (1955–2019): former Pakistani cricketer

David Gower (1957–): former British cricketer

Middle Stump: cricket terminology. Three wooden sticks called stumps are placed on either end of the cricket pitch. A batter stands in front of the stumps to face the pitch thrown at them by the bowler (pitcher)

Gundappa Vishwanath (1949–): former Indian cricketer

Courtney Walsh (1962–): former Jamaican cricketer, who represented the multi-national Anglo-Caribbean West Indies side in international cricket

Mike Brearley (1942–): former British cricketer

Sunil/Sunny Gavaskar (1949–): former Indian cricketer

Zahir Abbas (1947–): former Pakistani cricketer

Azharuddin (1963–): former Indian cricketer

Raman Lamba (1960–98): former Indian cricketer
Roy Gilchrist (1934–2001): former Jamaican cricketer, who represented the multi-national Anglo-Caribbean West Indies side in international cricket
Wes Hall (1937–): former Barbadian cricketer, who represented the multi-national Anglo-Caribbean West Indies side in international cricket
Pankaj Roy (1928–2001): former Indian cricketer
Eden: Eden Gardens, world renowned cricket stadium in Kolkata
Mango fish: freshwater fish native to Eastern South Asia. Usually served deep fried in a Bengal gram flour batter
Pankaj Udhaas (1951–): Indian singer specializing in gazals
Chitthi Ayee Hain: one of Pankaj Udhaas' most well-known songs
Gazal: a short poem consisting of rhyming couplets. Originating in seventh-century Arabia, the art form arrived in South Asia through Sufi mystics. The word's etymological roots translate as the 'wail of a deer,' and true to the root many of the poems in this style focus on unrequited love. Today it is most commonly presented as songs set in tune
Ma Tara: another name for Goddess Kali, a mother goddess anthropomorphized as a naked blue-skinned woman wearing a skull of heads around her neck
Tarapith: a temple town in West Bengal, 220 kilometres from Kolkata. Ma Tara, the goddess mentioned above is the presiding deity
Puja: ceremonial worship in Hinduism
Shrikanth (1959–): former Indian cricketer
Victor Trumper (1877–1915): former Australian cricketer
Kapil Dev Nikhanj (1959–): former Indian cricketer who led India to its first cricket world cup victory in 1983
Conrad Hunte (1932–99): former Barbadian cricketer, who represented the multi-national Anglo-Caribbean West Indies side in international cricket
Garfield Sobers (1936–): former Barbadian cricketer, who represented the multi-national Anglo-Caribbean West Indies side in international cricket
Durani (1934–): former cricket player for India, originally from Afghanistan
Nadkarni (1933–2020): former Indian cricketer

Afterword

Bratya Basu's work is pioneering and complex in his multifaceted approaches to subjectivity, language, culture and globalization. Yet, what draws us to Basu's work is the deeply personal approach that he takes as a playwright, director and producer. For him, theatre-making is an opportunity for personal talk and private venting made public and exposed. Basu (2017: 249) says, 'I think all my life I have been writing only one play. It has sometimes been about my life and at other times it has been about my experience, my understanding of the circumstances around me.' He feels that the uncontested usefulness of art is the space that it provides for an artist to express his soul by undertaking the journey of unfolding the multiple layers that lead to the soul by gradually tearing himself apart from within even if what the artist discovers is shocking, terrifying or disorienting. In an interview given in 2008 he shares that his motivation to tear himself apart is to respond to 'the cruelty of a material, hierarchical and violent world full of conceit that unnerves the mind of any artist' (ibid.: 365). He further says, 'I suppose I live in a world of ignorance. I am pretentious in the way I talk, in the way I live my life . . . Since I do not possess the required courage, enthusiasm, or excitement to grasp raw reality, I choose to analyze its cruelty by using hyper-reality in my plays' (ibid.). The hyper-real becomes a tool to both respond to the world and its various local and global entanglements and to examine and deconstruct the subjectivities of the self that remain hidden by hegemonies and taboos of language, culture and capital.

However, in 2011 Basu chose to enter the 'raw' and the 'real' world of parliamentary politics by contesting election as a member of the Trinamul Congress Party (TMC) in West Bengal. While his entry into this world of politics in a developing country like India had been rather sudden, he admits to having been enriched as an artist thereafter as he is in the process of 'discovering' the lived experiences, anxieties and challenges faced by different sections of society. For him, a collective art like theatre is not the ideal and ultimate source of power for social transformation, especially because of the way in which an artist becomes complacent in the privilege and comfort of middle-class citizenship.

Sandra Harding (1992: 567) critiques 'objectivity as neutrality' by reminding us about the less visible, less conscious ways in which power is exercised through the 'institutional structures, priorities, practices and the languages of the sciences'. In the theatrical context of West Bengal, Basu seems to lay bare the lens of 'objectivity as neutrality' adorned by middle-class intellectuals for rightfully critiquing institutions of the state. However, he reminds us that in their claim as 'pure' and 'critical' citizens and as the 'face' of the civil society, artists fail to be self-reflexive about the embodied power relations they (re)produce in their own lives (YouTube 2022). Basu goes on to explore the complex relation between an artist and the state by referring to the lives and experiences of international playwrights such as Bertolt Brecht (Basu 2022a), Sławomir Mrożek and Václav Havel (Basu 2022b), and Luigi Pirandello (Basu 2021b). While drawing on the trajectory and historical movement of Bengali theatre from colonial times his essays focus on the intricate relations of Bengali playwrights such as Girish Ghosh, Sambhu Mitra, Sisir Kumar Bhaduri, Ajitesh Bandyopadhyay and Utpal Dutt (Basu 2021a) with the state.

The multitude of subjectivities that unfold in the personal process of examination and deconstruction emerges out of the self-reflexive approach that is imperative to feminist and intersectional discourses, which embrace the affirmation that the personal is political. When the personal is allowed to be political, discourse becomes perpetual and playful as the multitudes of subjectivities of one subject tarry with other multitudes and hegemonies are demystified to be seen as powerful trends rather than unquestionable norms.

Basu's plays are exercises in creating spaces for perpetual and playful discourse that explores questions about gender, nationalism, zealotry, sexuality, globalization, caste, class, family, language, identity and the place of theatre itself. Basu is certainly not the first or only playwright to pursue such a path as a theatre-maker and yet he is one of the few, if not the only, theatre-maker(s) who has done so in the Kolkata group theatre scene, in Bengali, and with a mission to ensure theatre's survival in twenty-first-century India. With this collection, we hope to have introduced you to the discourses, ideas and aesthetics of his theatre. We hope that a large untapped and rich oeuvre of Basu's work will motivate us in taking forward his mission of creating more conversation between Kolkata, Bengali, Indian and global theatres in the interest of preserving local theatre voices within a global discourse.

References

Basu, Bratya (2017). *Sakkhatkar Sangraha* [Collection of Interviews]. Kolkata: Kolikata Letterpress.

Basu, Bratya (2021a). *Bangla Theatre: Oitijhya o Parampara* [Bengali Theatre: Tradition and Legacy]. Kolkata: Apan Path.

Basu, Bratya (2021b). *Nirbachito Probondho* [Selected Essays]. Kolkata: Karigar.

Basu, Bratya (2022a). *B.B.* Kolkata: Kopotakkh.

Basu, Bratya (2022b). Tango. *Krittibash*, pp. 66–78.

Harding, Sandra (1992). After the Neutrality Ideal: Science, Politics, and 'Strong Objectivity'. *Social Research* 59(3): 567–87.

YouTube (2022). *Bangla bonam Bangali* [Bangla vs Bengali] – An Interview with Bratya Basu. Accessed on 12 September 2022 at https://www.youtube.com/watch?v=b_z7OOavI-w.